ONE WEEK LOAN

Fixing Fuel Poverty

Challenges and Solutions

Brenda Boardman

publishing for a sustainable future

London • Sterling, VA

First published by Earthscan in the UK and USA in 2010

ISBN: 978-1-84407-743-4 hardback
        978-1-84407-744-1 paperback

Typeset by MapSet Ltd, Gateshead, UK
Cover design by Susanne Harris

For a full list of publications please contact:

Earthscan
Dunstan House
14a St Cross Street
London EC1N 8XA, UK
Tel:+44 (0)20 7841 1930
Fax: +44 (0)20 7242 1474
Email: earthinfo@earthscan.co.uk
Web: **www.earthscan.co.uk**

22883 Quicksilver Drive, Sterling, VA 20166-2012, USA

Earthscan publishes in association with the International Institute
for Environment and Development

A catalogue record for this book is available from the British Library

Library of Congress Cataloging-in-Publication Data

Boardman, Brenda, 1943-
Fixing fuel poverty : challenges and solutions / Brenda Boardman.
    p. cm.
  Includes bibliographical references and index.
  ISBN 978-1-84407-743-4 (hbk.) — ISBN 978-1-84407-744-1 (pbk.) 1. Poor—
Energy assistance—Great Britain. 2. Dwellings—Energy consumption—Great
Britain. 3. Energy consumption—Government policy—Great Britain. 4. Energy
policy—Great Britain. I. Title.
  HC260.P63B59 2010
  362.5'83—dc22
                                                                    2009031019

At Earthscan we strive to minimize our environmental impacts and carbon
footprint through reducing waste, recycling and offsetting our CO_2 emissions,
including those created through publication of this book. For more details of our
environmental policy, see www.earthscan.co.uk.

This book was printed in the UK by TJ International,
an ISO 14001 accredited company. The paper used
is FSC certified and the inks are vegetable based.

Mixed Sources
Product group from well-managed
forests and other controlled sources
www.fsc.org Cert no. SGS-COC-2482
© 1996 Forest Stewardship Council
FSC

Over many years, I have been indebted to John Chesshire for his support, wisdom and positive perspectives on the problems of fuel poverty – he read and commented favourably on Chapters 1 and 2 in June. His death in September 2009 has robbed the energy research community of a tireless champion for social justice. John's compatriot since 2003 on the Fuel Poverty Advisory Group for England was the redoubtable Peter Lehman, who died in November 2008. They were formidable advocates for the fuel poor, and I dedicate this book to the memory of both of them, in the hope that those of us who continue to battle on behalf of the fuel poor can replicate their commitment, compassion and perceptiveness.

Contents

Figures and Tables

Figures

Tables

Preface

This is my second book on fuel poverty. The first one, *Fuel Poverty: From Cold Homes to Affordable Warmth* (Boardman, 1991) identified the problem and proved that it existed – there was considerable political scepticism at the time. The book also contained the first quantified definition of fuel poverty: it occurs when a household is unable 'to have adequate energy services for 10 per cent of income' (Boardman, 1991, p227). This applies to heating, hot water, lighting and all the other energy services within the home, not just warmth.

That book differentiated between the causes and symptoms – otherwise too much emphasis is placed on the immediate problems, such as fuel debts, disconnections and cold homes, without solving the underlying reasons. While fuel prices and low incomes contribute, these are also problems for many people who are not fuel poor. With fuel poverty, the real differentiating cause is the energy inefficiency of the home as a result of insufficient capital expenditure on improving the calibre of the home. As a consequence, the home is expensive to heat and so some of the poorest people have to buy the most expensive warmth. This emphasis on capital expenditure is what differentiates fuel poverty from poverty. Raising incomes can lift a household out of poverty, but rarely out of fuel poverty.

That first book resulted from my doctoral thesis, completed in 1988, so much of the data in it are now over 20 years old, including the basis for the original – and continuing – definition of fuel poverty. It is an appropriate moment to reassess where we have got to and what policies are needed. This has been confirmed by the substantial growth in the numbers living in fuel poverty since 2004 as a result of rising fuel prices. Something is going badly wrong as about one fifth of all UK households are now living in fuel poverty.

Two other major influences have shaped this book: my work with the Lower Carbon Futures (LCF) team at the University of Oxford and with Friends of the Earth. The report *40% House* (Boardman et al, 2005) produced by the LCF team provided the background study on how to reduce the carbon emissions from the housing sector by 60 per cent by 2050. Then, early in 2007, I was commissioned by Friends of the Earth and The Co-operative Bank to look at the opportunities and policies for achieving an 80 per cent cut in the residential sector, together with the eradication of fuel poverty. This resulted in *Home Truths* (Boardman, 2007). I continued to work with Friends of the Earth on fuel poverty by providing the witness statements for the judicial review of the UK government's policies on fuel poverty, which it launched with Help the Aged in February 2008. The discipline, research focus and positive enthusiasm that have come from working with these two groups have been of enormous benefit to me.

A new imperative is the way in which fuel poverty is occurring in other countries. Back in 1991, the UK was the best-known example, with similar problems found in Ireland and New Zealand. Now, in Europe, it is the countries of the former Soviet Union where there is growing evidence of fuel poverty. As their planned economies change to liberalized energy markets and subsidies are removed, the cost of heating and energy are no longer negligible, but a major part of the weekly budget. It is to be hoped that the debates in this book on the lessons from the UK can be useful in other countries, where fuel poverty is, sadly, growing.

A final imperative that is influencing the coverage of this book is the debate about the way in which action on climate change and on fuel poverty can be synchronized and whether it is inevitable that conflicts will occur. The issue of fuel poverty has an important environmental dimension: the fuel poor tend to live in energy-inefficient properties and these are, per pound of fuel expenditure, the most polluting. Action to improve the homes of the fuel poor is action on climate change.

This book does not repeat the details in the former book – for instance, on the early history and evidence of fuel poverty; nor does it deal with the underlying science – for example, on the way in which heat is lost from homes and the efficiency of boilers. Neither book extends beyond the home into other forms of energy use (e.g. for travel).

What I am doing is reassessing the evidence on the causes of fuel poverty, the effectiveness of the policies that have been implemented and identifying some possible new initiatives. This is loosely for the period since 2000; but there is, sometimes, a gentle reaching back a bit further, to bridge the gap with the first book. The future perspective is strongly linked to the government's legal obligation to end fuel poverty by 2016, though the climate change debate has a much further horizon.

The majority of the evidence provided has come from government or respected academic sources – it is a synthesis of the evidence that is already out there and not new primary data. The justification is that this is a horribly interdisciplinary subject and it has taken me considerable effort to make any sense of the existing information. At times, I am clearly defeated; but this is not for want of trying. Perhaps some of the conundrums I have uncovered will be of assistance to your thinking. It would be wonderful if the government could simplify its definitions and policies in order to make the whole process of understanding fuel poverty easier. After all, it is a relatively simple concept.

One of the underlying themes is based on a memorable study that I used in the first book. In 1986, Karen Smith interviewed elderly private tenants in the London borough of Kensington and Chelsea about their housing conditions.

She gave this study the apt title of 'I'm Not Complaining'. It refers to some of those in society who live their lives in considerable hardship, but who prefer not to do anything that might jeopardize their quite fragile existence: they do not want to risk it getting worse, so they continue to suffer in silence. I believe that this group of people are likely to experience some of the worst fuel poverty; but we don't know about them. So I have consistently demonstrated where they could be found. A guess, but finding the hidden is never easy. This is what they said (Smith, 1986):

> *They won't do the repairs. They're just waiting for me to die.* (p24)

> *I don't say anything about the repairs. My main problem is being able to stay here ... the landlord wants to convert the house into luxury flats.* (p25)

> *I won't apply for a grant, because I have to ask for the landlord's permission. Even if I did something which is legal, he might put the rent up.* (p27)

> *My landlord grudges to pay out for repairs. But he never bothers me so I can't say that he is unreasonable.* (p34)

> *I'm frightened to go to the toilet in case I lose my balance and fall down the basement. But I've got used to it now. I'm not complaining.* (p37)

References

Boardman, B. (1991) *Fuel Poverty: From Cold Homes to Affordable Warmth*, Belhaven, London

Boardman, B. (2007) *Home Truths: A Low-Carbon Strategy to Reduce UK Housing Emissions by 80% by 2050*, Research report for the Co-operative Bank and Friends of the Earth, London, www.for.co.uk/resource/reports/home_truths.pdf

Boardman, B., Darby, S., Killip, G., Hinnells, M., Jardine, C. N., Palmer, J. and Sinden, G. (2005) *40% House*, Environmental Change Institute, University of Oxford, Oxford, UK, www.eci.ox.ac.uk/research/energy/downloads/40house/40house.pdf

Smith, K. (1986) *'I'm Not Complaining': The Housing Conditions of Elderly Private Tenants*, Kensington and Chelsea Staying Put for the Elderly Ltd in association with SHAC, London

Acknowledgements

Within the Lower Carbon Futures team at the Environmental Change Institute, I am particularly grateful to Nick Eyre, my successor, for his acute observations and to Noam Bergman, Sarah Darby, Tina Fawcett, Mark Hinnells, Chris Jardine, Gavin Killip and Allen Shaw for reading chapters and helping to develop my ideas.

At Friends of the Earth, my inspiration is Ed Matthew, with strong support from the legal team of Phil Michael and Laura Gyte.

Many other people have kindly given of their time and expertise to read some of the text and advise me on the intricacies and nuances of policy: William Baker; Ron Campbell; Martin Evans; Jack Hulme, Norrie Kerr; Jim Kitchen; Christine Liddell; Phil Matthews; Stephen McCulla; Douglas McIldoon; JohnMcMullan; Catherine Mitchell; Dick Moore; Chris Morris; Tim Nicholson; Ian Preston, Noel Rice, Simon Roberts; Les Shorrock; Steve Thomas; Joanne Wade; Damon Wingfield and Phil Wright.

My thanks to the two reviewers of the initial proposal to Earthscan, who both backed it and provided challenging observations. I hope I have lived up to their expectations.

Lastly, my ever-patient and supportive husband, John, has coped with being a book widower with great understanding and tolerance – we can now be sociable again.

Abbreviations

AHC	after housing costs
APPEEL	Awareness Programme for Policy-Makers in Energy Efficiency in Low-Income Housing
BEC	benefit entitlement check
BERR	UK Department for Business, Enterprise and Regulatory Reform (now BIS)
BHC	before housing costs
BIS	UK Department for Business, Innovation and Skills
BRE	Building Research Establishment
BREDEM	Building Research Establishment Domestic Energy Model
CCC	Climate Change Committee
CERT	Carbon Emissions Reduction Target
CESP	Community Energy Saving Programme
CFL	compact fluorescent light bulb
CH_4	methane
CHP	combined heat and power
CO_2	carbon dioxide
CO_{2e}	carbon dioxide equivalent
CRAG	carbon reduction action group
CSH	Code for Sustainable Homes
DCLG	UK Department for Communities and Local Government
DD	direct debit
DECC	UK Department of Energy and Climate Change
Defra	UK Department for Environment, Food and Rural Affairs
DETR	UK Department of the Environment, Transport and the Regions
DHS	Decent Homes Standard
DLA	disability living allowance
DOE	UK Department of the Environment
DOH	UK Department of Health
DSDNI	Department for Social Development in Northern Ireland
DSO	Departmental Service Order
DTI	UK Department of Trade and Industry (subsequently BERR)
DWP	UK Department for Work and Pensions

EAGA	Energy Action Grants Agency
EAPN	European Anti-poverty Network
ECE	Eastern and Central Europe
EEC	Energy Efficiency Commitment
EEPE	European Fuel Poverty and Energy-Efficiency Project
EFRA	Environment Food and Rural Affairs
EESOP	Energy Efficiency Standards of Performance
EHCS	*English House Condition Survey*
ENDS	Environmental Data Services
EPC	Energy Performance Certificate
EU	European Union
EU ETS	European Union Emissions Trading Scheme
EU-SILC	Eurostat Survey on Income and Living Conditions
EWD	excess winter death
FPAG	Fuel Poverty Advisory Group
FPI	Fuel Price Index
g	gram
GB	Great Britain (England, Wales and Scotland)
GHG	greenhouse gas
HBAI	households below average income
HECA	Home Energy Conservation Act
HEES	Home Energy Efficiency Scheme
HHSRS	Housing Health and Safety Rating System
ICT	information and computer technology
ISMI	income support for mortgage interest
kg	kilogram
kWh	kilowatt hour
LAA	Local Area Agreement
LCF	Lower Carbon Futures
LCZ	low-carbon zone
LED	light-emitting diode
LESA	Landlord's Energy Saving Allowance
LPG	liquid petroleum gas
LSP	Local Strategic Partnership
LZC	low- and zero-carbon technology
m	metre
MIS	minimum income standard
MP	member of parliament
NatCen	National Centre for Social Research
NHER	National Home Energy Rating
NHS	National Health Service
NI	National Indicator, with appropriate number (as in NI 187)
NI	Northern Ireland
NIAUR	Northern Ireland Authority for Utility Regulation
NIEES	Northern Ireland Electricity Energy Supply

ODPM	UK Office of the Deputy Prime Minister
OECD	Organisation for Economic Co-operation and Development
Ofgem	Office of the Gas and Electricity Markets
PG	Priority Group
Poca	Post Office card account
pph	people per household
PPM	prepayment meter
PSA	Public Service Agreement
RdSAP	reduced Standard Assessment Procedure
RO	Renewables Obligation
RPI	Retail Price Index
RSL	Registered Social Landlord
SAP	Standard Assessment Procedure
SC	standard credit
SDC	Sustainable Development Commission
SEEDA	South-east England Development Agency
SEG	socio-economic group
SHQS	Scottish Housing Quality Standard
SO	Supplier Obligation
SOA	Single Outcome Agreement
SSE	Scottish and Southern Electricity
TUC	Trades Union Congress
TWh	terawatt hour
UK	United Kingdom (Great Britain and Northern Ireland)
UNICEF	United Nations Children's Fund
VAT	value added tax
W	watt
WF	Warm Front
WFP	winter fuel payment
WHECA	Warm Homes and Energy Conservation Act 2000
WHO	World Health Organization
WZ	Warm Zone

1

Political Recognition

Fuel poverty is a recognized social problem that affects the poor, with its roots in the quality of the housing stock and cost of fuel. While this has been acknowledged by campaigners and academics since at least 1975, political acceptance has been slower. The following is not an extensive history, but includes some of the main events that occurred from 1991 (when my first book was published) to today's context. Many of the reports cited have covered fuel poverty in the context of energy policy, presumably because of the name 'fuel poverty'.

Fuel poverty as a policy issue

The Conservative government, in power until May 1997, dismissed fuel poverty as a recognizable problem (Boardman, 1991, p1). As a result, it was prepared to increase fuel prices, through government policy, with the imposition of value added tax (VAT) on household energy. Previously, domestic energy had been exempt from VAT in the UK, unlike most other European countries. The Chancellor announced in the budget on 16 March 1993 that value added tax would be imposed on household energy in two stages: 8 per cent from April 1994 and the full 17.5 per cent from April 1995. The furore that was generated by these proposals, particularly from the pensioner lobby and because of fuel poverty concerns generally, meant that the second increase was never imposed. Therefore, from April 1994, the price of household energy bills, for all households, increased by 8 per cent and there was no further increase a year later. The whole episode had been deeply unpopular because of fears about its regressive impact, with extensive media coverage.

All governments have consistently stressed the benefits of greater energy efficiency. The Conservative government introduced the Home Energy Efficiency Scheme (HEES) for low-income households in 1991 – a consolidation of the *ad hoc* policies that had existed since 1977 (Boardman, 1991, p74). The scheme was limited to the installation of basic energy efficiency measures (loft, hot water tank and pipes insulation and draught-proofing) and required a

£15 contribution from the recipients. It later became Warm Front, also funded by the government, and from April 1994, the utilities were supporting their own scheme, the Energy Efficiency Standards of Performance (EESOP). This new requirement introduced the concept of energy efficiency being funded by the energy companies.

The dismissal of fuel poverty by the Conservatives was somewhat circumvented by energy efficiency and housing publications referring to 'affordable warmth', the sub-title of my first book (someone is not in fuel poverty, if they have affordable warmth): '"Affordable warmth" targets can be set based on the likely income of the occupants to ensure they can afford to heat their homes' (BRECSU, 1995, p7). This subterfuge was continued with the *Energy Report* of the 1991 *English House Condition Survey* (EHCS), which had a short section on 'affordable warmth' – the first government document to use the phrase:

> The two central aims of energy efficiency policies – of achieving energy conservation, on the one hand, and affordable warmth, on the other – tend to affect very different sectors of the housing stock. Even moderate improvement in energy efficiency would yield very important benefits in terms of providing affordable warmth to the poorest households. (DOE, 1996, p247)

This was the nearest that any official document was allowed to get to the problem, as the phrase 'fuel poverty' could not be used (Moore, pers comm). By the time the 1996 EHCS *Energy Report* was published in 2000, the Labour government was in power, so there could be a whole chapter on fuel poverty (DETR, 2000, p119).

In 1997, the local authority housing sector was much diminished in size because tenants had been given the right to buy their homes at a discount. The remaining stock was, inevitably, the less attractive properties and contained a multitude of problems, as the minister stated:

> ... when we came to power in 1997, we faced a backlog of repairs with a value of £19 billion. Some 2 million homes were failing to meet the basic decency standards... We set a target in 2001 to make all social housing decent by 2010. (Hansard, 2009a)

Housing associations, now called registered social landlords, provided an increasing proportion of social housing:

> The social sector provides subsidized housing and allocates it on the basis of need... Housing for lower income households ... differs from other necessities, such as energy and food, in that government takes a strong proactive role in ensuring access and affordability. (Whitehead, 2008, p48)

When the Labour government was elected in May 1997, it focused on fuel poverty as a policy issue almost immediately in a radical change from the previous administration. This is despite the lack of any commitment on fuel poverty in the Labour election manifesto. Angela Eagle, the responsible minister at the Department of the Environment, Transport and the Regions (DETR), acknowledged the problem of fuel poverty and that the government would tackle it during the Labour Party Conference in September 1997. One of her first steps was to set up an informal interdepartmental group to examine the issue (Hansard, 1997).

The problem of fuel poverty was officially recognized by government when Angela Eagle stated:

> We will take an integrated approach across government to tackle fuel poverty and energy efficiency. We have to produce coherent policies that go to the heart of the problem. (Hansard, 1998)

Another early policy for the Labour government was to reduce VAT on domestic fuel to 5 per cent from 1 September 1997 – the lowest allowable under European rules.

In July 1997, the Chancellor had also introduced a windfall tax on the excess profits of the privatized utilities because of their undervaluation and under-regulation at the time of privatization. This raised a net £4.8 billion for social welfare policies and had public resonance as 'the utilities were regarded by New Labour, and its voters, to have profited unreasonably from privatization' (Smith, A., 2009, p71).

In the November 1997 pre-budget report, the flurry of action on fuel poverty continued:

> ... the Government is determined to help pensioners where they need help most: with winter fuel bills. For this purpose, a sum of £20 will be paid to pensioner households. Pensioner households who are receiving income support will be paid £50... About 7 million pensioner households will benefit... The cost will be £190 million for each of the next two years. (Treasury, 1997, para 5.04)

This was a precursor to what became the winter fuel payment and it set the precedent for a generous fuel poverty policy towards pensioners in all income groups. This may have been because of the impact upon all politicians of the backlash over VAT, which had involved a strong pensioner campaign. But the policy excluded, for instance, low-income families with children from the same assistance.

Even though it was now government policy to tackle fuel poverty, it took a private member's bill, introduced by David Amess, to galvanize the government into real progress. His bill became the 2000 Warm Homes and Energy

Conservation Act (WHECA), with the government's support. This made it a legal obligation in England and Wales to ensure that 'as far as is reasonably practicable, persons do not live in fuel poverty' by 2016 in England and 2018 in Wales, widely interpreted as 'eradicating' fuel poverty. This was followed by similar legislation in the Housing (Scotland) Act 2001 and a non-statutory policy commitment in Northern Ireland (DSDNI, 2004), both with 2016 as the end date. The definitions are similar, but with Scotland requiring warmer homes for the elderly and infirm.

The act required the government to prepare and publish a strategy within a year, identifying their policies for eliminating fuel poverty within 15 years. It also required the establishing of interim targets. As a result of the act and a consultation process, the government published *The UK Fuel Poverty Strategy* (DTI, 2001) for the period up to 2016. Although the 2000 WHECA does not apply to Scotland or Northern Ireland (fuel poverty is a devolved responsibility), *The UK Fuel Poverty Strategy* covered the whole of the UK, with detailed sections for the separate administrations. The government's sincere commitment to the strategy's aims was clear from the humane tone of the 'Ministerial Foreword': 'committing the government to end the blight of fuel poverty for vulnerable households by 2010' (DTI, 2001, p1).

The first estimates of the numbers in fuel poverty

Statistics on the numbers in fuel poverty had to wait for an agreed definition. In the absence of political acceptance of the problem, there could be no official definition and no official statistics. The definition of fuel poverty from my first book was derived *from the statistics*. It took some time before there were statistics for fuel poverty derived *from the definition*.

The first assessment of the numbers of fuel poor household came from the analysis of the *English House Condition Survey 1996: Energy Report* (DETR, 2000). In a deft piece of editing, this included a comparison with the 1991 numbers, as if they had been defined as fuel poverty rather than as affordable warmth. Importantly, the definition used was based on the amount of money needed to be spent, not just actual expenditure. This was an extension of my original definition, which had been based solely on existing expenditure:

> ... *the annual total fuel cost required to achieve a set heating regime, adequate lighting, cooking and running costs of typical domestic appliances, in any particular dwelling.* (DETR, 2000, p119)

This statement is confirmation that fuel poverty covers all uses of energy in the home, not just warmth and, importantly, indicates that the energy efficiency of the home includes the cost of providing these energy services. Energy efficiency is not just a technical definition. The analysis in the 1996 EHCS *Energy Report* on the housing conditions of the fuel poor has never been bettered and, though now out of date, still provides important evidence of where policy should be focused.

There were some definitional differences between the original 1991 and the 1996 data; but the trend was clearly down, with the numbers of fuel-poor households declining by about 26 per cent in England. The reasons for the decline varied with the intensity of fuel poverty:

> ... most of this reduction can be attributed to the combined effect of lower fuel costs and higher incomes. However, the greatest in-road into more serious categories of fuel poverty has come from improved energy efficiency and higher incomes, the rising fuel costs of this group actually reducing the overall improvement. (DETR, 2000, p144)

Because of this lack of comparability between 1991 and 1996, most official trends for the numbers in fuel poverty start in 1996, with 4.3 million households (in about 2005, this figure was increased to 5.1 million by the government to maintain comparability with later amendments to the definition). The EHCS was a five-yearly survey, so the next assessment was not until 2001. The preparation undertaken, albeit covertly, in the 1991 and 1996 EHCSs on the definition and analysis of fuel poverty (and affordable warmth) prepared the way for rapid action by Labour: the civil servants had the information on which to base policy.

The 1996 EHCS was the last survey with a detailed energy component. In 2001, the survey took a reduced format and was mainly aimed at assessing progress on the Office of the Deputy Prime Minister's Public Service Agreement (PSA) target for delivering decent homes (ODPM, 2003, p1). Since 2001, there have been annual estimates of fuel poverty, but these are based on an EHCS that no longer asks questions about fuel expenditure, temperatures in the home or energy consumption. The figures for the fuel poor are, therefore, modelled from the results of the annual surveys. This is why so much of the government's analysis refers back to 1996. Everything has been modelled from that point onwards.

By 2000, the number of fuel-poor households had fallen significantly from 1996 figures: 'the main reason for the fall in the numbers of fuel poor since 1996 has been reduced energy prices and improved incomes' (DTI, 2001, p37, para 4.29). Thus, over the whole period of 1991 to 2000, the reductions achieved in the number of fuel-poor households were declared to result from rising incomes and falling fuel prices. There had been a minimal effect of improved energy efficiency. This is somewhat counterintuitive as there had been the VAT price hike between April 1994 and September 1997 and most of the improvement in incomes did not start until the Labour government's policies were introduced, from 1997 onwards.

The policy-makers' support for energy-efficient housing was linked to policies on the worst housing – the homes that were unfit for human habitation. Considerable effort went into reducing the number of unfit properties, particularly those that failed on the grounds of thermal comfort. In England, between 1996 and 2001, 2.2 million homes had been improved (all tenures) so they no longer failed the thermal comfort criteria for unfitness. At an average cost of £7000 (ODPM, 2003, pp 41, 93), this represented a total of £3 billion per annum, from a range of funding sources, including the owners and occupants.

The UK Fuel Poverty Strategy

The UK Fuel Poverty Strategy was published in November 2001 and covered the entire UK, despite the varying responsibilities of the devolved administrations. Overall, the document is an honest statement of the situation and a valuable résumé of the various initiatives then in place. So, by 2001, the problem of fuel poverty was part of government policy. The strategy had to do one specific thing to comply with the 2002 WHECA: announce an interim target. In order to do this, the government chose that by 2010 fuel poverty among vulnerable fuel-poor households would be eliminated. It chose a wide definition of vulnerable households, going well beyond those on the lowest incomes or benefits.

The focus on the vulnerable was strongly correlated in the strategy with improved health: in the 158-page strategy, the word 'health' appears 238 times (Liddell, undated):

> *The first priority is ... to ensure that by 2010 no older house-holder, no family with children, and no householder who is disabled or has a long-term illness need risk ill health due to a cold home.* (DTI, 2001, p10, para 2.2)

As Christine Liddell has pointed out, human health could be construed as the main beneficiary.

The strategy was a major step forward, but it was only intended as a first attempt. There was an expectation that, as circumstances changed and experience was gained, the strategy would be revisited:

> *... it should not be seen as the last word, but representing the start of the road to the end of fuel poverty in the UK ... we remain ready to review and revise policies in the light of practical experience.* (DTI, 2001, p1)

In the *Executive Summary*, the government explained the importance of annual monitoring:

> *The intention is to produce a comprehensive picture of progress towards meeting the targets to enable the Government to assess whether any changes are required in policies to ensure the targets are met.* (DTI, 2001, p5)

The strategy did not provide for a clear series of outcomes – for instance, by which year fuel poverty had to be at a specified level – other than the two main targets. The policies discussed were in terms of a level of activity, or outputs, not as a required reduction in fuel poverty or outcomes. Nor did the strategy provide a business plan covering the measures necessary to achieve those outcomes over the whole period. The underlying assumption was that energy prices would fall, despite short-term rises in wholesale gas prices, because of the government's faith in the competitive market and new responsibilities given to the Office of the Gas and Electricity Markets (Ofgem) (DTI, 2001, pp17, 127). There would be 'continuing action to maintain the downward pressure on fuel bills' (DTI, 2001, p10), but no discussion of what would be required should prices rise, beyond that 'it might necessitate a review of policies and programmes' (DTI, 2001, p19, para 3.32).

The government's confidence in falling fuel prices is confirmed by the setting of a target to reduce average expenditure on fuel (as a percentage of income) for the lowest three income deciles to 5 per cent by 2003/04 (DTI, 2001, p125), a target that was quietly dropped.

In government pronouncements on energy efficiency, there is an unaddressed disconnect between assisting a household (i.e. with one or more measures) and eradicating fuel poverty: between doing something to the property and doing all that is necessary to bring the household out of fuel poverty:

> By 2004, it is expected that over 1.1 million UK households will have received improved heating and insulation through the specific fuel poverty programmes ... nearly all of the households receiving assistance will either be in, or at risk from, fuel poverty. (DTI, 2001, p10)

This obfuscation continues today, with the frequent use of words such as 'assistance' or 'measures' or 'insulation'. If nothing more, it creates confusion in the mind of the reader. The failure to tackle fuel poverty comprehensively, with the requisite range of measures tailored to each property, is rarely spelt out.

There is a similar problem about what is meant to be happening with fuel poverty. The act effectively talks about 'eradication', albeit with the caveat of 'when reasonably practicable'. However, the government can be inclined to discuss 'alleviation', particularly as the target dates become close (DECC, 2009, p24).

Progress on the strategy

All four governments set up Fuel Poverty Advisory Groups (FPAGs). In England, this was an advisory non-departmental public body sponsored by the Department for Environment, Food and Rural Affairs (Defra) and the Department of Trade and Industry (DTI). Its primary task is to report on the progress of delivery of the government's fuel poverty strategy and to propose and implement improvements to regional or local mechanisms for its delivery.

In February 2003, both the English FPAG and the government produced their reports on progress since *The UK Fuel Poverty Strategy* was launched in November 2001 – so neither could comment on the other's report. Subsequently, the FPAG's reports came out before the government's, so the latter could comment on the recommendations made by the FPAG. Without exception, the FPAG reports produced strong, useful and clear recommendations, and, again with virtually no exception, the government's responses were mild or dismissive. Many of the current problems with fuel poverty policy would have been avoided if the government had taken the FPAG's comments seriously and responded positively to the recommendations made by its own advisers. For instance:

- 'Current programmes, even if made more cost effective, and if continued to 2010 and beyond, will not on their own be adequate to meet the Government's 2010 targets' (FPAG, 2003, p2).
- 'The Government's commitment to the fuel poverty targets ... will turn out to be a meaningless one unless the resources are provided in the Spending Round' (FPAG, 2004, p2).
- 'The 2010 statutory target can only be met if there is determination from Government and Ofgem on energy prices, in general, and also on prices for low income customers; and if further resources are made available' (FPAG, 2006, p2).

As 2003 was the year of the lowest fuel prices, all of the FPAG reports and the government's responses deal with a period of rising fuel prices and increasing fuel poverty. Expenditure on fuel poverty was also, generally, increasing, but at a slower rate. The bulk of the money was spent on income support (e.g. winter fuel payments), some on energy efficiency funded through the government (e.g. Warm Front) and some on energy efficiency funded through the utilities and their customers (e.g. the Energy Efficiency Commitment, or EEC). The awareness of price rises, from 2003 onwards, ought to have triggered the government's monitoring in order to allow it 'to assess whether any changes are required in policies to ensure the targets are met', as promised in the strategy (DTI, 2001, p5). A policy based on falling fuel prices had less and less relevance and required adjusting.

But that is not how it has transpired. The government's successive annual fuel poverty reports continued to be 'reports', not amendments to the strategy. The strategy became a sacrosanct article, an end in itself, beyond the original intentions. According to the act, it had to be produced, it was produced, so the act had been complied with.

Broader government policies

There continued to be strong political recognition of the problem of fuel poverty when the government put access to affordable warmth as one of the four main goals of energy policy in the UK's 2003 Energy White Paper (DTI, 2003): 'to ensure that every home is adequately and affordably heated'. This was the pinnacle of hope for fuel poverty campaigners: the problem had political status and should result in strong action. The White Paper, however, did not contain many details of how its proposals were to be delivered, so the government subsequently produced a plan of action that was intended 'to meet the first of our fuel poverty targets in England – eradicating fuel poverty in vulnerable households by 2010' (Defra, 2004, p1). The government's advisers responded:

> This is, however, not a plan. There is no estimate of the resources required, no timeline to meet the 2010 and 2016 statutory fuel poverty targets, no consideration of the major obstacles and no assessment of the options available for overcoming them. (FPAG, 2005, p5)

From here onwards, the government's emphasis on fuel poverty wanes, as does its focus on demand reduction, energy efficiency and renewables. The priority becomes climate change. The coverage in the *Energy Review* sounded powerful:

> Saving energy is key to meeting our long-term energy challenges. It can help us reduce carbon emissions... At the same time, by allowing us to use less energy for the same level of output ... it can contribute to the security of our energy supply, to our economic growth (by lower bills for firms and consumers) and to tackling fuel poverty. (DTI, 2006, p36, para 2.1)

In reality, it was vague, without specific actions:

> The Energy Review *was extremely disappointing, with very little on fuel poverty ... the size and nature of the programmes to combat fuel poverty will be determined by the Energy White Paper.* (FPAG, 2007, p2)

When the 2007 Energy White Paper was published: 'Our goal remains to ensure that every home is adequately and affordably heated' (DTI, 2007, p23), and yet no new measures were announced. The government explained the reasons behind the increase in fuel poverty from 1.2 million households in 2004 to 2.4 million households in 2006. The rise in fuel prices had:

... driven up total fuel poverty levels by around 1.6 million households in England alone, with income improvements offsetting this by around 300,000 households and energy efficiency improvements by a further 100,000 households... It is clear that households remaining in fuel poverty will need to receive additional assistance if we are to meet our targets. (DTI, 2007, p77, para 2.1.7)

The figures indicate the very limited effectiveness of the government's energy-efficiency improvements in terms of alleviating fuel poverty in comparison with the negative effects of fuel price rises: the ratio is +1 to −16.

In the White Paper, the government predicted some possible future fuel price scenarios and their likely effect on fuel poverty numbers (Figure 1.1). Before 2002, the real price of fuel had been dropping, which led to a decrease in the numbers of fuel-poor households. The real price increases since 2003 resulted in a doubling of the fuel poor from 1.2 million households in England in 2003 to 2.4 million in 2006. The three projections beyond this date were based on the price of oil being high (US$80 per barrel), central (US$52.5 per barrel) or low (US$20 per barrel) in 2020 (BERR, 2008, p4). In all cases, even in 2007, the government was predicting the continuing existence of some fuel-poor households, thus failing to achieve the eradication of fuel poverty among the vulnerable by 2010 or for all fuel-poor households by 2016, as required by legislation and its own strategy. The government's policy appears, to a large degree, to rely on falling fuel prices resulting in fuel poverty numbers dropping again.

Importantly, the White Paper concluded (in relation to fuel poverty):

Next steps will be set out in the UK Fuel Poverty Strategy Fifth Annual Progress Report... *The report will outline action taken by the Government on a range of factors impacting [upon] the fuel poor. It will provide further analysis of our current position and outline action required to deliver on our objectives.* (DTI, 2007, p81)

In December 2007, the government published its *5th Annual Progress Report* (Defra, 2007a). However, the promised action was not forthcoming and the required 'additional assistance' did not materialize. The government appeared to have given up on trying to combat rising fuel poverty or to comply with the statutory targets.

Not only was there a failure to provide extra money, the government announced a large cut to Warm Front funding (from £350 million per annum to £267 million per annum, approximately a cut of 30 per cent in real terms). That cut was made despite a very strong recommendation by FPAG in its previous progress report that it was 'essential' that the level of Warm Front funding was 'at least maintained in 2008–2011 at the 2007/08 level of around £350 million [per annum]' (FPAG, 2007, p3).

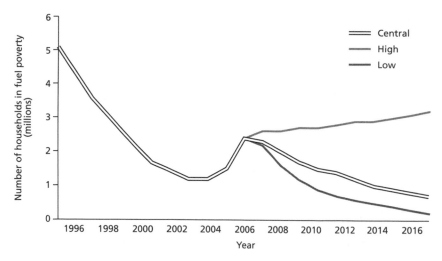

Source: DTI (2007, p77)

Figure 1.1 *Households in fuel poverty, England (1996–2016)*

In the same year, another publication, the *UK Energy Efficiency Action Plan* (Defra, 2007b) had only four paragraphs on fuel poverty out of 100 pages, despite its strong emphasis on energy efficiency as the way to achieve carbon dioxide reductions. As a result, according to FPAG: 'the 2016 target is challenging but attainable... The 2010 target remains very difficult' (FPAG, 2007, p2).

Some of the shift in emphasis in energy policy might be explained by other issues attaining prominence, particularly climate change from 2000 onwards and worries about energy security, from 2007, as the UK became a major energy importer again. However, on both counts, strong action on fuel poverty would assist with these goals: more energy-efficient households emit less greenhouse gases and, as they are consuming less energy, there is less need to import fuel. Somehow, the concern for social justice evidenced by the government between 1997 and 2003 had petered out:

> *The decade from 1997 was favourable to an egalitarian agenda in several ways: the economy grew continuously; the government ... aspired to creating 'a more equal society'; and public attitudes surveys suggested pent-up demand for more public expenditure. Ominously, the government actually found it harder ... in the period after 2003, when overall living standards grew much more slowly, even before the credit crunch. The politics of redistribution with growth are far easier than those of redistribution without growth – the world in which we currently find ourselves... Gains are possible, but they require continuous and intensive efforts to be sustained. (Hills, 2009)*

Effectiveness of policy

There are very few statements about the effectiveness of individual policies at reducing fuel poverty. This is not entirely surprising, as it will inevitably be problematic to give the net result of two moving targets: policies pushing down the numbers in fuel poverty, whereas rising energy prices are increasing the size of the problem. The numbers, when quoted, are always to the nearest 100,000 and never linked to the underlying assumptions (e.g. what is assumed about fuel prices). The majority of statements relate to energy-efficiency improvements and are usually in relation to expectations, rather than findings:

- The 'first four years of the Warm Front programme – with a budget of approximately £600 million over the period 2000 to 2004 – should contribute to a small, but significant, reduction in the fuel poverty gap among private sector vulnerable households in the order of 7 per cent or a reduction of around 60,000' (Sefton, 2004, pvii).
- 'Despite expenditure of around £765 million, the first phase of Warm Front (June 2000–May 2005) will have lifted about 150,000 vulnerable households out of fuel poverty... An abysmally low number' (Boardman, 2005, p12).
- 'The government anticipates that 150,000 households will be removed from fuel poverty between 2001 to 2005 by Warm Front' (Defra, 2004, p16).
- 'A total of 100,000 households in Great Britain could be removed from fuel poverty through energy-efficiency measures by the suppliers over 2002 to 2011' (Defra, 2007a, p19) (i.e. at a rate of 10,000 per annum).
- 'Around 100,000 households in England (and around 200,000 in the UK as a whole) were taken out of fuel poverty in 2006 by winter fuel payments' (Defra, 2008, p8). This statement is based on the false assumption that pensioners will use all the winter fuel payment for energy bills just because it is called a winter *fuel* payment. In reality, it is received as a cash payment and will be used in the same proportions as other income (i.e. spending 10 per cent of it on fuel).
- 'The Energy White Paper 2007 proposals will take an additional 200,000 households out of fuel poverty by 2010' (DTI, 2007, p81) – a small dent in the 4 million households thought to be in fuel poverty and only sufficient to offset a 7 per cent rise in fuel prices.
- The measures planned 'can reduce fuel poverty in the UK by around 200,000 households' (Defra, 2007a, p52), of which Carbon Emissions Reductions Target (CERT) is anticipated to play a modest role. The *Executive Summary* of the report gives a figure of 300,000 for England alone (i.e. 100,000 more than quoted in the main body of the report). The reason for this difference is not clear (Defra, 2007a, p5).

These seven assessments, two academic and five government, are the full set; they are not a sample. No other statements are known that link policy with the resultant reduction in fuel poverty. Nor are there any government trajectories showing how the targets could be reached, only how they will be missed. There is no sense that the targets were taken as being important and that policy was designed to fulfil them (e.g. through a process of back-casting). In addition, the tone of *The UK Fuel Poverty Strategy* was open and relaxed, as if inviting collaboration. Subsequently, government documents have become more defensive and categoric, as if debate and failure could not be envisioned.

2008 and the judicial review

The expected failure of the government to achieve the 2010 target of eradicating fuel poverty for vulnerable households led Friends of the Earth and Help the Aged to request a judicial review of the policies in February 2008. They were not alone in their concerns. In March 2008, the FPAG concluded that:

> ... *the Government's policies over a period have now made it impossible to meet the 2010 target and this will result in a shortfall, greater than necessary. The Government has recently taken some important steps, but has not yet, in our judgement, done everything which is reasonably practicable to meet the targets.* (FPAG, 2008, p2)

To which the government responded in October:

> ... *whilst the current mix of fuel poverty measures will not totally eradicate fuel poverty amongst vulnerable households by 2010, the package announced on 11 September underlines the Government's commitment to doing all that is reasonably practicable to ensure that such households do not live in fuel poverty. We remain committed to doing all that is reasonably practicable to eradicate fuel poverty in all households by 2016.* (Defra, 2008, para 2.3, p6)

In September 2008, the prime minister announced a new package of fuel poverty measures worth £1 billion, of which about 90 per cent was to be funded by the utilities.

The judicial review was held in October 2008 and, at its core, dealt with the tension between a decision by parliament (through the 2000 WHECA) to eradicate fuel poverty and the government's failure to find sufficient money to implement the act. For a judge, this requires the careful balancing of legal and policy issues: only the former is his concern.

The judicial review required a clarification of what is meant by the statement in the act of 'as far as is reasonably practicable'. Prior to the judicial review, there had been no government definition as to whether this was based on a cost-benefit analysis or some other assessment. There was an agreement at the judicial review that there can be some monetary limit on expenditure (i.e. the act does not require the eradication of fuel poverty, whatever the expense). However, further than this, the legal arguments at the judicial review (and subsequent appeal) have not clarified the definition of 'as far as is reasonably practicable'. During the discussion of the original bill and early policy (Defra, 2004, p12), some of the caveats were to do with the problems of physically gaining access to a building (the householder would not let the installer into the house), so assistance was refused. The government's defence at the judicial review was linked to budgetary constraints though the government has never defined cost effectiveness in relation to fuel poverty. There are numerous policies that the government could have implemented that would be cost effective under many definitions; but the government has chosen not to implement them. 'The applicants argued that while cost effectiveness was a relevant factor, budgetary restraint could not be, otherwise budgets would dictate legal duty rather than the other way round' (Macrory, 2008, p57).

The main reason that the judicial review was unsuccessful was the judge's ruling that the act required the publication of a strategy, with target dates. As this had occurred with *The UK Fuel Poverty Strategy* in 2001, the government had fulfilled its obligations under the act. The fact that the strategy might be inadequate, provisional and out of date was not discussed. According to the judge, the task of eradicating fuel poverty had been subsumed into the publication of the strategy and confirmation that the government is making an 'effort' to achieve targets rather than a guarantee that targets will be reached (FOE, 2008).

One of the reasons that the judicial review of fuel poverty is important is that the government has framed two other major pieces of policy in similar statutory terms: the eradication of child poverty by 2020 and the 2008 Climate Change Act, committing the UK to an 80 per cent reduction in greenhouse gas emissions by 2050. The latter does not contain a clause about 'reasonably practicable'; the former has not yet been drafted. But in all three cases there is a delicate balance between an absolute commitment, in an Act of Parliament, and its subsequent political interpretation and budgetary priority by a government.

Thus, by the end of 2008, progress on eradicating fuel poverty was completely overshadowed by the combined effect of inadequate policies and rising fuel prices. Despite all the good intentions of the Labour government when it came into power in 1997 and despite £20 billion being spent since 2000, the actual outcome was heartbreakingly insufficient: more households are slipping into fuel poverty than are being removed from it by present policies. Fuel poverty in the UK in 2009 is thriving.

Fuel poverty elsewhere

The European Union (EU) is the leading international player on climate change, so it is committed to firm policies to be achieved by 2020: the so-called 20/20/20 package requires, in relation to 1990, cutting greenhouse gases by 20 per cent, producing 20 per cent of primary energy from renewables, and improving energy efficiency by 20 per cent. The renewable energy target carries the most weight – there are financial penalties if it is not achieved – and for the UK this means producing 15 per cent of our energy (all types) from renewable sources by 2020. This target is measured in energy, not carbon.

At the same time, there is some action on fuel poverty. The situation for low-income households in Europe has been deteriorating, particularly as a result of the energy liberalization strategies of the former Soviet Union countries in Eastern and Central Europe (ECE). Here, during the communist era, heat and often other forms of power were included in the rent as a social necessity, leading to heavy subsidies to keep prices affordable. This policy also resulted in a lack of attention to the energy efficiency of the dwelling, no meters to monitor the amount of electricity or heat used, and an absence of awareness of its importance in the population, among architects and planners. As a result, the combined effect of the collapse of communism in 1989 onwards, international monetary policy and applications to join the EU have meant the removal of energy subsidies and an attempt to convert the utilities into commercial concerns. The rise in costs at the household level has resulted in the creation of 'energy poverty' (Buzar, 2007), comparative studies across most of Europe (Healy, 2004) and to reports from the World Bank covering Eastern Europe and Central Asia (Lampietti and Meyer, 2002). As ten of the ECE countries have joined the EU (e.g. Bulgaria, Czech Republic, Hungary, Poland, Romania and Slovenia), the problem of fuel/energy poverty (they mean the same thing) has, at last, become an EU concern.

In May 2009, the third energy package was adopted by the European Parliament. The package contains three regulations and two directives, one of which is the third Electricity Directive (2009/72/EC) – a revision of Electricity Directive 2003/54. The regulations contained in the package will enter into force 20 days after their publication in the *Official Journal*. It is thought that publication will occur within the subsequent five or six months. Member states then have 18 months to transpose the directives into national law (Smith, H., 2009). The revised Electricity Directive contains special protection measures for vulnerable energy consumers. EU countries should take 'appropriate measures' to address energy poverty such as National Energy Action Plans or benefits in social security systems to guarantee necessary energy supply to vulnerable customers or energy-efficiency improvements. This would mean that by mid 2011, all member states have to start producing reports on fuel poverty in their country.

There is action in several other countries of the world, though accurate comparative studies are difficult to find. The Eurostat Survey on Income and

Living Conditions (EU-SILC) has supporting statistics and, in Canada, résumés of fuel poverty in several countries around the world, including the US and Australia, have been provided (Ontario, 2008). The Organisation for Economic Co-operation and Development's (OECD's) definition is:

> ... lacking affordable warmth *(a term used in 20 countries coordinated by the Organisation for Economic Co-operation and Development). In most regions of the world,* lacking affordable warmth *is measured through household surveys, with items scoping how often households go without heating on cold days, whether other needs are left unfulfilled in order to heat the home, and whether the home energy supply has been disconnected because of debt.* (Liddell, undated)

These international comparisons are fraught because of different definitions. For instance, in Ireland, fuel poverty appears to be assessed in relation to warmth only. The energy for other uses in the home is excluded (Healy, 2004, p106), which would approximately halve the number suffering in comparison with a UK definition.

Present situation

The 2008 Climate Change Act has set the UK a target of reducing greenhouse gas emissions by 80 per cent by 2050. The government's advisers, the Climate Change Committee (CCC), have proposed that the residential sector should be zero carbon by 2050 (i.e. a 100 per cent cut in emissions (Turner, 2009)). The UK government has recognized that this is helped by reducing the demand for energy. Hence, the debates about renewable energy sources, climate change and demand reduction are all coming together. However, 'despite all the policy debate, very little has actually happened in terms of increased renewable energy installation or reduced demand' (Mitchell, 2008, p59).

Fuel poverty is rising because fuel price increases have rapidly outstripped the modest impact of policy interventions. The government has announced a review of fuel poverty policy, coming out of the Department of Energy and Climate Change (DECC), with initial findings due in summer 2009 (Hansard, 2009b):

> *The review is examining whether existing measures to tackle fuel poverty could be made more effective. It is also considering whether new policies should be introduced to help us make further progress towards our goals, particularly in light of market conditions and our aims to reduce carbon emissions.*

The fuel poverty review is desperately needed, as the government is not on course to meet the 2010 target, by its own admission (Figure 1.1):

Looking at the central energy price and income scenario, these projections show that around 1.6 million households in England will remain in fuel poverty in 2010, of which around 1.3 million are vulnerable. (Defra, 2007a, p38)

Meanwhile, there have been announcements on fuel poverty from the prime minister (11 September 2008), on measures to support energy efficiency in the pre-budget report (November 2008) and in the budget (April 2009). The November statement included £100 million of new funding for low-income households; but the April budget was more general: 'Mr Darling announced £435 million for energy efficiency measures in "homes, businesses and public buildings"' (Treasury, 2009).

The 2010 target is now unobtainable; but there are parallel worries about the achievability of the 2016 target. Thus, in mid 2009, the level of fuel poverty in the UK is high and is probably still growing, despite considerable expenditure and a catalogue of reports and statements. There is a risk that the requirements of the 2000 Warm Homes and Energy Conservation Act (WHECA) cannot be met, though the government is still saying that it is committed, as the minister stated: 'We intend to put ourselves on a trajectory to meet the 2016 target' (HC 37, 2009, Ev 75, Q319).

The situation in relation to fuel poverty is akin to policy on renewable energy (Mitchell, 2008, p135):

The renewable energy policy in the UK is rather like a chimera. Successive governments have always been very supportive of renewable energy in public. However, at no point has any government ever seriously addressed renewable energy deployment.

How has the UK reached this stage?

There is now clear political awareness of the problem of fuel poverty and between 2001 and 2004 it received good political support, particularly on paper. This support was relatively cost free as fuel prices were dropping and appearing to solve the problem. There was useful kudos to be obtained from claiming the credit for something that was being cured by external factors – world fuel prices. Subsequently, the rhetoric has continued; but the political emphasis has diminished as fuel prices have risen: policy is both demonstrably less effective and much more expensive.

While there is clearly a problem with political will and vision, there are also some fundamental questions about the lack of past progress. Through an examination of these issues, sometimes going back to basic principles, it is hoped that future policy will be more successful. One cautionary note is required from the start: there is a circular argument that is endemic to the book – the data and the definition are inextricably linked. The only data that are available are based on the existing definition, so this limits the scope for analysis of new definitions. However, this book addresses some of the major questions to expose the challenges and indicate possible solutions:

- Is the definition of fuel poverty appropriate (Chapter 2)?
- How could policy be targeted more effectively (Chapters 2 and 3)?
- How much could higher incomes contribute to reducing fuel poverty (Chapter 3)?
- How much fuel poverty has been caused by utility policies (Chapter 4)?
- Where are there synergies and where are there conflicts between climate change policy and fuel poverty policy (Chapter 5)?
- Who lives in the most energy-inefficient homes and are they the poorest people? How much has been achieved by the various energy-efficiency programmes (Chapter 6)?
- Who are the most vulnerable to the health implications of cold homes? What are the cost implications for the National Health Service (NHS) of greater action (or inaction) on fuel poverty (Chapter 7)?
- Who has responsibility for delivering the eradication of fuel poverty and what layer of government could be held responsible? Where should higher levels of expenditure come from and what would be the size of the budget (Chapter 8)?
- What are some possible solutions (Chapter 9)?

The book examines these questions to establish what might be involved in fixing fuel poverty. The chapters are individual, but also part of a cumulative story: this is an interactive problem that requires coherent policies.

One of the best insights into why the UK is failing on fuel poverty comes from a statement in 1976 by an early campaigner, Marigold Johnson, when commenting on the rise in fuel prices after the first oil crisis in October 1973. The cause, she believed, was 'society's failure to plan for an age of high-cost fuels' (cited in Boardman, 1991, p25). If only those 33 years had been used more wisely.

References

BERR (Department for Business, Enterprise and Regulatory Reform) (2008) *Updated Energy and Carbon Emission Projections*, URN 07/947X, for Energy White Paper, BERR, www.berr.gov.uk/files/file39580.pdf

Boardman, B. (1991) *Fuel Poverty: From Cold Homes to Affordable Warmth*, Belhaven Press, London

Boardman, B. (2005) 'Falling short', *Energy Action*, NEA, Newcastle, March

BRECSU (1995) *Energy Efficient Refurbishment of Existing Housing*, BRECSU Best Practice Guide 155, www.feta.co.uk/rva/downloads/gpg155.pdf

Buzar, S. (2007) *Energy Poverty in Eastern Europe: Hidden Geographies of Deprivation*, Ashgate, UK

DECC (Department of Energy and Climate Change) (2009) *Annual Report and Resource Accounts 2008–2009*, HC 452, July

Defra (Department for Environment, Food and Rural Affairs) (2004) *Fuel Poverty in England: The Government's Plan of Action*, Defra, London

Defra (2007a) *The UK Fuel Poverty Strategy: 5th Annual Progress Report*, Defra, London, December

Defra (2007b) *UK Energy Efficiency Action Plan*, Defra, London

Defra (2008) *The UK Fuel Poverty Strategy: 6th Annual Progress Report*, Defra, London, October

DETR (Department of the Environment, Transport and the Regions) (2000) *English House Condition Survey 1996: Energy Report*, DETR, London

DOE (Department of the Environment) (1996) *English House Condition Survey 1991: Energy Report*, DOE, London

DSDNI (Department for Social Development, Northern Ireland) (2004) *Ending Fuel Poverty: A Strategy for Northern Ireland*, DSDNI, Northern Ireland, November, www.dsdni.gov.uk/ending_fuel_poverty_-_a_strategy_for_ni.pdf

DTI (Department of Trade and Industry) (2001) *The UK Fuel Poverty Strategy*, DTI, London, November, www.berr.gov.uk/files/file16495.pdf

DTI (2003) *Our Energy Future – Creating a Low Carbon Economy*, Energy White Paper, Cm 5761, DTI, London, www.berr.gov.uk/files/file10719.pdf

DTI (2006) *The Energy Challenge: Energy Review – A Report*, DTI, London, July, www.berr.gov.uk/files/file31890.pdf

DTI (2007) *Meeting the Energy Challenge*, White Paper on Energy, Cm7124, DTI, London, May, www.berr.gov.uk/files/file39387.pdf

FOE (Friends of the Earth) (2008) *Government Taken to High Court over Fuel Poverty*, www.foe.co.uk/resource/local/planning/news/fuel_poverty_judgement_16028.html

FPAG (Fuel Poverty Advisory Group) (2003) *Fuel Poverty Advisory Group for England: First Annual Report – 2002/3*, Department of Trade and Industry, London, February

FPAG (2004) *Fuel Poverty Advisory Group for England: Second Annual Report – 2003/4*, Department of Trade and Industry, London

FPAG (2005) *Fuel Poverty Advisory Group for England: Third Annual Report – 2004/5*, Department of Trade and Industry, London

FPAG (2006) *Fuel Poverty Advisory Group for England: Fourth Annual Report – 2005*, Department of Trade and Industry, London, March

FPAG (2007) *Fuel Poverty Advisory Group for England: Fifth Annual Report – 2006*, Department of Trade and Industry, London, April, www.berr.gov.uk/files/file38873.pdf

FPAG (2008) *Fuel Poverty Advisory Group for England: Sixth Annual Report – 2007*, Department for Business, Enterprise and Regulatory Reform, London, March

Hansard (1997) HC Written Answer (Session 1997–1998), vol 302, col 629, 11 December

Hansard (1998) HC Deb (Session 1997–1998), vol 304, col 306, 14 January

Hansard (2009a) HC Deb (Session 2008–2009), vol 489, col 1202, 20 March, Joan Ruddock, Minister for Fuel Poverty, DECC

Hansard (2009b) HC Written Answers (Session 2008–2009), vol 492, col 658, 12 May

HC 37 (2009) *Energy Efficiency and Fuel Poverty*, Third report of session 2008–2009, Environment, Food and Rural Affairs Select Committee, Stationery Office, London

Healy, J. (2004) *Housing, Fuel Poverty and Health: A Pan-European Analysis*, Ashgate, Farnham, UK

Hills, J. (2009) 'In a fair state?', *The Guardian*, 25 February, www.guardian.co.uk/society/2009/feb/25/social-exclusion-policy/print

Lampietti, J. and Meyer, A. S. (2002) *Coping with the Cold: Heating Strategies for Eastern Europe and Central Asia's Urban Poor*, World Bank, Washington, DC

Liddell, C. (undated) *Tackling Fuel Poverty and Impacts on Human Health: A Review of Recent Evidence*, University of Ulster, Coleraine Campus, Northern Ireland

Macrory, R. (2008) 'Failed fuel poverty claim questions enforceability of climate Bill goals', *ENDS Report*, Environmental Data Services, 406, November, London

Mitchell, C. (2008) *The Political Economy of Sustainable Energy*, Palgrave Macmillan, Basingstoke, UK

Moore, R., EHCS and fuel poverty energy consultant, pers comm

ODPM (Office of the Deputy Prime Minister) (2003) *English House Condition Survey 2001: Building the Picture*, ODPM, London, July

Ontario (2008) *Appendix A, Country Specific Low-Income Energy Programs*, www.rds.oeb.gov.on.ca/webdrawer/webdrawer.dll/webdrawer/rec/81017/view/LowIncomeConsultation_Appendix%20A_CountrySummaries_20080905.pdf

Sefton, T. (2004) *Aiming High: An Evaluation of the Potential Contribution of Warm Front towards Meeting the Government's Fuel Poverty Target in England*, Centre for Analysis of Social Exclusion Report 28, London, November

Smith, A. (2009) 'Energy governance: The challenges of sustainability', in I. Scrase and G. MacKerron (eds) *Energy for the Future: A New Agenda*, Palgrave Macmillan, Basingstoke, UK

Smith, H. (2009) *The EU's Third Energy Package: Tighter Control over Europe's Transmission Control Businesses*, Energy e-bulletin, 12 May 2009, Herbert Smith LLP, www.herbertsmith.com/NR/rdonlyres/43EB840A-0495-4AAF-B8F4-B71DF73D5434/11131/EUthirdenergypackage120509.html

Treasury (1997) *Pre-Budget Report 1997*, www.hm-treasury.gov.uk/prebud_pbr97_rep05.htm

Treasury (2009) *The Budget – Building Britain's Future*, http://budget.treasury.gov.uk/building_a_low_carbon_recovery.htm

Turner, A. (2009) Powerpoint presentation to UCL, 20 May, http://hmccc.s3.amazon-aws.com/UCL%20Lecture%2020%20May%2009.ppt#262,8

Whitehead, C. (2008) 'Housing' in S. Thomas (ed) *Poor Choices: The Limits of Competitive Markets in the Provision of Essential Services to Low-Income Consumers*, Energywatch, www.psiru.org/reports/PoorChoices.pdf

2

Finding the Fuel Poor

Now that fuel poverty is politically accepted as a real problem, there are some difficult definitional issues to consider. All of these are compounded by the circular argument: who is fuel poor depends on the definition; but the definition depends on who you want to focus on and this involves political judgement. Some of the answers just have to be pragmatic. Some may be government decisions, based on an underlying philosophy, though this is rarely made explicit and may not be sufficiently coherent. For instance, there are various definitions of a vulnerable household, so why did the government choose this one for fuel poverty? What are the relative political priorities for pensioners compared with families with young children (different definitions of fuel poverty favour them separately)?

The starting point is the current definition of fuel poverty in order to identify what is known about the social characteristics of the fuel poor. This helps to establish what aspects of the definition most need to be reassessed or questioned and is part of the process of trying to establish to what degree the failure of fuel poverty policy is linked to an inappropriate or incorrect definition.

Fuel poverty occurs because of a combination of low income and energy-inefficient homes. The definition of energy efficiency used, here and by government in relation to fuel poverty, includes both the quantity of energy used in the home and its cost (i.e. it is not just a technical definition of efficiency). Therefore, all of the three main components – income, fuel prices and energy efficiency – are included in the relationship. Other contributory factors are the absence of savings and living in rented accommodation, both of which limit an occupant's opportunities to improve the property.

Current definitions

The current definition of fuel poverty has accumulated and evolved since 1991 and a little bit of history is needed to provide the background situation. As stated in the Preface to this book, the original definition of fuel poverty was that it occurred when a household could not 'have adequate energy services for 10 per cent of income' (Boardman, 1991, p227). This was based on 1988 data when household average expenditure on energy for use in the home was 5 per cent of the weekly budget, and the 30 per cent of households with the lowest income did, indeed, spend 10 per cent. The figure of 10 per cent was, therefore, in some sense 'affordable' for the poorest households. It was what they were spending, although they were often cold as well. Another reason for taking 10 per cent was that work by two economists at the Department of Health and Social Security had stated that expenditure at a level equivalent to twice the median is 'disproportionate' (Isherwood and Hancock, 1979). For households, this only occurred with expenditure on housing and with fuel. There were – and are – policies designed to assist with housing costs and thus reduce the impact (e.g. housing benefit). For fuel poverty, the hardship was not amelio-rated, indicating that the fuel poor needed assistance. Policies to tackle fuel poverty specifically could be justified. There was another useful synergy between the two approaches: the Isherwood and Hancock (1979) definition of twice the median indicated that it was the households in the lowest three deciles who had disproportionate fuel expenditure, which confirmed the approach that I had taken. The 'catchment' area for the fuel poor was not the lowest two deciles or some other proportion, but the 30 per cent of households with the lowest incomes.

There are several components to the definition of fuel poverty (Table 2.1) and these have been defined at different times by a variety of sources. They are predominantly linked to technical, quantifiable factors, rather than social ones, such as self-assessed comfort or ability to pay the fuel bill. All four administra-tions have roughly the same definition, with the exception of some variation in Scotland with living room temperatures, the definition of sick and disabled, and what qualifies as under-occupancy. In Scotland and Northern Ireland, household income is restricted to that of the two main adults, not all household occupants, as in England.

The first two components in Table 2.1 are based on World Health Organization (WHO) standards. The temperatures shown for whole house heating roughly approximate to a 24-hour mean internal temperature of 16°C to 17°C, less in really energy-inefficient homes, where the temperature drops quickly when the heating is off. Scotland uses a higher temperature of 23°C in the living room for elderly (60+), disabled and infirm households (self-reported) and 18°C elsewhere, for 16 hours a day (SHCS, 2006, p1).

Proportion of the house: there has been no debate about the reduction for under-occupation, although this is likely to mean that anyone who is under-occupying and is in fuel poverty is, in reality, in severe fuel poverty: their situation is much worse than calculated because it is often difficult to close off half the house (Sefton and Chesshire, 2005, p28). Scotland does not use the half-house approach (Hulme, pers comm).

All energy services: the definition of fuel poverty has always included all energy services in the home, not just heating, although this is not always made

Table 2.1 *Constituent parts of the definition of fuel poverty*

Component	Description	Source
Temperature	21°C in the living room;* 18°C elsewhere	England: DOE (1996, pp129, 83) UK: DTI (2001, p6)
Hours of heating	9 hours a day for those at work or in full-time education; 16 hours for those likely to be at home all day	England: DOE (1996, pp129, 83)
Proportion of house	All rooms, unless under-occupied (i.e. more space and bedrooms than the Parker Morris standard), in which case only half the space is heated*	DTI (2001, p144) England: Defra (2006, p15)
Energy for all energy services	Based on Building Research Establishment Domestic Energy Model (BREDEM), related to number of people and/or size of dwelling	England: DOE (1996, pp379–380); DTI (2001, p30)
Need to spend	Calculated in the fuel poverty model	UK: DTI (2001, p6)
Proportion of income	10% of income (however income is defined)	Boardman (1991, p227) UK: DTI (2001, p6) England: DTI (2001, p30)
Definition of income	Full income, including housing benefit and income support for mortgage interest (ISMI). Scotland only includes up to two household members	England: DTI (2001, pp30, 108) Scotland: DTI (2001, p50); Hulme (pers comm)
Vulnerable	Householders aged 60+, families with children, disabled or with a long-term illness	UK: DTI (2001, pp8–9)

Note: * Scotland uses a higher temperature of 23°C for the elderly and infirm and does not adjust for under-occupancy.

explicit, even in government documents. Undoubtedly, some of the confusion has been encouraged by the phrase 'affordable warmth'. However, households need hot water, lighting, cooking and all the other uses of energy in the home, and this is recognized. For other uses of energy, there is less precision on the standard to be achieved than for heating, partly because there have been few attempts at defining adequate hot water, lighting or other energy uses. The figures used, therefore, are based on average consumption, not needed use (Sefton and Chesshire, 2005, p38).

Need to spend: although implicit in the original definition, this has been clearly stated subsequently in order to include those that are restraining expenditure and are cold.

Proportion of income: the 10 per cent figure has stayed the same as in my first book, though that was calculated on the basis of the proportion of the weekly budget (the only statistics available) in 1988. It has subsequently, and correctly, been redefined as 10 per cent of income. For the poorest households, there is rarely any difference: they spend all their income and do not save. For better-off households the difference is important as their income is often considerably larger than their expenditure. Using the proportion of income means that richer households are rarely included, which is appropriate.

Income: this part of the definition has remained controversial, particularly in relation to housing costs, and is discussed below.

Vulnerable: the definition of eligible groups is now debated.

Vulnerable and non-vulnerable households

An issue that would benefit from some greater political transparency is the definition of vulnerable households. The government introduced the vulnerable as a subcategory of the fuel poor in *The UK Fuel Poverty Strategy* and gave 2010 as the target date for taking them out of fuel poverty – this was a requirement of the original act. Vulnerable households are defined as 'older householders, families with children and householders who are disabled or suffering from a long-term illness' (DTI, 2001, p11, para 2.8).

In reality, the government chose an extremely broad definition of vulnerability. This may have been encouraged because the numbers of fuel poor were falling at the time the strategy was published: it looked feasible to be generous. The definition is linked to the characteristics of the household rather than being based on anything to do with income levels, receipts of benefits or condition of the home. Importantly, the definition was not consistent with those used by other departments. For instance,

- 'Vulnerable households are those in receipt of at least one of the principal means tested or disability related benefits/tax credits. This applies to households of any tenure, unless specific reference is being made to communities and local government's Departmental Service Order (DSO) indicator group, which relates to private-sector vulnerable households only' (DCLG, 2008, p173).
- Under the gas and electricity acts, the definition of vulnerable households given to the Office of the Gas and Electricity Markets (Ofgem) does not include those with children.
- Vulnerable is often used in a generic sense (e.g. Sykes et al, 2005; NAO, 2009, p7, para 15) just as is the phrase 'disadvantaged'.

The government chose an extensive definition and reconfirmed the importance of health:

> *Whilst amending the eligibility criteria to exclude those on non-means tested benefits may improve targeting to the fuel poor, we feel it is important to continue to provide assistance to those whose health may be affected by the cold.* (Defra, 2004, p39)

Table 2.2 *Vulnerable and non-vulnerable households (millions) and fuel poverty, England (2006)*

	Not fuel poor	Fuel poor	Total	Percentage of fuel poor
Non-vulnerable group	5.5	0.5	6	20
Vulnerable group	13.3	1.9	15.2	80
Total	18.8	2.4	21.2	100

Source: BERR (2008a, Table 23)

This extensive category both enlarges the total number of households in fuel poverty and ensures that the vulnerable represent about 80 per cent of all fuel-poor households. The definition of vulnerable is so wide and generous that it potentially encompasses 72 per cent of all households: 15.2 million out of 21.2 million households (Table 2.2). As 80 per cent of the fuel poor are vulnerable, the earlier 2010 target for the government was much tougher than the 2016 target. With this definition, there is no natural cut-off point for the numbers in fuel poverty as fuel prices rise further, as there would be with claimants. The problem with the definition is demonstrated in 2006, as the risk of being in fuel poverty among vulnerable households was 13 per cent and only 8 per cent among non-vulnerable households, both relatively small proportions.

There are social benefits from a wide definition, particularly in relation to energy efficiency: if receipt of the improvements is dependent only on means-tested benefits, then householders can refuse the intervention as it marks them out as 'in poverty'. The breadth of the government's vulnerability definition for fuel poverty overcomes this but causes considerable practical problems – it is easy to identify a pensioner, but not a pensioner in fuel poverty, so many richer households receive unnecessary assistance. What is really curious is that the government has taken a broad, inclusive approach, but failed to make political capital from it.

There are only two groups in society: the vulnerable and the non-vulnerable. The non-vulnerable fuel poor are healthy, below retirement age and with no children at home and represented 0.5 million households in 2006 (Table 2.2). Of these, about two-thirds were unemployed, whereas the remaining third were in work (Palmer et al, 2008, p17). For the non-vulnerable, the risk of fuel poverty decreases substantially as the hours of work increase: there are barely any who are working full time and in fuel poverty (Palmer et al, 2008, p23). With the present recession, this indicates that there will be a growing number of non-vulnerable fuel poor as a result of additional unemployment.

For all households, not just the vulnerable, if fuel poverty had been restricted to those on a means-tested benefit, tax credits, attendance allowance or disability living allowance (DLA), there would have been a 42 per cent reduction in the fuel poor, from 2.4 million to 1.4 million in 2006 in England (BERR, 2008a, Table 26).

The scale of fuel poverty

The numbers of households in fuel poverty in England and the UK are set out in Table 2.3 on the basis of the government's own reports.

There was a steady decline in the numbers of fuel-poor households until 2003; but since 2004 the numbers of fuel-poor households have risen consistently every year. The figures for England in 2007 and 2008 are government projections, as the data post-2006 have not yet been analysed. The figures for UK are *pro rata* extensions based on 69 per cent of the fuel poor being in England, the average of the previous years. The uncertainty about all fuel poverty figures means that they have to be treated with caution.

Based on the government's projections, there were 5 million households in fuel poverty in the UK in 2008. The number is double the figure for 2001, when *The UK Fuel Poverty Strategy* was introduced. It is also about the same level as when the Labour government came to power in 1997. The government is stating that the trend in the number of fuel-poor households is continuing upwards, despite the target of eradicating fuel poverty for all vulnerable households by 2010. The government has indicated that at least 1.3 million vulnerable households will still be in fuel poverty by 2010, in a scenario of central energy prices and incomes (DTI, 2007, p77) (Figure 1.1 in Chapter 1). This may be an optimistic assessment in relation to how the numbers are brought down to this level.

The data on the size of the four UK countries are provided to gauge the importance of subsequent statistics. The UK comprises England, Scotland, Wales and Northern Ireland, with the bulk of the households in England (Table 2.4); Great Britain excludes Northern Ireland. As a rough rule of thumb, Scotland has 10 per cent of the households in England, Wales has half of Scotland's and

Table 2.3 *Numbers of households (millions) in fuel poverty, UK (1996–2008)*

Year	England Vulnerable	England Non-vulnerable	England Total	UK Total
1996	4.0	1.1	5.1*	6.5
1997	No figures found			
1998	2.8	0.6	3.4	4.75
1999	2.5–2.6	0.5–0.6	3.1	
2000	2.2–2.4	0.4–0.6	2.8	3.7
2001	1.4	0.2	1.7	2.5
2002	1.2	0.2	1.4	2.25
2003	1.0	0.2	1.2	2
2004	1.0	0.3	1.2	2
2005	1.2	0.3	1.5	2.5
2006	1.9	0.5	2.4	3.5
2007	2.5	0.6	3.1	4.5**
2008	2.8	0.7	3.5	5.0**

Notes: Fuel poverty is based on the full-income definition.
* Originally 4.3 million, but increased by the government in 2005 for consistency. ** *Pro rata.*
Source: Defra (2008, pp8, 57) for England 1996–2008 (most years, except 1999 and 2000); BERR (2008b, p4) for UK 1996–2006

Table 2.4 *Numbers of households (millions), by country (2000–2008)*

	England	Scotland	Wales	Northern Ireland	UK total
2000	20.332	2.177	1.20	0.648	24.3
2004	21.062	2.249	1.25	0.681	25.24
2007	21.23	2.313	1.28	0.705	25.53
2008					26.41
Percentage of UK in 2007	84%	9%	5%	2%	

Source: DCLG (2009c, live Table 401) for England, Wales and Scotland 2000 and 2004; MTP (2009) for UK totals; GRO (2009) for 2007 Scotland; WAG (2009) for Wales; NIHE (2007, p18) for Northern Ireland

Northern Ireland has half of the households in Wales. The housing stock is growing each year in order to accommodate more people and more households. The growth of the housing stock comes mainly from new construction or conversions, and only a small proportion is to replace demolished properties.

The proportion of UK fuel-poor households that are in England has varied from 78 per cent in 1996 to 60 per cent in 2003 and 2004 – a surprisingly large range that underlines the uncertainty over the numbers. Fuel poverty is worse in the devolved administrations (Table 2.5), although again a consistent set of numbers and proportions in fuel poverty for the four countries is elusive. The number of households in fuel poverty has risen since 2004 in each country, with Northern Ireland having the highest proportion of fuel poor and England the lowest.

The higher temperatures used in the Scottish definition are one reason why the level of fuel poverty is greater in Scotland. The situation in Northern Ireland results from other factors, notably high fuel prices, lower average wages and a greater dependence on oil for heating. Otherwise, the differences are a result of climate, affluence and housing costs.

The target dates are similar, but not identical, across the four countries (Table 2.6). Scotland does not have a target for 2010; but the other three countries appear certain to miss their targets.

Table 2.5 *Fuel poverty by country, UK (millions of households) (2000–2008)*

	England	Scotland	Wales	Northern Ireland	UK total
2000	2.8	0.6	0.181	0.203[*]	3.7
2004	1.2	0.419	0.13	0.146	1.9
2006	2.5	0.543	0.25	0.226	3.5
2008	3.5	0.85	0.45	0.32	5.0
Percentage of all households in fuel poverty, 2008	≈16%	≈35%	≈35%	≈45%	19%
2000:2008	+25%	+25%	+150%	+80%	+35%

Note: * (2001). All of these figures are indicative, so trends and proportions are approximate and numbers may not sum.
Source: various sources, including Table 2.3, some extrapolated from previous years: PIU (2002, p29) for 2000; DSDNI (2007, p3), NIHE (2007, p101), McMullan (pers comm) for Northern Ireland; Roberts (pers comm) for Wales; Kerr (pers comm) for Scotland

Table 2.6 *Target dates for eradicating fuel poverty, by country*

	England	Scotland	Wales	Northern Ireland
Interim target	2010 for vulnerable	None	2010 for vulnerable	2010 for vulnerable and all in social-rented sector
An end to fuel poverty	2016	2016	2018	2016

Source: DTI (2001) for England and Wales; Scottish Executive (2002, p1) for Scotland; DSDNI (2004, p3) for Northern Ireland

Modelling

The government's first assessment of the numbers in fuel poverty in England came from the 1991 and 1996 *English House Condition Surveys* (EHCSs). Subsequently, the numbers in fuel poverty are modelled and come from the Building Research Establishment (BRE) model of fuel poverty. This is described in Defra (2006) and based primarily on annual EHCSs. House condition surveys, or similar, take place periodically in the devolved administrations and these are combined into their own models – for instance, BRE produces indicators on fuel poverty for Northern Ireland and Wales; Scotland's model is also based on BRE Domestic Energy Model (BREDEM) 12. There is no overall UK model of fuel poverty.

The BRE model for England tries to take a precautionary approach so that it does not underestimate the numbers in fuel poverty (Defra, 2006, p10). The procedure is updated (BERR, 2007, 2008c), for instance, to reflect amendments to the core model, BREDEM. A recent change has been to place greater reliability on what the occupants say about incomes and benefits. Most of the information comes from the EHCS, but is validated against other sources, such as the *Family Resources Survey*. There is no link between the fuel poverty model and the Standard Assessment Procedure (SAP) described in Chapter 6, although both are based on BREDEM and they differ in some important ways. The English fuel poverty model includes:

- seasonally-weighted averages of fuel prices over the period of April to March of the year that the EHCS was taken, so the fuel costs are updated each year and are current to the year of the survey;
- a calculation of the energy required for all energy uses – none is collected by the EHCS; this estimate is related to the number of occupants for water heating and cooking, and the number of occupants and the floor area for lights and appliances (these are the actual number of occupants within the household, not some theoretical number derived from the floor area);
- calculations for the nine regions in England.

Once modelled for the year, there is a wealth of information about the different characteristics of groups of fuel poverty sufferers (e.g. BERR, 2008a, 2008b).

These are by far the best source of data on the fuel poor – though the model is not made available. The delay in producing statistics, however, is a serious obstacle to planning successful policies. Because the data are two years behind, when the numbers are provided in 2012 for the target year of 2010, it will be too late to adjust policy.

Many of the nuances involved in the model can have an effect on both the numbers and distribution of the fuel poor (Sefton and Chesshire, 2005); but amendments to the fuel poverty model seem to occur slowly.

Income and housing costs

The definition of income, as used in my first book, was derived from household expenditure, which meant that it came out of disposable income, net of any deductions of income tax and national insurance. With the switch to income and away from expenditure, the model still uses net income in all of its definitions (Defra, 2006, p2).

The possible definitions of income in relation to housing costs were considered in detail in *The UK Fuel Poverty Strategy* (DTI, 2001, pp107–108) and subsequently updated (Defra, 2008, p40). For England these are:

- *Basic income:* includes all income, but excludes income related directly to housing (i.e. after housing costs, or AHC).
- *Full income:* the basic income plus all benefits relating to housing, including housing benefit, income support for mortgage interest (ISMI) and council tax benefit (i.e. before housing costs, or BHC).

There are further implications from the use of the different definitions and these would include altering the 10 per cent proportion in order to contain the numbers affected.

The government decided to use full income as the appropriate definition because excluding all housing costs risked including too many richer households. The basic income definition only excluded housing costs for those on benefits and this was seen as inconsistent and unfair to the fuel poor who were not on benefit. However, the use by the government of full income does create some unfortunate anomalies.

Many low-income households on means-tested benefits are in receipt of housing benefit, which pays a proportion of their rent, tapering down as income increases. If a household in receipt of housing benefit has a rent increase (of £20 per week) and the amount of housing benefit rises by the same amount, then so does the household's full income (Table 2.7). Thus, a household can be taken out of fuel poverty as a result of a rent rise.

With both housing benefit and another benefit related to housing (council tax benefit), the money may go direct from the government to the landlord or local authority and not through the purse of the recipient. The fuel-poor household cannot, in reality, use the money in any budgeting sense, so there is an

Table 2.7 *Effect of a rent rise on fuel poverty qualification (data are per week)*

	Original – in fuel poverty	After rent increase – not in fuel poverty
Housing benefit	£40	£60
Other income	£60	£60
Total income	£100	£120
Fuel costs	£11.50	£11.50
Percentage of total income on fuel	11.5%	9.6%

Source: Author

argument that the definition of income should be one that excludes housing costs. But if housing costs are excluded, as in the basic income definition, different distortions are introduced – for example, maintenance is included in the landlord's costs and covered by rent, so this would often be excluded. However, maintenance for owner occupiers would remain as an included item.

The use of full income particularly affects the number of fuel poor in high rent areas, such as London. Overall, the difference between including and excluding housing costs occurs in the switch between outright owners and renters. Those who own outright have a capital asset, even if they are income poor. Most are probably pensioners. The decision about housing costs is eventually a political decision primarily about who should be helped most and can, crudely, be summarized as a debate about the political priorities of some capital-rich pensioners (BHC, full income) and children (AHC, basic income). Even then, it is not quite so simple:

> *Households in income poverty who own their properties outright need to spend, on average, around 5 per cent more on fuel than other household types. This is because they tend to live in larger and less energy-efficient houses ... and due to the large proportion of single-person households, in this case pensioner singles, in this group.* (Palmer et al, 2008, p28)

However, 'there is no intention to change the fuel poverty definition to an after housing costs basis' (Defra, 2008, p65).

More detail of who is affected if the definition is switched from full income to basic income is provided in Table 2.9. The excellent analysis of the existing definition (Sefton and Chesshire, 2005) introduced many of the issues, most of which were accepted by the government (BERR, 2005). They highlighted that the present method of dealing with housing costs for fuel poverty is different from that used by the Department for Work and Pensions (DWP) in the official statistics on households below average income (HBAI). The differences between AHC and BHC are real and acknowledged; what is needed is a debate linked to a stated philosophy on political priorities.

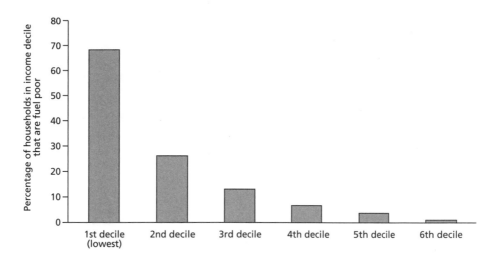

Source: Defra (2008, p54)

Figure 2.1 *Households in fuel poverty, by income decile, UK (2006)*

Alternative income definitions

There is no doubt that low income is an important component of fuel poverty: in 2006, 89 per cent of the fuel poor (2.1 million) were in the 30 per cent of households with the lowest incomes (Figure 2.1). There are virtually no fuel-poor households above median income, although some are only just below, in the fourth and fifth deciles.

The original definition of fuel poverty was based on data for the 30 per cent of households with the lowest incomes (Boardman, 1991, p46). The use of the lowest three deciles seems still to be appropriate in England. A similar distribution occurs in Northern Ireland, where 75 per cent of those with an income below £7000 were in fuel poverty (NIHE, 2007, p106).

Poverty can be measured in a variety of ways, other than by income deciles. As explained above, there are varying definitions of income and what should or should not be included. Apart from actual levels of income, there are relative measures. For instance, an international approach is for income poverty to be defined as below 60 per cent of average household income. In addition, quite a few of the major income surveys use equivalized incomes, which means that the income of the household is adjusted to account for the size of the family: a one-person family on £10,000 per annum has greater resources than a two-person family on the same income (Sefton and Chesshire, 2005, p47).

These two approaches are combined in the government's definition of 'income poverty' (Palmer et al, 2008, p14) and the numbers compared with those in fuel poverty, also on an equivalized basis (Figure 2.2). Of the 3 million households in fuel poverty in England in 2007, nearly two-thirds (1.9 million) were in both income and fuel poverty, whereas the remaining 1.1 million were in fuel

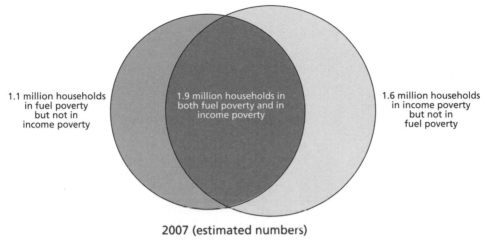

1.1 million households in fuel poverty but not in income poverty

1.9 million households in both fuel poverty and in income poverty

1.6 million households in income poverty but not in fuel poverty

2007 (estimated numbers)

Note: A household is deemed to be in income poverty if its disposable income, before deducting housing costs, is less than 60 per cent of median household income; all incomes are adjusted (equivalized) to take account of differences in household size and composition.
Source: Palmer et al (2008, p15)

Figure 2.2 *Relationship between fuel poverty and income poverty, England (2007)*

poverty, but received an income above 60 per cent of the average. Importantly, there are 1.6 million households in income poverty, but not in fuel poverty. By implication, they are living in fairly energy-efficient homes. As prices rise, the future fuel poor come mainly from this group.

Using two different definitions and adjacent years, the evidence from Figures 2.1 and 2.2 confirms, respectively, that:

- 89 per cent and 63 per cent of the fuel poor are on a low income;
- 34 per cent and 46 per cent of the poor are fuel poor;
- 11 per cent and 37 per cent are fuel poor who are not on a low income.

Locating the fuel poor is both difficult and definition dependent. Poverty and fuel poverty are linked, but not synonymous concepts.

Equivalent incomes are useful when undertaking fairly sophisticated analyses of trends over time, despite changing demographics. However, they may not be entirely appropriate for fuel poverty analysis – this is an open debate (e.g. Palmer et al, 2008, p38, footnote 38). For instance, they could not be used on the doorstep when checking if a household is eligible for a free energy-efficiency improvement. The passport benefits have to be used. The major effect of equivalizing incomes is to make it appear that small households have a higher income and that large families have less.

There is a further debate about how to equivalize, if it is to be undertaken. The normal process requires a somewhat arbitrary allocation of resources to adults and children. For instance, the allocation is independent of total family

Table 2.8 *Indices of per capita energy use, floor space and equivalized income, by household size (people per household, or pph)*

	1pph	2pph	3pph	4pph	5pph
Gas	100	65	47	39	35
Electricity	100	69	55	45	38
Floor space	100	64	45	36	29
Income equivalization*	100	75	66	62	60
Income equivalization**	100	75	60	52	48

Notes: * Assuming only adults and children above 14. ** Assuming up to two adults and children under 14.
Source: Fawcett et al (2000, p12); Boardman et al (2005, p29); Palmer et al (2008, p13)

size. This can be compared with actual data on the use of energy and floor space in households of different sizes (Table 2.8) where the additional energy used by an extra person diminishes as the household grows in size. For fuel poverty purposes, equivalization of incomes should reflect the amount of energy used, which is not the case at the moment.

The factors involved and the process of equivalization may cause as many problems as they solve:

> *Even if it makes sense conceptually, a fuel poverty threshold of 10 per cent of a household's equivalized income is not very intuitive and may possibly overcompensate in favour of larger households. It would, in any case, require a significant change in the definition of fuel poverty, which ministers are not prepared to consider. We therefore do not recommend any action at this stage in terms of the equivalization of incomes. Nevertheless, the case for equivalization reinforces the conclusion ... that the current way of defining fuel poverty will tend to under-state problems of fuel affordability among larger households relative to smaller households.* (Sefton and Chesshire, 2005, p48)

It is often difficult to know whether the data are actual incomes or adjusted ones. The EHCS definition, used in its poverty statistics and for income quintiles, is, surprisingly, 'households with equivalized income below 60 per cent of the median household income (BHC – before housing costs)' (DCLG, 2008, pp173, 191).

Another method of measuring poverty is through establishing a minimum income standard (MIS) of what needs to be spent by a particular household type to achieve what members of the public think is a socially acceptable standard of living (Hirsch et al, 2009). This has been used to identify the numbers in fuel poverty and demonstrates that there would be more households in fuel poverty than under the government's full income definition (including housing costs) or using income poverty (excluding housing costs) (Moore, pers comm). Perhaps it would be appropriate to use the MIS approach as a form of equivalization and to see the effect that this has. But, eventually, the method chosen and the groups prioritized are a political, not academic, decision.

There are therefore several methods of defining income, with varying attributes, levels of fuel poverty and inclusion of different groups of households:

> *Although probably more by chance than judgement, the government's definition of fuel poverty is effectively biased towards single elderly households in two ways:*
> * *by making no attempt to equivalized household incomes, it is biased towards single households, the majority of whom are aged 60 years or over; and*
> * *by including housing costs in income, it is also biased towards households who own their homes outright, nearly two-thirds of whom are single or elderly couples.*
>
> (Moore, pers comm)

Bringing energy use and income together

Although improved energy efficiency has had a minimal effect on the numbers of fuel poor (Defra, 2008, p48), it is the reduced need for energy that is the most permanent solution to the problem, as confirmed by the government (DTI, 2006, para 5.10). The relationship between income, energy efficiency and fuel poverty can be demonstrated using data from the 1996 EHCS (Figure 2.3). In 1996, there were 4.3 million households in fuel poverty in England, which is similar to the 2009 level, so the principles and proportions are likely still to be entirely relevant. The three dimensions – energy efficiency, income and dwelling size – are subdivided into quintiles (though not all are shown here), so each box represents 0.8 per cent of households. One of the benefits of this approach is that it allows both the energy efficiency (cost per square metre) and the full energy cost (total cost of the dwelling, whether large or small) to be considered.

All of the poorest households (in the lowest quintile) are in fuel poverty, and severe fuel poverty occurs in all five energy-efficiency quintiles (across the rows), even the most efficient, if a large property. For the second income quintile, the relationship between size (and total energy costs) and energy efficiency (energy costs per square metre) is demonstrated: total energy costs have to reduce sufficiently to take the household out of fuel poverty. Large properties have to be really energy efficient for their occupants to avoid fuel poverty, whereas it is easier for households in small properties to avoid fuel poverty, even when the home is energy inefficient. There is only one group suffering from fuel poverty in the middle-income quintile – those in large energy-inefficient homes. So, fuel poverty occurs in only the top three income quintiles, but in all five energy-efficiency quintiles, indicating the importance of the total fuel bill: 'Net income is clearly a dominant factor in determining fuel

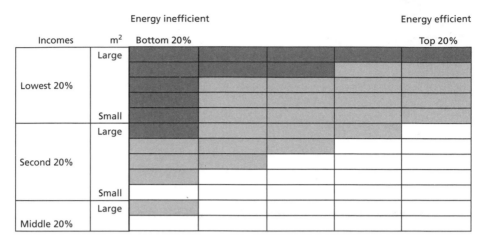

Note: In the dark-shaded boxes, households would have to pay >20 per cent of their income, and in the lighter-shaded boxes, 10 to 20 per cent on fuel. The boxes that are not shaded represent households spending <10 per cent.
Source: based on DETR (2000, p129)

Figure 2.3 *Risk of fuel poverty, England (1996)*

poverty, but ... energy efficiency and dwelling size are of almost equal importance' (DETR, 2000, p129).

Severe fuel poverty exists when a household would have to pay more than 20 per cent of its income to have adequate energy services. In England, one third of fuel-poor households were in severe fuel poverty in 1996 and they are grouped in the least energy-efficient homes (Figure 2.3); but this had dropped to 15 per cent by 2006 (BERR, 2008a, Table 7). In Scotland, in 2007, it was 29 per cent of the fuel poor (SHCS, 2008, Table 19). In all cases, these households are suffering dreadful hardship and are likely to be extremely cold.

One thing that becomes eminently clear from Figure 2.3 is confirmation that fuel poverty is, indeed, caused by the interaction of low income and the energy inefficiency of the home. The government's definition of fuel poverty only focuses on the income of the household; it should take into account the calibre of the property.

The relationship between the different components of fuel poverty can be summed up, as in Figure 2.4. There is an absence of fuel poverty if the household has affordable warmth (and all other energy services). It is possible to define what is meant by affordable and the 10 per cent of income (based on 1988 data) is still being used. There are accepted definitions, for instance from WHO, of what is meant by warmth, as here. The standards for the other uses of energy are more difficult to define but have to be included. If the amount of money that is affordable is fixed, as is the case in the short term, at least, and there is a defined standard of energy services to be obtained, then the only way these can be brought together is through the energy efficiency of the home and the equipment inside. This means that the lower the income of the household,

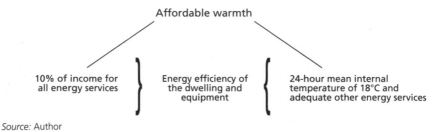

Source: Author

Figure 2.4 *Relationship between incomes, energy efficiency and affordable warmth*

the more energy efficient the property has to be to ensure that they are not in fuel poverty. Although counter-intuitive, the poorest people should have the most energy-efficient homes. This is certainly not the situation in 2009.

Who are the fuel poor?

With uncertainty about the definition of fuel poverty (e.g. is income before or after housing costs?) and the numbers in fuel poverty varying so much in the last few years (e.g. trebling between 2004 and 2008), getting a clear description of who the fuel poor are is difficult. In addition, the picture in England does not necessarily describe those in fuel poverty in the devolved administrations, where there are higher proportions in fuel poverty (Table 2.3). There is also the problem of deciding what the statistics are telling you and what is most important. For instance, in Scotland in 2007 (SHCS, 2008, Table 21):

- 54 per cent of all single pensioners are fuel poor (190,000 out of 349,000).
- 32 per cent of all the fuel poor are single pensioners (190,000 out of 586,000).
- 15 per cent of all households are single pensioners (349,000 out of 2.314 million).
- 8 per cent of all households are fuel-poor pensioners (190,000 out of 2.314 million).

The first statistic tells you that within the group, there is a high risk of fuel poverty affecting about half of all single pensioners. The second statistic identifies that single pensioners are nearly one third of all the fuel poor, so that for fuel poverty policy they are an important group. The third statistic confirms that single pensioners are a reasonably sized group of households and the final statistic demonstrates that any general policy would be unlikely to help the fuel-poor single pensioners. Confirming which of these is the most relevant statistic requires some care and concentration.

Using the two definitions of fuel poverty (full and basic), the main social characteristics of the fuel poor can be identified for England in 2006 (Table 2.9). This is the first of a trio of tables and fits with Tables 4.6 (Chapter 4) and

6.11 (Chapter 6), all based on the fuel poverty model. These social characteristics combine three categories of factors. For the full income definition (the one that the government prefers), these are:

- characteristics fairly similar to the rest of the population (i.e. they are within 90 per cent of the average; rows 2, 7);
- those where the fuel poor are disproportionately likely to have the characteristic (rows 1, 3–6, 8, 10);
- those where the fuel poor are disproportionately unlikely to have the characteristic (row 9).

One implication of the figures in Table 2.9 is that the vulnerable definition being used by the government is not particularly useful: it does not help to identify the fuel poor from the majority of the population. In Scotland, as in England, the two social factors that particularly characterize the fuel poor are low income (below £200 per week in 2007) and being a single-person household (SHCS, 2008, Table 21).

The main differences between the full and basic definitions are that with the basic income definition, the proportion of households on means-tested benefits, who rent and have a child in the family all increase, whereas the number of fuel poor who are elderly reduces. Otherwise there is relatively little difference. Thus, part of the debate about the appropriate social definition is likely to be a political one, covering the relative needs of elderly households, who probably own their home outright, versus those who are renting and have children.

The role of children and their risk of fuel poverty is important, not least because of the government's strong policy commitment to eradicating child poverty. The risk of fuel poverty for lone parents is much greater than that for couples with children (Table 2.10); but the situation in Northern Ireland, for both groups, is considerably worse. For lone-parent families in Northern Ireland, there was a 30 per cent increase just between 2004 and 2006 (Liddell, 2008, p7). Overall, Northern Ireland has the highest level of fuel poverty of the four countries listed – three times that of England (Table 2.5).

Analysis of the risk of being in fuel poverty for those on a low income in England found that, in addition to the known risks of poverty and energy-inefficient homes, the greatest risks are for:

- Single-person households because, while 'their estimated fuel costs tend to be a *bit* lower (25 per cent) than those for other household types, their household income tends to be a *lot* lower (50 per cent). In other words, fuel costs tend to be a bigger burden, relative to incomes, for single-person households than for larger households' (Palmer et al, 2008, p8). This applies to single households of working age or older, in all four countries, though the risk in Scotland and Northern Ireland is greater for pensioners than for working-age singles (Palmer et al, 2008, p10).

Table 2.9 *Social characteristics of fuel-poor households, England (2006)*

	Characteristic	Percentage of fuel poor (full income)	Percentage of fuel poor (basic income)	National average (%)	Sources from BERR (2008a)
1	Household with lowest 30% of incomes	90	91	30	Tables 34, 70
2	Vulnerable (fuel poverty definition)	80	82	72	Tables 23, 59
3	Household on means-tested benefit, disability living allowance or tax credit	58	71	31	Tables 26, 62
4	One adult (i.e. one source of income)	54	54	26	Tables 18, 54
5	Household contains at least one person over 60	50	45	31	Tables 15, 51
6	Long-term disability or illness	38	41	29	Tables 21, 57
7	Living in rented accommodation	32	49	29	Tables 13, 49
8	At least one person aged 75 or over	24	22	13	Tables 17, 53
9	Child under 16	16	21	30	Tables 16, 52
10	Needing to spend more than 20% of income on fuel	15	16	2	Tables 7, 8

Note: Several categories overlap, for instance many of the vulnerable are in households with the lowest 30 per cent of incomes.
Source: BERR (2008a)

- Rural low-income households, who 'tend to live in larger and less energy-efficient properties, [but with] no offsetting factor in terms of higher incomes'. The more rural the area, the more concentrated the fuel poverty (Palmer et al, 2008, pp9, 10). There are higher levels of rural fuel poverty in Scotland, Wales and Northern Ireland than in England (Palmer et al, 2008, p86).

As a result, the challenge for those researching and campaigning on fuel poverty is:

> *... to ensure that government policy-makers understand that progress on fuel poverty will be limited unless broader government policy adequately addresses the problems of income poverty among both single-person households of working age and the rural poor.* (Palmer et al, 2008, p11)

Low-income single people, whether of working age or pensioner, 'were more likely than not to be in fuel poverty' (Palmer et al, 2008, p23). Any single person is vulnerable as they are dependent solely on their own resources and circumstances: the costs of sickness or unemployment are immediate and are not shared with anyone else. Most working-age adults who have not been in work for five years or more are in receipt of incapacity benefit, which means

Table 2.10 *Fuel poverty for households with children, by country (2006)*

Percentage fuel poor	Northern Ireland	Scotland	England	Ireland
Couples with children	21	10	4	7
Lone parents with children	48	14	14	37

Note: Comparable data not available for Wales.
Source: Liddell (2008, p6)

that they are disabled or have had a long-term illness. Thus, policies to reduce fuel poverty in this group would ideally focus on increasing incapacity benefit (Palmer et al, 2008, p24).

Part of the problem is that single-person households 'face higher relative housing costs than other family types', partly because they live on their own (Palmer et al, 2008, p31). Thus, the way in which the definition of fuel poverty treats housing costs has a considerable impact on the numbers of single-person households in fuel poverty. In England in 2007, there were 6 million single people living on their own (29 per cent of all households). This is a large and growing group, comprising both people of working age and pensioners, predominantly outright owners and tenants in social housing (DCLG, 2009b, Table S109).

Tenure

The relationship between income and tenure (Table 2.11) shows that the high-income group is those with a mortgage. The groups most likely to be in fuel poverty are the privately rented and perhaps the owner occupiers outright. The lowest incomes are in the social sector; but this sector has a slightly below expectations risk of being in fuel poverty.

The tenure distribution of those households known to be spending more than 10 per cent on fuel – not including those who are spending less than 10 per cent but need to be warmer – has changed in the five years from 2001/2002 to 2006/2007 (Table 2.12). The growth in the numbers of households spending more than 10 per cent of their income on fuel is much faster

Table 2.11 *Relationship between income, tenure and fuel poverty, England*

	Percentage with income <£300 per week (2004/05)	Median income of whole group (£ per week 2004/05)	Group as percentage of households all (2007)	Percentage in fuel poverty (2006)
Own outright	40	363	31	69
Buying with mortgage	10	699	39	
Privately rented	39	398	13	16
All private	41	533	82	84
All social	59	212	18	16
All households	34	454	100	100

Source: DCLG (2009b, Tables S114, S101); BERR (2008a, Table 13)

Table 2.12 *Tenure of households spending 10 per cent or more on fuel, England (2001/2002 – 2006/2007)*

	2001/02		2006/07	
	Households (thousands)	Percentage	Households (thousands)	Percentage
Own outright	506	33	725	41
Buying with mortgage	258	17	266	15
Privately rented	187	12	246	14
All private	**951**	**62**	**1237**	**70**
Social rented: council	421	27	345	20
Social rented: housing association	158	10	185	10
All social	**579**	**38**	**530**	**30**
Total	**1531**	**100**	**1768**	**100**

Source: DCLG (2009a, Table 903)

than the growth in the total number of households (Table 2.4): 15 per cent instead of 4 per cent. This confirms the general increase in fuel poverty (Table 2.3) particularly in private households (+ 30 per cent). These house-holds are spending out of their disposable income (i.e. after tax). They are some, but not all, of those in fuel poverty: there were 2.4 million households in England in fuel poverty at that time (Table 2.2), 0.6 million more than in this table. The assumption is that all of these 1.8 million are in fuel poverty as they already spend more than 10 per cent of their income on fuel and a further 0.6 million households are under-spending and cold. The high proportion of households who own their properties outright is important – these are often single pensioners who are capital rich and income poor – and this category is increasing in absolute and relative terms. In contrast, the number and proportion of council tenants in fuel poverty have declined, perhaps partly because of transfers to housing associations. Even when all social tenants are grouped together there has been an overall decline of 8 per cent (from 38 to 30 per cent), demonstrating the effectiveness of programmes such as decent homes.

Households buying with a mortgage are not expected to be in fuel poverty, but they are undoubtedly a growing group with the effect of the recession and as unemployment increases: 'the low overall risk of fuel poverty among mortgage holders masks a high risk among low-income mortgage holders' (Palmer et al, 2008, p25).

Combined effects

Not surprisingly, the greatest risk of fuel poverty occurs when several precipi-tating factors come together in one household. One particular package is when a single-person household has a low income and lives in a property of below average energy efficiency, taken to be a rating of SAP<50 (Chapter 6). When

Table 2.13 *Risk of fuel poverty*

Household	Risk of fuel poverty at 2005 fuel prices	Risk of fuel poverty at 2007 fuel prices
On a low income	6%	19%
+ Either single person or energy-inefficient house	30%	62%
All three factors	82%	97%

Source: Palmer et al (2008, p30)

these three attributes are combined, the cumulative effect is dire (Table 2.13): almost no one escaped fuel poverty with fuel prices at 2007 prices.

The cumulative effect of these triggering factors is much greater than a sum of their parts. Just improving the energy efficiency of the home to SAP>50 (which, in reality, is not very high) would have reduced the risk of fuel poverty from 97 to 62 per cent in 2007 (i.e. it would have more than counteracted the increase in fuel prices that occurred between 2005 and 2007). This demonstrates the pernicious and substantial effect of fuel price rises for households in energy-inefficient homes.

Another package occurs when a low-income household is in a large house (>110 square metres), which they are under-occupying. By 2007, almost all of these households 'were likely to be in fuel poverty' (Palmer et al, 2008, p71).

Trends

There are definite changes that can be foreseen and some of these are likely to have an effect on the numbers in fuel poverty. As already mentioned, the numbers of households are growing as a result of population increases. This is partly immigration and partly the ageing population. There are now more people of pensionable age in the UK than children under six, with the over-80s as the fastest-growing age group (Travis, 2008). The number of people of state pensionable age – currently over 65 for men and over 60 for women – rose by 1.9 per cent in 2008 to 11.58 million. These increases refer to people, but the effect will be similar for households. Another factor influencing fuel poverty is the growing level of unemployment, part-time working and reduced overtime as a result of the recession. The effect is likely to be a rise in the number of fuel poor. There is little evidence that the government is planning for such pressure from the social characteristics of the population, though demographic change was incorporated within the Climate Change Committee's (CCC's) projections of the numbers in fuel poverty by 2022 (Hulme, 2008).

By 2016, one-person households are predicted to have grown to over 35 per cent of all households, in comparison with 32 per cent in 2006. Most of the change in the age distribution is in retired householders – a trend that is likely to continue until at least 2031 (DCLG, 2009d). Demographic changes occur much more quickly than the housing stock can adapt, so the growth in the numbers of single-person households means that under-occupancy and fuel poverty increase together, in an unhelpful way, and have done since 2003 (BERR, 2008b, p21).

Conclusions

There are two major problems with the definition of fuel poverty: the vulnerable group is too big and there is no recognition of the calibre of the home. These combine to make the present definition inaccurate as a method of identifying the fuel poor in practice.

The government chose a wide definition of vulnerability in order to identify who should be the subject of the 2010 interim target. This target is now impossible, so it would seem sensible for the government to drop any definition of vulnerability – it is no longer relevant. If a household is fuel poor, it is fuel poor. Across both groups, only 8 to 13 per cent were fuel poor, so that the vulnerable definition was not helping with identification.

The residual definition relates to households on a means-tested benefit. This does focus policy on the low-income fuel poor; but households in receipt of a means-tested benefit, tax credit or disability living allowance (DLA), only represent 58 per cent of the fuel poor (Table 2.9). Targeting benefit-recipients solely does not solve the problem. When the quality of the home is introduced into the debate, there is a clear relationship between the energy inefficiency of the property and low income (Figure 2.3). The overlap between energy inefficiency and receipt of the qualifying benefits is not known, but is likely to be strong and to be useful in indicating those in severe fuel poverty. This is similar to the approach being used by the government in assessing the national indicator on fuel poverty (NI 187; p200). However, at least 42 per cent of the fuel poor would still be excluded. The choice appears to be between a definition that is too wide and poorly focused (the present one) and an alternative that is too narrow, but accurately targeted.

The definition of fuel poverty is needed for two other purposes: to establish which groups need the most financial help and to monitor what is happening to the numbers in fuel poverty, in general. It will be a political decision if financial help is to be refocused. This is clearest with the inclusion or exclusion of housing costs from the definition of income. At heart this is a debate about the priorities of low-income pensioners who own their homes outright and are, therefore, income poor but capital rich. Many of these are single-pensioner households. The beneficiaries of leaving out housing costs would be those who rent in high-cost areas, such as the south, and families with children, particularly lone-parent families. The government's strong emphasis on eradicating child poverty should mean that the synergies with fuel poverty give a new impetus to removing housing costs from the definition, so that both priorities (fuel and child poverty) have the same definition.

For monitoring, the complexity of minimum income standards, equivalized incomes, poverty-related to 60 per cent of average incomes, and BHC or AHC provide a rich area for sophisticated analysis, once the government has defined its relative priorities. This monitoring has to identify when policy is failing and improvements are needed. The solutions proposed in Chapter 9 do not depend on further clarification of the definition.

Otherwise, most of the components of the definition seem secure – the 10 per cent of income will be examined in the next chapter. The treatment of under-occupying homes may be too harsh and, if this is revisited, it would imply that more pensioner households will become fuel poor. With the current definition, single people are more at risk of fuel poverty than had previously been acknowledged because their much lower incomes are insufficient to cover their slightly lower fuel costs.

The combined effect of packages of trigger factors are particularly dire – for instance, a poor single-person household, living in an energy-inefficient home, had a 97 per cent risk of being in fuel poverty in 2007.

Although there is a circular argument between the definition and the number and types of fuel poor, it is evident that fuel poverty is again rising. Using government statistics, as many as 5 million households were in fuel poverty in the UK in 2008 – nearly 20 per cent of all households. The 2010 target of eradicating fuel poverty in vulnerable households is unachievable. The government is still intent on reaching the 2016 target. In order to make rapid progress now, it is action, not debate, that is needed.

References

BERR (Department for Business, Enterprise and Regulatory Reform) (2005) *The Government Response to the Peer Review of the Methodology for Calculating the Number of Households in Fuel Poverty in England*, www.berr.gov.uk/files/file16567.pdf

BERR (2007) *Updates and Modification to Fuel Poverty Methodology for the 2005 Fuel Poverty Analysis*, URN 07/P34, BERR, London

BERR (2008a) *Fuel Poverty Statistics, Detailed Tables 2006*, Annex to Fuel Poverty Strategy Report, 2008, URN 08/P33, BERR, www.berr.gov.uk/files/file48038.pdf

BERR (2008b) *Fuel Poverty Statistics, Background Indicators, 2008*, Annex to Fuel Poverty Strategy Report, 2008, URN 08/P31, BERR, www.berr.gov.uk/files/file48037.pdf

BERR (2008c) *Updates to the Fuel Poverty Methodology for 2006*, Annex to Fuel Poverty Strategy Report, 2008, URN 08/P34, BERR, www.berr.gov.uk/files/file48039.pdf

Boardman, B. (1991) *Fuel Poverty: From Cold Homes to Affordable Warmth*, Belhaven Press, London

Boardman, B., Darby, S., Killip, G., Hinnells, M., Jardine, C. N., Palmer, J. and Sinden, G. (2005) *40% House*, Environmental Change Institute, University of Oxford, Oxford, UK, www.eci.ox.ac.uk/research/energy/downloads/40house/40house.pdf

DCLG (Department for Communities and Local Government) (2008) *English House Condition Survey Full Report 2006*, DCLG, London

DCLG (2009a) *Household Expenditure on Electricity, Gas and Other Fuels*, DCLG, Live tables, www.communities.gov.uk/housing/housingresearch/housingstatistics/housingstatisticsby/housingfinance/livetables/

DCLG (2009b) 'Housing, Table S101: Trends in tenure'; 'Table S109: Number of people per household'; 'Table S114: Gross weekly income of household by tenure', www.communities.gov.uk/housing/housingresearch/housingsurveys/ surveyofenglishhousing/sehlivetables/trendstenure/; www.communities.gov.uk/documents/housing/xls/139286.xls

DCLG (2009c), 'Housing, Table 401: Household estimates and projections, United Kingdom, 1961-2031', Live tables, www.communities.gov.uk/housing/ housingresearch/housingstatistics/housingstatisticsby/householdestimates/ livetables-households/

DCLG (2009d) *Household Projections to 2031, England,* Housing statistical release, DCLG, www.communities.gov.uk/documents/statistics/pdf/1172133.pdf

Defra (Department for Environment, Food and Rural Affairs) (2004) *Fuel Poverty in England: The Government's Plan for Action,* Defra, London, November

Defra (2006) *Fuel Poverty Methodology Documentation,* URN 06/1261, Defra, www.berr.gov.uk/files/file29694.pdf

Defra (2008) *The UK Fuel Poverty Strategy: 6th Annual Progress Report,* Defra, London, October

DETR (Department of the Environment, Transport and the Regions) (2000) *English House Condition Survey 1996: Energy Report,*
DETR, London

DOE (Department of Environment) (1996) *English House Condition Survey 1991: Energy Report,* DOE, London

DSDNI (Department for Social Development in Northern Ireland) (2004) *Ending Fuel Poverty: a Strategy for Northern Ireland,* DSDNI, Belfast, www.dsdni.gov.uk/ending_fuel_poverty_-_a_strategy_for_ni.pdf

DSDNI (2007), *Tackling Fuel Poverty: A Strategy for Northern Ireland,* Inter-departmental Group on Fuel Poverty, Annual Report 2007, DSDNI, www.dsdni.gov.uk/dsd_fuel_pov_1.pdf

DTI (Department of Trade and Industry) (2001) *The UK Fuel Poverty Strategy,* DTI, London, November, www.berr.gov.uk/files/file16495.pdf

DTI (2006) Energy – Its Impact on the Environment and Society, DTI, URN 06/441, July, www.berr.gov.uk/files/file32546.pdf

DTI (2007) *Meeting the Energy Challenge,* White Paper on Energy, Cm7124, DTI, London, May, www.berr.gov.uk/files/file39387.pdf

Fawcett, T., Lane, K. and Boardman, B. (2000) *Lower Carbon Futures for European Households,* Research report 23, Environmental Change Institute, University of Oxford, Oxford, UK

GRO (General Register Office for Scotland) (2009) *Estimates of Households and Dwellings in Scotland, 2007,* GRO, www.gro-scotland.gov.uk/statistics/ publications-and-data/household-estimates-statistics/estimates-of-households-and-dwellings-in-scotland-2007/list-of-tables.html

Hirsch, D., Davis, A. and Smith, N (2009) *A Minimum Income Standard for Britain in 2009,* Joseph Rowntree Foundation, www.jrf.org.uk/publications/minimum-income-2009

Hulme, J., Senior Consultant, Building Research Establishment, Garston, UK, pers comm

Hulme, J. (2008) *The Effect of the Committee on Climate Change's Proposed Carbon Budgets on Fuel Poverty,* Building Research Establishment, Garston, UK, www.theccc.org.uk/pdf/The%20effect%20of%20the%20CCC's%20proposed%20carbon%20budgets%20on%20fuel%20poverty%20(BRE).pdf

Isherwood, B. C. and Hancock, R. M. (1979) *Household Expenditure on Fuel: Distributional Aspects*, Economic Adviser's Office, DHSS, London

Kerr, N., Director, Energy Action Scotland, pers comm

Liddell, C. (2008) *The Impact of Fuel Poverty on Children*, Policy briefing for Save the Children, Belfast

McMullan, J., Chair, FPAG NI and CEO Bryson Charitable Group, pers comm

Moore, R., EHCS and fuel poverty energy consultant, pers comm

MTP (2009) *Household and Population Figures 1970 – 2020*, Briefing Note, Cross-Sector, 25 (BNXS 25), Market Transformation Programme, www.mtprog.com/cms/product-strategies/subsector/cross-sector

NAO (National Audit Office) (2009) *Department for Works and Pensions: Communicating with Customers*, NAO, HC421, May

NIHE (Northern Ireland Housing Executive) (2007) *Northern Ireland House Condition Survey 2006 – Full Report*, NIHE, www.nihe.gov.uk/housing_conditions_survey_2006.pdf

Palmer, G., MacInnes, T. and Kenway, P. (2008) *Cold and Poor: An Analysis of the Link between Fuel Poverty and Low Income*, New Policy Institute, www.npi.org.uk/reports/fuel%20poverty.pdf

PIU (Performance and Innovation Unit) (2002) *The Energy Review*, PIU, Cabinet Office, London, February

Roberts, R., Chair, FPAG Wales, pers comm

Scottish Executive (2002) *The Scottish Fuel Poverty Statement*, www.scotland.gov.uk/Resource/Doc/46951/0031675.pdf

Sefton, T. and Chesshire, J. (2005) *Peer Review of the Methodology for Calculating the Number of Households in Fuel Poverty in England: Final Report to DTI and DEFRA*, www.berr.gov.uk/files/file16566.pdf

SHCS (Scottish House Condition Survey) (2006) *Technical Note: Definition and Measurement of Fuel Poverty in SHCS Reports*, The Scottish Government, Scottish House Condition Surveys, www.scotland.gov.uk/Resource/Doc/1125/0048118.pdf

SHCS (2008) *Scottish House Condition Survey, Revised Key Findings 2007*, www.scotland.gov.uk/Resource/Doc/933/0079066.pdf

Sykes, W., Hedges, A., Ward, K., Melvin, K. and Bose, M. (2005) *Understanding the Service Needs of Vulnerable Pensioners: Disability, Ill-Health and Access to the Pension Service*, Research Report 263, Department for Work and Pensions, www.dwp.gov.uk/asd/asd5/rports2005-2006/rrep263.pdf

Travis, A. (2008) 'Pensioners outnumber under-16s for the first time', *The Guardian*, 22 August

WAG (2009) (Welsh Assembly Government) (2009) *Stats Wales Household Estimates for Wales by Measure 1991–2007*, www.statswales.wales.gov.uk/TableViewer/tableView.aspx?ReportId=10366

3

Income as a Cause

With some understanding of who the fuel poor are, it is now possible to examine what is known about their expenditure, income levels and sources of income. This will inform the debate about how much fuel poverty could be reduced by additional income and at what cost. Thus, a discussion about the effectiveness of current policies has to encompass the relationship between actual income (from benefits and other sources) and fuel poverty. This is part of the income debate. The discussion on expenditure in this chapter relates to the total energy budget; the amount of fuel and warmth that is bought is dealt with in Chapter 5. From the previous chapter, for England in 2006:

- Low income correlates strongly with fuel poverty.
- Most of the fuel poor are on a low income but, depending on the definition, up to a third of the fuel poor are not.
- Only 58 per cent of the fuel poor receive means-tested benefits, disability living allowance (DLA) or tax credits; the other 42 per cent do not (Table 2.9).

These findings have different implications for tackling fuel poverty, when combined with the targeting of existing programmes, and help with the unravelling of why policies are so poorly focused.

As discussed, there are various definitions of poverty. There is also a range of political concerns about the extent to which poverty in society matters. The initial drive by the Labour government towards greater social equality peaked at around 2003, as reported in Chapter 1, just when fuel prices started to rise quickly: 'After 1995/96, inequality began to rise again, reaching a peak in 2001/02 – at a level very similar to that in 1990. Between 2001/02 and 2004/05, income inequality fell before rising again' (Jones, 2008, p38).

The political philosophy on social justice is crucial in determining levels of state support for benefits, the extent of taxation imposed on the poorest households and the importance of a more equal society generally. If the incomes of the richest households are several multiples of the poorest households, it could cause great social disquiet and dysfunction (Wilkinson and Pickett, 2009). The issue becomes a concern for all, therefore. The present horror and anger at the levels of greed in high places, with the bonuses paid to bankers and the excessive expenses claims of members of parliament (MPs), may indicate that in the UK in 2009 the pendulum has swung too far in favour of *laissez faire* policies towards the rich. This chapter identifies some of the evidence and ways in which interventions could and should occur to help the fuel poor have higher incomes.

Household expenditure on fuel

Everyone needs to purchase fuel to provide essential energy services, such as warmth, hot water and lighting. These are not discretionary purchases, but absolute necessities.

For the 30 per cent of households with the lowest incomes, the figures of actual expenditure on fuel have varied considerably since 2000, with a range from 4.6 to 6.1 per cent of the weekly budget between 2004 and 2007: a rise of one third in three years (Table 3.1). These proportions compare with the original figure of 10 per cent based on actual expenditure by the 30 per cent of households with the lowest incomes in 1988 (Boardman, 1991, p46). The proportions being spent echo the drop in the numbers of fuel-poor households during this central period, in both cases because of changes in fuel prices. Between 2000 and 2007, the government's index of fuel prices rose by 62 per cent in real terms (Table 4.1 in Chapter 4) – faster than any household expenditure increases. Thus, for none of the household groups in Table 3.1 has expenditure on fuel kept pace with fuel price inflation and the gap is largest for the 30 per cent of households on the lowest incomes. On average, everyone is purchasing less energy.

The government has kept the 10 per cent definition despite very substantial variations in fuel prices. At times of low prices, when fuel was typically 3 per cent of average weekly expenditure, a payment of over 10 per cent represented extremely harsh conditions. Even when translated into the necessary level of expenditure, as opposed to actual (which this is), the statement would still be true. Even in 2007, the average fuel expenditure was under 4 per cent, so that the government continues to exert downward pressure on the numbers of fuel poverty sufferers by taking a fixed definition, despite changing circumstances.

This raises the question as to whether fuel poverty is an absolute or relative concept. With an absolute definition, there is an assumption that fuel poverty can be abolished, as in the Warm Homes and Energy Conservation Act (WHECA) 2000. In this case, the 10 per cent fixed payment level can be used despite varying fuel prices, levels of income or demographics. If, however, the level of fuel poverty is affected by all of these elements and is relative to the norms of society, then the definition required is variable and linked to what other households are spending. The original definition was defined both in relation to actual expenditure levels, but also to a declaration that 'twice the median' represented

Table 3.1 *Weekly expenditure on fuel (£ and percentage of expenditure), UK (2000–2007)*

	30% of households with lowest income		Other 70%		Average of all households	
	£	%	£	%	£	%
2000	9.93	6.0	12.74	2.7	11.9	3.1
2001	9.2	5.3	12.77	2.6	11.7	2.9
2002	9.03	5.2	12.84	2.5	11.7	2.9
2003	9.1	5.1	13.24	2.5	12.0	2.9
2004	9.4	4.6	13.83	2.6	12.5	2.9
2005	10.43	5.2	15.39	2.8	13.9	3.1
2006	12.23	5.9	17.47	3.1	15.9	3.5
2007	12.73	6.1	19.14	3.4	17.22	3.8
2000:2007	+28%		+50%		+45%	

Note: This is actual expenditure from disposable income.
Source: various family expenditure surveys (e.g. ONS, 2008a)

disproportional expenditure (Isherwood and Hancock, 1979). Neither component of the original definition implied that the proportion should be fixed, at 10 per cent or any other number. For practical policy, it is obviously easier to have a fixed proportion. The need to spend 10 per cent of income on fuel as the fixed trigger for fuel poverty has been a major reason for the decline in the numbers in fuel poverty since 1988, when fuel prices were falling. A debate is needed about the merits of a relative versus absolute definition for fuel poverty. Setting objectives for poverty in relative terms creates the difficulty of a 'moving target' – a threshold that changes with national prosperity.

Interestingly, the government's main poverty policy, to halve child poverty by 2010 and eradicate it by 2020 (in relation to 1998/99) is based on a relative definition as it refers to the number of children living in a household with an income below 60 per cent of the median – a target that is moving much more slowly than fuel prices. The government series on households with below average incomes also normally provides the information both before and after housing costs. The precedents are there for fuel poverty monitoring, should the government choose to follow them, and closer linkages between the targets on fuel poverty and child poverty would seem to be eminently sensible.

The data in Table 3.1 and in Table 2.12 (Chapter 2) show what people are actually spending, not what they need to spend in order to obtain an adequate level of energy services. The 30 per cent of households with the lowest incomes spent £12.73 per week on fuel, or £660 per annum. The extent to which this was sufficient for the fuel poor will be discussed in Chapter 6 in relation to the homes occupied. At least 25 per cent of the fuel poor are known to be underspending. While only a partial window onto the problem of fuel poverty, the tables demonstrate another of the concerns: the awkward relationship between proportions and absolute sums of money. Between 2000 and 2007, the weekly fuel bill of the poorest 30 per cent increased by £2.80, whereas for the better-off households (the remaining 70 per cent) it rose by £6.40, well over double.

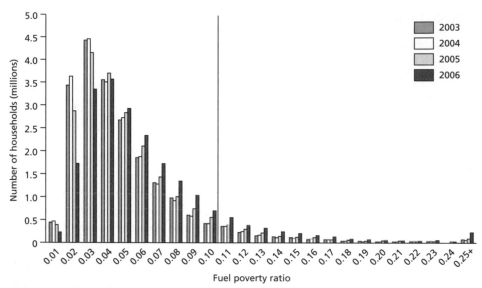

Note: Ignore the blip at 0.25+ for 2006: it is due to definitional issues. The fuel poverty ratio is effectively the proportion of income that needs to be spent on fuel – hence the 10 per cent line, at 0.10, identifies that the households to the right of the line are in fuel poverty.
Source: Defra (2008, p46)

Figure 3.1 *Fuel poverty ratios – required household spend on energy as a proportion of income, England (2003–2006)*

The continuing emphasis on proportions hides a growing disparity in the levels of absolute expenditure. But the latter is equally important.

One of the important characteristics of expenditure on fuel is the way in which, as a proportion of income, it is a skewed distribution, with most households bunched at one end, below 5 per cent, but a long tail of households paying more than this and up to 25 per cent of income (Figure 3.1). The existence of this long tail was used as part of the government's confirmation that 10 per cent was the appropriate maximum (DETR, 2000, p115). As fuel prices have risen since 2003, the distribution of all households has flattened and pushed more into fuel poverty: 'The effect of this is that a 1 per cent increase in prices would now push more people into fuel poverty than it would have done in 2003' (Defra, 2008, p46).

The impact of a fuel price rise on fuel poverty is not a fixed linear relationship, but an escalating one. The next 10 per cent increase in fuel prices would bring about 700,000 households into fuel poverty, whereas a further 10 per cent increase beyond that would affect another 1 million households. This questions the government's projection that the level of fuel poverty would increase from 2.4 million households in 2006 to 3.5 million in 2008, in England (Table 2.3 in Chapter 2). Over this period, fuel prices rose by about 19 per cent in real terms (Table 4.1 in Chapter 4). So the government's projections could be an underestimate and the increase is more likely to be from 2.4 million in 2006 to over 4 million in 2008.

Total income over time

Actual expenditure on fuel by the poorest households is increasing more slowly than that for better-off households; but how is this affected by what is happening to their incomes as a whole? Over the period of 1999/2000 to 2007/08, there have been two distinct periods for the changes in real incomes (Table 3.2). The first occurred in the four years of 1999/2000 to 2003/04 and saw an increase of about 2 per cent per annum or more in all the groups listed. The second period was the four years from 2003/04 to 2007/08, where the pattern was mixed. Real incomes fell for households in the lowest decile, were stable for the second decile, but increased slightly for the third decile and increased by 5 per cent more for the average. Over the whole eight-year period, the poorest decile had a real weekly increase of only £7, in comparison with £62 for the average. In total incomes, the lowest three deciles were all below 60 per cent of the average annual income of £15,324. So the fuel expenditure of the poor is not only increasing more slowly than for better-off households (Table 3.1), but for many it is based on a shrinking relative income.

The average equivalized income of the three lowest deciles was £11,000 in 2007/08 (Table 3.2) and was virtually the same from Table 3.1 (£12.73 is 6.1 per cent of £209 per week, or £10,870 per annum) in 2007.

The Climate Change Committee (CCC) confirmed that average incomes in Great Britain (including housing costs) grew at 1.9 per cent per annum during 1999/2000 to 2006/2007, whereas those of the poorest 5 and 10 per cent grew much less: 0.8 per cent and 1.6 per cent, respectively (CCC, 2008, p400).

As John Hills stated in a review of ten years of Labour (Hills, 2009):

> In several key respects, the UK had become a more equal society after ten years of a Labour government. Away from the very top and very bottom of distribution, income differences narrowed. There were notable reductions in child and pensioner poverty. The relative position of disadvantaged neighbourhoods improved... But at the same time, incomes at the very top – especially the top 1 per cent, and the best off within it – grew much more rapidly than the average, while incomes of the

Table 3.2 *Income levels, UK (1999/2000–2007/08) (2007/08 prices)*

	First decile		Second decile		Third decile		Average (mean)	
	£/week	Change	£/week	Change	£/week	Change	£/week	Change
1999/2000	140		193		231		425	
2003/04	152	+9%	218	+13%	263	+14%	466	+10%
2007/08	147	-3%	219	0	268	+2%	487	+5%
1999/2000 to 2007/08	7	+5%	26	+13%	37	+16%	62	+15%
2007/08 (£ per annum)	7644		11,388		13,936		25,324	

Note: These data are before housing costs (i.e. housing costs are included), in equivalized income.
Source: HBAI (2009, Table 2.1)

poorest tenth grew more slowly. Wealth inequality continued to grow... Looking across a range of official indicators ... trends have improved since 1997 compared with the period before for nearly half of them, but they deteriorated for a quarter.

Where significant policy initiatives were taken, the outcomes generally moved in the right direction, if not always as rapidly as policy-makers and others might have hoped. This included the clearly redistributive tax and benefit changes between 1996/7 and 2004/5 (but not since then) ... and the wide range of programmes aimed at poor neighbourhoods... The experience is not one where nothing was tried or where nothing worked. Rather, many things were tried and most worked.

The problem is that the scale of action was often small relative to the underlying inequalities; problems were often harder to tackle than the government appears originally to have assumed, and less amenable to a one-off fix. As growth in living standards as a whole slowed, even before the current recession, and public finances became more constrained, policy momentum gained by the middle of the period had often been lost by the end of it. (Hills, 2009)

Sources of income

Fuel-poor households receive their income from:

- state benefits/tax credits – both means tested and universal (the latter includes the state pension and child benefit);
- government grants in the form of money – including winter fuel payments and cold weather payments (both non-taxed);
- private income – includes occupational pensions, rent from lodgers, work.

The government's main responsibility here is to maintain employment levels and the minimum wage as this provides people with higher incomes than can come from benefit. Otherwise, private incomes are the responsibility of the private individual, although this may be the only source of income for non-vulnerable households (the healthy adults) who are not on a means-tested benefit. In relation to the working poor: 'there have been no obvious fuel poverty initiatives focused on them' (Palmer et al, 2008, p10).

With both state benefits and government grants, it is possible to consider both the level of payment and the number of recipients to establish whether the fuel poor could be receiving more income assistance.

Social security benefits (which combine both means-tested and universal benefits) provide about three-quarters of the income of the households in the lowest income quintile (Figure 3.2) and around 40 per cent of the income for the next quintile. All households in 2007 in the first income quintile had an

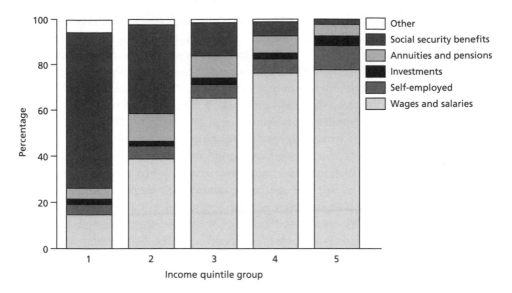

Source: ONS (2008a, p30)

Figure 3.2 *Sources of income, by gross income quintile, UK (2007)*

income of below £149 per week (£7750 per annum) and the household contained 1.2 people, on average. The income level is lower than that in Table 3.2 because of the effect of equivalizing income. The income range for the next quintile was £150 to £223 (i.e. up to an annual income of £11,600, with an average household size of 1.7 people).

By definition, receipt of a means-tested benefit means the household's income and assets have been assessed and are confirmed as below a specified amount (this amount varies with the different benefits). According to some government definitions, the household has been shown to be poor. The other main group of benefits are universal benefits, such as child benefit and the state pension, which everyone is entitled to (although the amount of the latter may depend on contributions). The importance of state benefits is clear. These benefits are both a lifeline and part of government policy to reduce income inequality:

> *Taxes and benefits therefore reduce income inequality. In 2006/07, before taxes and benefits, the top fifth of households had an average income ... around 15 times as great as ... the bottom fifth. After taking account of taxes and benefits, [this became] a ratio of four to one.* (Jones, 2008, p1)

For the 6.6 million individuals (not households) with an income below £10,000 in 2005/06 in the UK, the majority of people did not pay any income tax and for those who did, it was below 6 per cent of income (ONS, 2008b, p121). Therefore, few of the fuel poor pay income tax, although they contribute through other taxes such as value added tax (VAT). This is important when considering how to fund policies and whether the money should be found by the Exchequer, from tax, or whether it should come from the utilities. All the fuel poor have utility bills and thus would be contributing to the funds for these programmes, such as the Carbon Emissions Reduction Target (CERT), whereas a smaller proportion would be supporting the programmes through taxation. The least regressive route should be chosen.

The complexity of contributory and non-contributory benefits, universal and income-related benefits, and vulnerable and non-vulnerable households makes it tortuous to clarify the sources of incomes of the fuel poor. Suffice to say, the levels of state benefits are crucial in improving equality for the poorest people in the UK. Therefore, the level of benefits and their relationship with costs and fuel prices are important, as demonstrated by minimum income standards. The extent to which the government promotes redistributive policies, decisions on the amount paid in benefit, eligibility conditions and publicity about take-up are highly relevant for the fuel poor: 'While income poverty is a longstanding government concern, policy developments to reduce it are not currently closely associated with the issue of fuel poverty' (Palmer et al, 2008, p31).

State benefits

Means tested

The reason that the main means-tested (sometimes known as income-related) benefits are so important in the context of fuel poverty is that they are the 'passport' to the main energy-efficiency programmes (Warm Front and the Priority Group with the Energy Efficiency Commitment (EEC), now CERT). In a literal sense, to qualify for these improvements, households have to show their benefit books or paperwork to prove that they qualify. The receipt of these means-tested benefits is not otherwise linked to fuel poverty: there is no extra money provided with the weekly benefit for any group of the fuel poor. There were, prior to 1988, heating additions (Boardman, 1991, pp21, 29) for those in hard-to-heat homes; but these have long since ceased. Now, benefit levels are standard and no part of any benefit is related to the actual or potential energy costs, or to the condition of the home in terms of its energy efficiency.

The main means-tested benefits are, by value, income support; housing benefit; council tax benefit; and pension credit. The qualifying conditions vary between the different benefits so that the cut-off for one (e.g. pension credit) may be much more generous than for another (e.g. income support). The recipients of means-tested benefits are not all equally poor. A cut-off point of about £15,000 of capital (apart from the home) is usually taken for fuel poverty statistics (ONS, 2008b, p140).

Benefits that are not means tested

The two main universal benefits are child benefit and the pension – these are given to a household on the basis of the age of one of the occupants, independently of the household's income. For pensioners, the qualifying age is 60 for women and 65 for men (6.5 million households in England in 2006 – 31 per cent of all households). There were 7.5 million families receiving child benefit (for children under 16) at the end of August 2007 (HMRC, 2008, p1). Income is also ignored if people are disabled (and receive the DLA) or long-term sick (and receive incapacity benefit).

Levels of benefit take-up

Means-tested benefits have to be claimed; they are not given as of right. This means that not everyone claims. Apart from losing vital income, the non-claimant is also not eligible for Warm Front or EEC/CERT Priority Group programmes as they do not have the necessary passport. The Department for Work and Pensions (DWP) estimates for 2006/07 the take-up of the five main income-related benefits in Great Britain. Taking all of these together, there was between £6180 million and £9990 million left unclaimed; this compared to £34,630 million that was claimed through these five benefits and represents take-up of between 78 and 85 per cent of expenditure (Table 3.3).

In addition to the £6 to £10 billion unclaimed income-related benefits, Her Majesty's Revenue and Customs figures revealed that around £5 billion of working tax credit and child tax credit goes unclaimed annually: there is only a 21 per cent take-up with some types of working tax credits (Evans, pers comm). This makes a total of up to £15 billion a year that those in greatest need of support are not receiving (CPAG, 2006).

Of the 6.5 million households in receipt of means-tested benefits, tax credits or DLA in England in 2006, 1.4 million (22 per cent) were in fuel poverty (BERR, 2008, Table 26). As shown in Table 2.9, 58 per cent of the fuel

Table 3.3 *Estimates of some unclaimed benefits, Great Britain (2006/07)*

Benefit	Amount unclaimed (millions)	Number of people not claiming (millions)	Take-up, by value of benefits	Recipients (millions of people)	Payments made per annum (millions)
Income support (non-pensioners)	£530–£1300	0.24–0.5	87–95%	2.09	£9060
Housing benefit	£1250–£2280	0.57–0.95	86–92%	3.96	£13,740
Council tax benefit	£1480–2060	2.25–2.99	65–72%	5.05	£3740
Pension credit	£1960–2810	1.26–1.82	69–76%	2.62	£6370
Jobseekers' allowance	£1040–1700	0.42–0.64	52–64%	0.62	£1840
Total	£6180–£9990		78–85%		£34,630

Note: Does not include non-take-up of tax credits; numbers of people cannot be summed as there would be some double-counting (these are people, not households).
Source: DWP (2008)

poor are in receipt of a means-tested benefit, tax credit or DLA. These are, therefore, both good and bad ways of targeting the fuel poor. If all the £15 billion unclaimed benefits were taken up, roughly £3.3 billion might go to fuel-poor households. It is not possible to identify how much of this would go to brand new claimants or how much would top up the income of existing claimants. However, increasing take-up would seem to be an excellent route for reducing fuel poverty.

In order to help people get their entitlement, become eligible for free energy-efficiency improvements and, through both routes, reduce fuel poverty, there is growing emphasis on offering a benefit entitlement check (BEC), particularly through the energy-efficiency programmes, such as Warm Front and Warm Zones. Not every household will participate – some people still prefer to keep their finances private. And of those who do go through the process, some are found not to qualify for any additional payments as the Minister Joan Ruddock stated:

> *Since April 2008, over 65,000 benefit entitlement checks have been completed. A new or additional benefit eligibility has been identified in 45 per cent of cases, which has resulted in an average weekly increase in household income of £31 per applicant, or £1600 per year.* (Hansard, 2009)

For these 30,000 households, £1600 is a substantial increase in income. However, this is a slow rate of progress in comparison with at the least 3 million households that could be claiming. It is important that the BEC process takes the householder right through to claiming the additional money and does not leave them knowing that they have an entitlement, but not helping with the form filling. Some of these forms are easily 16 pages long, so it is a daunting process, particularly if the householder has limited literacy, English or self-confidence. It would, therefore, have been more comforting if Joan Ruddock had used 'obtained' rather than 'identified' in her statement.

Poverty is decreased when eligible households claim their benefit entitlement, and a BEC is an appropriate and quick way to get additional income to people. There has been a proactive campaign from the Social Security Agency in Northern Ireland to ensure that people claim the benefits to which they are entitled. The first round found that confirming their eligibility for people was not sufficient (only 6 per cent actually got extra money); so in future there will be more attention given to helping people complete the necessary paperwork and ensuring that the benefit is received (McMullan, pers comm). It is not clear what proportion of the 42 per cent of the English fuel poor, who are not able to receive free energy-efficiency improvements, could be brought into the fold through a BEC. According to the Fuel Poverty Advisory Group (FPAG), 'everything possible' should be done to maximize benefit take-up (FPAG, 2008, p31).

Some of those who might be most affected are the 'I'm not complaining' group of households – people who do not push themselves forward and probably equate claiming benefits with accepting charity. A sympathetic interviewer could persuade them, through a BEC, to claim and get enrolled in at least part of the system.

Benefit rates over time

For those who are in receipt of a means-tested benefit, it is important that it keeps pace with the cost of living, particularly as, for many households, benefits represent the bulk of their income. All benefits, whether means tested or universal, are increased annually, in April, according to certain rules. Most increases are based on the Retail Price Index (RPI) for the 12 months up to the previous September. This means that all price changes take some time to feed through into the new benefit levels. The price rises over October 2007 to September 2008 were not fed through into increased benefits until April 2009 onwards. Thus, for up to 18 months, claimants have had to bear the cost of additional fuel price rises, with no assistance from the basic benefits.

The RPI is the basis for benefit increases; but this underestimates the importance of what has been happening to fuel price rises for the fuel poor. The RPI component for fuel and light is weighted according to average household expenditure – equivalent to 3.8 per cent of weekly expenditure in 2007 (Table 3.1), as that is the proportion of the average budget that is spent on fuel. This considerably underestimates the importance of fuel costs in the budget of low-income households, where it is typically about twice the level of the average. Thus, a benefit increase includes a delayed and a reduced effect of fuel price increases as they have actually affected the recipient. This causes particular hardship at a time of rapidly rising fuel prices, as since 2004 (Chapter 4).

It is commonly thought that the 'state benefits are protected in real terms' (Reeves, 2009). This is, unfortunately, not true. Between 2000 and 2007, the RPI increased by 22 to 29 per cent (depending on which month of the year you take), whereas the main state benefits went up by 13 to 29 per cent (based on ONS, 2008b, Table 10.4). The pension, the biggest benefit in terms of recipients and cost, went up by 29 per cent from 2000 to 2007, whereas child benefit, incapacity benefit and disability allowance went up 21 per cent and jobseekers' allowance and income support by 13 per cent. For many claimants, their benefits are not keeping pace with inflation, let alone fuel prices. The government is making fuel poverty worse through inadequate welfare policy.

Housing benefit provides support for householders with their rent. It is the largest of the five main income-related benefits in terms of the money paid out. It has been increasing both in the numbers of recipients and the average payment and, therefore, the cost to the Treasury (Whitehead, 2008, p77). Housing benefit is a tapered allowance: reducing as household income increases. This is a sensible precedent where large sums of money are involved, as with rent or energy-efficiency improvements. For those tenants receiving housing benefit, their average rent was £74 per week and they paid £11 per week, with housing benefit paying the remaining £63 (DCLG, 2009, p17). The other housing-related benefit is council tax benefit, averaging £14 per week. These are households whose weekly expenditure is only just over £200 (Table 3.1), so that the £77 is a large extra proportion. It is becoming clear why the definition of housing costs affects large numbers of households.

There is one final aspect of being a claimant to examine – the extent to which people move in and out of poverty and, thus, the extent to which the numbers to be treated should include many of the nearly poor. In 2005, over 40 per cent of the people in the lowest quintile had been in the lowest quintile in 1999, and over two-thirds stayed within the lowest two quintiles over the period: for many people, poverty is an enduring situation (DWP, 2007, p28).

Specifically for the fuel poor, there was a range between the 75 per cent of pensioner households who remained in fuel poverty over the five years of 1991 to 1996, the most persistent group, and 36 per cent of couples with children, the group with the greatest rate of change, sometimes called churn (Sefton, 2004, p442). Thus, there is annual movement, with some households going in and out of poverty and/or fuel poverty, quite frequently; but for many it is a lifetime sentence.

The amount of any individual benefit is the same throughout the UK. In Northern Ireland, benefits are more important as incomes are lower: average earnings are 15 per cent lower and fuel poverty is growing fastest among working households.

Total cost to the Exchequer

The total cost to the Treasury of these various social security payments (means tested, universal, etc.) is over 11 per cent of the UK's gross domestic product (GDP): a total £150 billion in 2006/07. The main items of expenditure are (ONS, 2008b, p161):

- just over one third goes in pensions (£54 billion);
- income support (£16 billion);
- income tax credits and relief (£14 billion);
- child benefit (£10 billion);
- disability benefits (£9 billion);
- incapacity benefit (£7 billion).

This £150 billion does not include housing benefit (£14 billion; Table 3.3) and council tax benefit (nearly £4 billion), or winter fuel payments (nearly £3 billion, Table 3.4), so the total cost in 2006/07 is likely to be around £170 billion. If there is a successful benefits entitlement campaign, this should increase further by some proportion of the £15 billion thought to be unclaimed.

The DWP is the funding department for many of these social security payments, but it does not appear to have any publications or statements on its website in relation to fuel poverty. The only mention is in relation to its obligations (Public Service Agreement (PSA) 9) on child poverty. This is somewhat curious as up to 10 per cent of this money (£17 billion) is likely to be going on the fuel bills of the fuel poor or other low-income households. Because the DWP does not have any policies on fuel poverty and because none of the benefit payments are linked to fuel costs or the energy efficiency of the home, then the DWP has no particular interest in reducing fuel poverty: it would not recoup any expenditure or be able to cut it back when a household has an energy-efficient home. As there is no support for the costs of fuel, the fuel poor are left to cope with rapidly rising prices, without much government assistance. The only group that is helped are pensioners through the winter fuel payment.

Fuel poor who are non-claimants

As stated, 42 per cent of the fuel poor do not receive a means-tested benefit, DLA or tax credit in England in 2006 (BERR, 2008, Table 26). About half (0.5 million) of these households are non-vulnerable, of working age and perhaps in work (Table 2.2 in Chapter 2). In Northern Ireland, 27 per cent of the fuel poor are in work. The less hours a week someone works, the greater the risk of fuel poverty (Palmer et al, 2008, p23). For those with work, the minimum wage is vital – and cheap for government; but it has only increased recently by 4 pence an hour to £5.77 and has been falling below inflation for two years. 'Inequality will grow unless the minimum wage rises a bit above inflation every year – yes, even in the hard years' (Toynbee, 2009).

It is not clear how many of the fuel-poor non-claimants would be eligible for benefits and how many are in a policy void. But, in total, it is quite a substantial number of households: 1 million in England in 2006.

Pensioners

Pensioners are one of the largest groups of fuel poor – about half of all fuel-poor households in England in 2006, using a full-income definition (Table 2.9 in Chapter 2). If housing costs are deducted, the pensioner proportion of the fuel poor declines as more of them are owner occupiers than renting.

Many pensioners do have extremely low incomes: 1.2 million pensioners (in an unknown number of households) have no income other than the state retirement pension and state benefits. The basic state pension for a single person in January 2009 was £105 per week (£5460 per annum) and £94 per week (£4888 per annum) per person in a married couple. As a result, about 50 per cent of single pensioners live off less than £6000 per annum and should have annual fuel bills below £600.

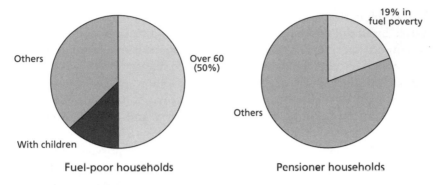

Source: adapted from BERR (2008, Table 15)

Figure 3.3 *Targeting fuel-poor pensioners, England (2006)*

Poverty does increase with age, particularly once retired. Because of this, the government extended the CERT Priority Group to include all those over 70, regardless of income, as the minister explained:

> *Among householders aged 70 or more who do not claim benefit, the average fuel poverty level is around 50 per cent higher than in the overall population. That is why we have expanded the priority group to include not just low-income customers, but all elderly customers aged 70 or over.* (Hansard, 2009)

The situation with regard to pensioners illustrates the fuel poverty targeting problem well: pensioners are the biggest group of the fuel poor, representing about half of all fuel-poor households in England in 2006 (Figure 3.3) and a similar proportion in Northern Ireland. However, these 50 per cent represent only 19 per cent of all pensioner households. Thus, a policy targeted at pensioners would appear to be a sound approach from a fuel poverty perspective, but not from a general targeting and cost-effectiveness viewpoint. This is one of the problems with winter fuel payments.

The proportion of pensioners in the population and in fuel poverty is similar in Scotland.

Government income grants

There are two government grants provided during the winter: the winter fuel payment for pensioners and cold weather payments. Both payments are made automatically to eligible households – they do not have to be claimed.

Cold weather payments

These are provided retrospectively when the weather has been below freezing for a specific geographical area for seven consecutive days or more. A household is eligible if it is in receipt of an income-related (as opposed to housing-related) benefit, and with certain other conditions, such as having a child under five or a disabled child. The qualifying benefits are:

- income support;
- employment and support allowance;
- income-based jobseekers' allowance;
- pension credit.

This is seen as complementary to the winter fuel payment, so few pensioners qualify. The amount used to be £8.50 per qualifying week; but the government increased it to £25 per week in the prime minister's 11 September 2008 statement. This was fortunate for the fuel poor as there were some severely cold periods during the winter of 2008/09. As a result, a total of £210 million was distributed in 8.4 million payments across Great Britain (DECC, 2009, p38).

Winter fuel payments

The winter fuel payment is the main fuel poverty policy through which the government increases income. It is not related to weather conditions. From 1999/2000, the payments were for all aged 60 and over, and around 8 million households benefited from the beginning (DTI, 2001, p117). The payment is an income supplement given each December to all pensioners as a single payment of £100, £200, £300 or £400 (depending on the year and age of recipient). It is not taxed. It is an indiscriminate payment – it goes to all pensioners, no matter what their income, as the minister has stated:

> ... this is a measure that was decided upon as a means of giving confidence to elderly people ... so ... a very large swathe of the population ... have a bit of extra money and, therefore, they can keep the temperature up or increase it if they need to ... it is based on a concept which is somewhat different from simply tackling fuel poverty. (HC 37, 2009, Ev 83, Q380, 383)

There are as many pensioner households in receipt of winter fuel payments in the top income decile as in bottom decile and 100,000 households with total annual income above £100,000 (HC 1099, 2008, pp53, 57–8).

The cost of winter fuel payments has been substantial from the beginning and rose to at least £2.75 billion in 2008, perhaps more as a result of the prime minister's announcement on 11 September 2008 (Table 3.4). Since 2000 it has involved a total expenditure of over £18 billion. The increasing cost is mainly a result of more generous payments, rather than additional pensioners.

The government likes the policy as it is relatively cheap to administer – pensioner households are known and are just given the extra money. However,

Table 3.4 *Winter fuel payments, UK (2000–2008)*

Year	Amount (£ millions)
2000	1800
2001	1731
2002	1755
2003	1966
2004	2004
2005	2050
2006	2050
2007	2050
2008	2750
Total	18,156

Source: Campbell, pers comm; McMullan, pers comm

it is poorly targeted. Only about 19 per cent of the money went to fuel-poor pensioners in 2006 (Figure 3.3) (i.e. £380 million out of £2 billion). Yet the government still insists on including all of the winter fuel payment in the statistics for expenditure on fuel poverty. This was effectively cheating the really fuel poor out of an expenditure of £1.62 billion in 2006 or £2.2 billion in 2008, if the targeting stayed the same.

As the fuel poor only spend 10 per cent of their income on fuel (by definition), they will only use £10 out of every £100 given as winter fuel payments on their fuel bills. Thus, 1.9 per cent of the total of £18 billion has actually been spent on the fuel bills of the fuel poor in England (19 per cent of households spent 10 per cent of it on fuel) or £345 million. Much better targeting of this money is an essential priority. Winter fuel payments are a policy that requires recurring expenditure every year and is not a long-term solution to the problem; most of it is given to people who are not, and are unlikely ever to be, in fuel poverty. The winter fuel payment is effectively a pension supplement for all pensioners every winter and should be renamed 'winter payments' in recognition of this (Fuel Poverty Charter, 2008). This policy is the best example of the problems of the vulnerable category: it is just too wide, as it is unrelated to both income and the energy-efficiency of the home.

Another of the major criticisms of the winter fuel payment is that it should include the non-pensioner fuel poor (Scottish Fuel Poverty Forum, 2008, p10). If the WFP was also paid to the households who are eligible for cold weather payments, this would extend the cost by about £320 million (Hansard, 2008).

Access to capital

Almost by definition, many of the fuel poor, and certainly those on income-related benefits, have no or little capital; they have virtually no savings. For pensioners, what savings they have are often thought of as a funeral fund. And capital is essential for expenditure on energy-efficiency improvements. This is why they cannot pay for their own improvements or contribute even relatively small amounts of money as 'top up' for existing grants. If required to find capital, they are quite likely to refuse the improvement. It is also why they buy second-hand inefficient appliances, rather than new efficient ones.

The fuel poor are a large proportion of the 53 per cent of people who do not save regularly and the 21 per cent of those who do not save at all (NS&I, 2008). Worse still, these households are unlikely to have a bank account or a building society account. This makes it difficult for them to obtain a conventional loan for capital improvements. The alternative, of a loan shark, is not recommended:

> *According to the government there were 3 million adults (13 per cent of the adult population) without a bank account, and this rises to 35 per cent in deprived areas. It had increased by 100,000 on the previous year, and many predict this rise to continue. The picture is very different in Western Europe, where banking exclusion averages between 1 and 5 per cent.* (Rahman, 2009)

Many of those without a bank account do have a Post Office card account (Poca):

> *Nationally, 5 million people have a Poca and the 13,000 post office branches (compared to 10,000 bank and building society branches) across the UK make them an accessible, comforting choice for many.* (Rahman, 2009)

There are proposals to make the Post Office into a bank, which would assist low-income households without capital to save and obtain small loans and to access direct debit energy deals.

At the other end of the scale of the fuel poor are some households with either high incomes or who have some capital. The amount of capital that an individual or a household can have, before being ineligible for a benefit, varies considerably. The cut-off point for pension credit is savings up to £16,000 and housing benefit tapers down to zero for households with £20,000 of savings.

Eligibility for energy-efficiency grants

The main energy-efficiency programmes and their effectiveness are described in Chapter 6. The two main programmes for the fuel poor are Warm Front and the EEC. Since April 2008, the latter has become CERT and 40 per cent of the benefit has to be received by households in the Priority Group – it was 50 per cent under EEC. The importance of these two programmes is that the grants are intended to be 100 per cent of the costs for eligible households. The rest of CERT does not normally cover the whole cost and is, therefore, not considered a fuel poverty programme here. Eligibility for Warm Front and the Priority Group is complex, as it combines tenure and receipt of various benefits to prove eligibility:

First, not all the qualifying benefits are means tested; around a third of grant recipients qualify because they are in receipt of tax credits or a non-means-tested benefit and may be relatively well off – for instance, in the top half of the income distribution. Second, some low-income households are receiving one of the means-tested benefits, but do not qualify for Warm Front because they are not in one of the 'vulnerable' categories, including working age adults without dependent children. Third, the receipt of a means-tested benefit is an imperfect proxy for low household income. Some low-income households are entitled to a means-tested benefit, but are not claiming it, while other low-income households may be (just) above the income threshold or may fail the assets test (savings over £8000 usually mean that you cannot receive income support). (Sefton, 2004, p15)

Those eligible for the EEC Priority Group were the largest fuel poverty category in England in 2006, as it covers all tenures and any household on a means-tested benefit and affects 1.4 million households: 58 per cent of the fuel poor (Table 3.5). Warm Front covers a subset of these same households because it is only for private households, who have to be both vulnerable and on a means-tested benefit (0.847 million households – 35 per cent of the fuel poor). Therefore, of the fuel-poor households:

- 35 per cent were eligible for both Warm Front and the EEC Priority Group.
- 58 per cent were eligible for the EEC Priority Group.
- 42 per cent were not eligible for either of these free energy-efficiency programmes.

This demonstrates one of the major problems with the present energy-efficiency programmes for the fuel poor: there are a large number of households without access to either programme and a nearly equivalent number who are eligible for both. The system has not been well designed to be coherent and inclusive. The cause is that both the two main grant schemes are targeted at those on a means-tested benefit, which does not match well onto the definition of fuel poverty. There is a mismatch between the definition of fuel poverty and programme design.

The 1.1 million fuel-poor households who are not on means-tested benefits, DLA or tax credits are not eligible for either programme though they may be entitled to benefits and just not claiming. About half of them are vulnerable and half are not. The non-vulnerable fuel poor are the 'healthy adults', such as people below 60, with no children.

Table 3.5 *Eligibility for main fuel poverty energy-efficiency grants, England (2006)*

Eligible for this programme	In receipt of a means-tested benefit, DLA or tax credits	Have to be in vulnerable category for eligibility	All tenures	In fuel poverty (million households)
Warm Front	Yes	Yes	No, private sector only	(0.847 also eligible for EEC PG)
EEC PG*	Yes	No	Yes	1.413
Neither programme	No	Yes	Yes	0.534
Neither programme	No	No	Yes	0.485
Total				2.432

Note: * EEC PG = Energy Efficiency Commitment Priority Group.
Source: adapted from BERR (2008, Tables 23, 28, 29)

Targeting

The problem of targeting is endemic to fuel poverty, though the winter fuel payment is one of the worst examples. As will be clear from the above, defining the fuel poor is difficult. Being able to identify a fuel-poor household, particularly on the doorstep (when offering practical measures), poses additional problems – hence the reliance on the passport benefits, where receipt can literally be proved. The problems of poor targeting have been known for several years and many were clearly identified by the National Audit Office (NAO, 2003) in relation to the delivery of Warm Front grants. These include the recipients who were not in fuel poverty to start with, as well as those for whom the interventions they needed were not available. The general message is still correct: identifying the fuel poor is a complex process, as their needs are variable, and the four UK governments are not very good at identifying them. Due to poor targeting, money (ostensibly for the fuel poor) is being spent on the non-fuel poor, mostly through winter fuel payments (Table 3.6). There are similar problems with the targeting of the free energy-efficiency programmes. As a result, in 2006, under one quarter of the government's fuel poverty expenditure actually went to fuel-poor households.

When fuel poverty is rising and millions more households are suffering considerable hardship, this misalignment of policy, funds and need borders on negligence: £2210 million went to non-fuel poor households in error, as a result of poor definition, not to fulfil a policy. And this is a situation that has been identifiable for several years, representing UK£ billions of wasted money. The omission of any criterion based on the calibre of the home is one of the primary reasons.

This is not just an English problem. The devolved administrations are not doing much better. In Northern Ireland, 31 per cent of homes helped by the Fuel Poverty Strategy were unlikely to have been fuel poor in the first place, according to the Northern Ireland Audit Office review in 2008. Only 10 per cent of Northern Ireland's fuel poverty budget has gone into homes containing children (Liddell, pers comm). The majority of the expenditure is through

Table 3.6 *Fuel poverty expenditure and the fuel poor, England (2006)*

	Percentage going to non-fuel poor	Percentage for which fuel poor are eligible*	Annual expenditure (millions)	Maximum expenditure on fuel poor (millions)
Warm Front, Warm Deal, HEES, Warm Homes (UK)	75%	25%	£477	£119
EEC PG**	78%	22%	£506	£111
Winter fuel payment (GB)	81%	19%	£2750	£523
Total	80%	20%	£3733	£753

Note: * The number receiving, as opposed to being eligible for, is not known. This is, therefore, a maximum figure.
** EEC PG = Energy Efficiency Commitment Priority Group (now CERT), provides free energy-efficiency measures.
Source: BERR (2008a, Tables 15, 28, 29) for the first two columns; Tables 3.4 and 6.13 for remainder

income support and the winter fuel payments. In Wales, only 54 per cent of fuel-poor households are eligible for the Home Energy Efficiency Scheme (HEES) and of the households helped, during March 2001 to January 2004, only 29 per cent were in fuel poverty. However, half of these were removed from fuel poverty by HEES (NEA, 2008, p19), which is undoubtedly a higher proportion than is achieved with Warm Front in England, partly because the maximum grant was higher in Wales (£3600 instead of £2700).

Future policy

Better targeting is promised as a result of data sharing between the DWP and the utilities. The 2008 Pensions Act now contains provisions to enable government to share data on pension credit recipients (i.e. low-income pensioners) with energy suppliers. It is expected that this can take place from winter 2009/10 onwards (Ofgem, 2008, p28). It is to be hoped that it will be done through a neutral third party, as otherwise the energy companies might introduce discriminatory policies, to the detriment of the low-income pensioners, as they have done in other circumstances (Chapter 4).

The utilities are probably going to offer benefit entitlement checks with CERT for Priority Group customers, in future. Again, this is both helpful and risky, as it will enable the company to have considerable information about its customers, which it must not use to their detriment.

A beneficial development is that the government is committed to raising the state pension in line with average earnings from 2012 – the link was removed in 1980. The Trades Union Congress (TUC) is asking for the link to be restored sooner (Haurant and Dunn, 2009). Reinstating this link with average earnings would mean that pensions increase faster than occurs with the present link to RPI, although, paradoxically, benefits increased by 5 per cent in April 2009 because of the time lag in the system and the higher rate of inflation in September 2008 – an unusual bonus. If the link to average earnings is brought forward, it might be an appropriate time to rethink the winter fuel payment and transfer it to a pension policy. It is not, in reality, a fuel poverty policy.

There has been no evident debate about a new strategy that would link expenditure on incomes paid by the DWP and the level of energy-efficiency improvements undertaken in the Department of Energy and Climate Change (DECC). There is no way, therefore, that larger expenditure by the latter could go towards reducing the commitments of the former. That would be really joined-up government; but it would require several radical new policy approaches and an income supplement linked to the energy rating of the home.

There is ambiguity about the extent to which the Labour government wishes to institute redistributive policies. There has been a curious dichotomy between the concerned and often-stated policy to reduce child poverty by half by 2010 and the empty rhetoric in relation to the 2010 target to eliminate fuel poverty for the vulnerable. What is evident, in relation to the child poverty reduction, is that it is extremely difficult to bring about large social changes, even when the government is really trying.

Conclusions

The mismatch between poverty and fuel poverty is duplicated in the misalignment of fuel poverty and receipt of the qualifying benefits (means tested, DLA and tax credits): only 58 per cent of the fuel poor receive these benefits and only 22 per cent of these benefit-recipients are fuel poor. Similarly, the 50 per cent of the fuel-poor households who are pensioners are only 19 per cent of all pensioner households. In every category examined, the fuel poor are a minority. This demonstrates the problems of using social characteristics or income levels as the main indicators of fuel poverty.

It is theoretically possible to eradicate fuel poverty by raising incomes sufficiently so that no household would have to spend more than 10 per cent of its income on fuel, no matter how energy inefficient the home. This would require a strong political emphasis on redistributive policies. For instance, if the 5 million households in fuel poverty in the UK in 2008 were to be able to spend an extra £4.50 per week on fuel, this would bring them up to the level of average household expenditure (Table 3.1). They might still be cold. But to spend £4.50 a week on fuel would require the household to have £45 per week extra in total, as only 10 per cent goes on fuel. An extra £45 per week, for 5 million households is £11.7 billion per annum, every year, over four times the current expenditure on income support (i.e. winter fuel payment) shown in Table 3.6. The flaw in this debate is that the 5 million cannot be identified, so bringing households out of fuel poverty through extra incomes alone seems an unlikely and expensive scenario.

There are several improvements to the present system of paying benefits that could help the fuel poor; but the effect cannot be estimated. For the 20 per cent of households on the lowest incomes, social security benefits provide about three-quarters of their income, so the role of the state is crucial in determining their standard of living. These improvements would include:

- Redistributive policies are stated as important to the government, but they are not being achieved in practice: for the poorest 10 per cent of households, poverty is increasing in absolute terms. This is almost exclusively because of the failure of means-tested benefits to match, let alone improve on, changes in average incomes.
- Ensure that fuel price increases are reflected in higher benefit levels more quickly than at present, when there can be a delay of 18 months. The amount of the increase is based on the lower proportion spent by an average household, thus further penalizing the fuel poor who pay twice as much as a proportion of income.
- Have a national campaign to increase benefit take-up rates and get some of the unclaimed £15 billion into the pockets of the poor and the fuel poor. Receipt of these benefits provides a double bonus for the fuel poor, as it both increases their income and proves eligibility for energy-efficiency programmes.
- Introduce a new system of benefits that recognizes the energy inefficiency of the home in order to compensate those in the properties that are phenomenally expensive to heat: the energy-inefficiency supplement. If an appropriate housing-related definition could be found, this could be extended to include the 1.1 million households who are in fuel poverty but not on a means-tested benefit.
- Either redesign the whole system of winter fuel payments, so that they are targeted effectively on the fuel poor, whatever their age (i.e. beyond pensioners), or scrap it and use the money for more targeted help – for instance, the proposed energy-inefficiency supplement.

All of these could have the effect of increasing the incomes of the fuel poor and, therefore, reducing the impact of fuel poverty. However, 42 per cent of the fuel poor do not receive any means-tested benefit, tax credit or DLA. Finding these people is nearly impossible, so they are not being helped through the major policies (unless they happen to be a pensioner and get the winter fuel payment). Too many of the fuel poor are excluded from policy.

In addition, the present misalignment of fuel poverty policy and definitions is leading to the majority of fuel poverty policy expenditure being misdirected. Too much fuel poverty money (75 per cent) is being spent on the non-fuel poor.

The present methods of targeting the fuel poor, mainly through the poorest households, are not working well. In this context, the debate about definitions is somewhat peripheral: radical changes in eligibility and definition are needed, rather than tinkering.

The government has two poverty targets, both of which are linked to eradication by specified dates: child poverty (2020) and fuel poverty (2016). An informed debate about appropriate synergies between these two policies, despite their different definitions, would be helpful.

References

BERR (Department for Business, Enterprise and Regulatory Reform) (2008) *Fuel Poverty Statistics, Detailed Tables 2006*, Annex to Fuel Poverty Strategy Report, 2008, URN 08/P33, BERR, www.berr.gov.uk/files/file48038.pdf

Boardman, B. (1991) *Fuel Poverty: From Cold Homes to Affordable Warmth*, Belhaven Press, London

Campbell, R., Head of Campaigns, Policy, Research and Information, National Energy Action, newcastle, pers comm

CCC (Committee on Climate Change) (2008) *Building a Low-Carbon Economy: The UK's Contribution to Tackling Climate Change*, First report, CCC, December, www.theccc.org.uk/pdf/TSO-ClimateChange.pdf

CPAG (2006) *£13 Billion of Means-tested Benefits Fails to Reach those in Poverty*, Press release, 26 October, 2006, Child Poverty Action Group, www.cpag.org.uk/press/261006.htm

DCLG (Department for Communities and Local Government (2009), *Survey of English Housing Preliminary Report 2007–08*, Housing Statistics Summary No 28, 2009, www.communities.gov.uk/documents/statistics/pdf/1133551.pdf

DECC (Department of Energy and Climate Change) (2009) *Annual Report and Resource Accounts 2008-09*, HC 452, July, www.decc.gov.uk/en/content/cms/publications/annual_reports/2009/2009.aspx

Defra (Department for Environment, Food and Rural Affairs) (2008) *The UK Fuel Poverty Strategy: 6th Annual Progress Report*, Defra, www.berr.gov.uk/files/file48036.pdf

DETR (Department of the Environment, Transport and the Regions) (2000) *English House Condition Survey 1996: Energy Report*, DETR, London

DTI (Department of Trade and Industry) (2001) *The UK Fuel Poverty Strategy*, DTI, London, November, www.berr.gov.uk/files/file16495.pdf

DWP (Department for Work and Pensions) (2007) *Low-income Dynamics 1991–2005 (Great Britain)*, http://research.dwp.gov.uk/asd/hbai/low_income/Low_income-dynamics_1991-2005.pdf, p.11

DWP (2008) *Income Related Benefits Estimates of Take-Up in 2006–07*, DWP, June, www.welfarerights.net/takeup.doc.pdf

Evans, M., Senior Research Fellow, Department of Social Policy and Social Work, University of Oxford, pers comm

FPAG (Fuel Poverty Advisory Group) (2008) *Sixth Annual Report – 2007*, London, April, www.berr.gov.uk/files/file45365.pdf

Fuel Poverty Charter (2008) Supported by a coalition of Age Concern; Association for the Conservation of Energy; Barnardo's; Centre for Sustainable Energy; Child Poverty Action Group; Disability Alliance; energywatch; Friends of the Earth; Help the Aged; National Energy Action; National Right To Fuel Campaign; WWF, www.foe.co.uk/resource/press_releases/Fuel_Poverty_Charter_08092008.html

Hansard (2008) HC Written Answers (Session 2007–2008), vol 474, col 186, 26 March

Hansard (2009) HC Deb (Session 2008–2009), vol 489, col 1202, 1204, 20 March

Haurand, S. and Dunn, S. (2009) 'Link pensions to pay again – TUC', *The Guardian*, 1 January

HBAI (2009) *Households Below Average Income 2007/8*, Department for Work and Pensions, www.dwp.gov.uk/asd/hbai/hbai2008/chapters.asp

HC 37 (2009) *Energy Efficiency and Fuel Poverty*, Third report of session 2008–9, Environment, Food and Rural Affairs Committee, Her Majesty's Stationery Office, London

HC 1099 (2008) *Energy Efficiency and Fuel Poverty*, Fifth Special Report of session 2007–8, Environment, Food and Rural Affairs Committee, Her Majesty's Stationery Office, London

Hills, J. (2009) 'In a fair state?', *The Guardian*, 25 February, www.guardian.co.uk/society/2009/feb/25/social-exclusion-policy/print

HMRC (Her Majesty's Revenue and Customs) (2008) *Child Benefit Quarterly Statistics, August 2007*, HMRC, February, www.hmrc.gov.uk/stats/child_benefit/aug-07.pdf

Isherwood, B. C. and Hancock, R. M. (1979) *Household Expenditure on Fuel: Distributional Aspects*, Economic Adviser's Office, DHSS, London

Jones, F. (2008) 'The effects of taxes and benefits on household income, 2006/07', *Economic & Labour Market Review*, Office for National Statistics, vol 2.7, July, pp37–A27, www.statistics.gov.uk/elmr/07_08/downloads/ELMR_Jul08_Jones.pdf

Liddell, C., Professor of Psychology, University of Ulster, Coleraine Campus, Northern Ireland, pers comm

McMullan, J., Chair, PAG, NI and CEO Bryson Charitable Group, pers comm

NAO (National Audit Office) (2003) *Warm Front: Helping To Combat Fuel Poverty*, NAO, HC 769, The Stationery Office, London, www.nao.org.uk/publications/nao_reports/02-03/0203769.pdf

NEA (National Energy Action) (2008) *The Wrong Direction: How UK Fuel Poverty Policy Lost Its Way – Sixth Year Report*, NEA, Newcastle, May

NS&I (National Savings and Investments) (2008) 'Brits maintain savings – but almost half are less likely to save in the coming months', press release, 12 December, www.nsandi.com/press-room/press-releases/pr2004404.jsp

Ofgem (Office of the Gas and Electricity Markets) (2008), *Sustainable Development Report*, Ofgem, www.ofgem.gov.uk/Sustainability/Documents1/SDR%202008%20-%20Master%20-%20FINAL.pdf

ONS (Office for National Statistics) (2008a) *Family Spending: A report on the 2007 Expenditure and Food Survey*, Rachel Skentelbery (ed), Palgrave Macmillan, ONS, www.statistics.gov.uk/downloads/theme_social/Family_Spending_2007/FamilySpending2008_web.pdf

ONS (2008b) *Annual Abstract of Statistics*, Ian Macrory (ed), Palgrave Macmillan, Office for National Statistics, www.statistics.gov.uk/downloads/theme_compendia/AA2008/AA2008.pdf

Palmer, G., MacInnes, T. and Kenway, P. (2008) *Cold and Poor: An Analysis of the Link between Fuel Poverty and Low Income*, New Policy Institute, London, www.npi.org.uk/reports/fuel%20poverty.pdf

Rahman, F. (2009) 'Banking at local post offices could widen inclusion', *The Guardian*, 22 April, p6

Reeves, R. (2009) In search of the truth about equality in Britain, *The Observer*, 5 April, p25

Scottish Fuel Poverty Forum (2008) *Towards 2016 – the Future of Fuel Poverty Policy in Scotland*, a report, www.scotland.gov.uk/Resource/Doc/240939/0066903.pdf

Sefton, T. (2004) *Aiming High: An Evaluation of the Potential Contribution of Warm Front towards Meeting the Government's Fuel Poverty Target in England*, Centre for Analysis of Social Exclusion Report 28, LSE, London, November

Toynbee, P. (2009) 'No ideas, no fight, no breath of life. But still – no regrets', *The Guardian*, 2 May

Whitehead, C. (2008) 'Housing' in S. Thomas (ed) *Poor Choices: The Limits of Competitive Markets in the Provision of Essential Services to Low-Income Consumers*, Energywatch, www.psiru.org/reports/PoorChoices.pdf

Wilkinson, R. and Pickett, K. (2009) *The Spirit Level: Why More Equal Societies Almost Always Do Better*, Allen Lane, London

4

Fuel Prices and Policy

The many and substantial increases in household energy prices that have occurred since 2003 have focused attention on the 'fuel' part of fuel poverty. As a result, it might appear that fuel poverty is caused by these rapid changes and that they provide the key to solving the problem of fuel poverty. While they are clearly important, the thesis in this book is that the primary cause is energy-inefficient homes. This still means that it is important to identify what it is about fuel price rises that causes such concern and hardship. It is also necessary to examine whether sufficient effort is made to ensure that the poorest households pay the lowest prices and how much fuel poverty has been caused by utility policies and how much the energy companies can be expected to reduce the problem.

The majority of energy used in British homes is either electricity or gas, and for both of these fuels in the UK the companies are privatized, their various processes commercially separate (unbundled), the markets liberalized and the regulator is primarily concerned with economic issues. For all of these reasons, there are limited opportunities for government to intervene and divert the market into helping the fuel poor – or even being fair to them. But it is important to establish how much different utility policies could reduce fuel poverty and whether current utility policies are creating fuel poverty.

The effect of world energy prices

The world price of oil directly affects the price of gas in the UK – there is commonly a contractual link between the two in the UK and the European Union (EU) (DTI, 2001, para 3.25, p17; Rutledge and Wright, 2008) – and the price of gas indirectly affects the price of electricity as it is one of the main fuels used for generating. Hence, as oil becomes a scarcer resource – the peak-oil situation – then the long-term expected trend is for residential gas and electricity prices to rise. Because of these linkages, this has been predictable for many years, though the speed and scale of change has probably been greater than anticipated. Although predictable, the UK government has not noticeably

Table 4.1 *Residential fuel and retail price indices, UK (1998–2008)*

Year	Fuel Price Index (FPI)	Annual change (%)	Retail Price Index (RPI)	Annual change (%)	Real fuel price increase (%)
1990	100		100		
1998	107.8		129.1		
1999	107.4	–0.3	131.2	+1.6	–2.0
2000	107.0	–0.3	135.0	+2.9	–3.2
2001	107.8	+1	137.4	+1.8	–1.0
2002	111.1	+3	139.7	+1.7	+1.4
2003	112.4	+2	143.8	+2.9	–1.7
2004	121.4	+7	148.0	+2.9	+4.9
2005	137.8	+14	152.2	+2.8	+10.4
2006	171.8	+25	157.1	+3.2	+20.8
2007	184.0	+7	163.8	+4.3	+2.7
2008	218.9	+19	170.3	+4.0	+14.4
2000:2008		**+105%**		**+26%**	**+62%**

Source: BERR (2009)

factored the issue into practical policies to protect the population, particularly the fuel poor.

For several years up to 2000, world energy prices as well as overcapacity in the UK gas and electricity markets (Rutledge and Wright, 2008, p6) lowered UK prices in real terms. Residential fuel prices can be tracked via the Fuel Price Index (FPI), an official government component of the Retail Price Index (RPI) (Table 4.1). Between 1990 and 2001, residential energy prices fell by nearly 30 per cent in real terms, as compared to the RPI (137.4–107.8). As a result, for the period of 1996 to 2003, 22 per cent of the reduction in fuel poverty was due to falling prices (DWP, 2007) and this might be an underestimate.

Subsequently, fuel prices have risen and at a faster rate than the RPI during every year since 2003. The size of the increases in 2005, 2006 and 2008 has been particularly severe. Overall, there has been an increase of 105 per cent in residential fuel prices since 2000. When set against a RPI increase of only 26 per cent, this represents a real fuel price increase (i.e. above the rate of inflation) of 62 per cent.

By February 2009, the FPI was at 244.1 and the RPI had fallen to 167.6, demonstrating that household energy prices were still rising in real terms. This means that, in real terms, residential fuel prices in the UK have effectively increased by 84 per cent between 2000 and February 2009 for the average household. For the fuel poor this will be close to doubling.

Generally, the price increases have occurred for all household fuels. The rise in gas prices has been greater than that for electricity (Table 4.2), although gas was cheaper to start with – and still is (Chapter 5).

In 2008, residential prices, including value added tax (VAT), rose in real terms by 28.3 per cent for electricity and 48.2 per cent for gas (DECC, 2009b, p10). These continuing and huge price increases, in just one year, cause great hardship for households on fixed incomes and with tight budgets, as demon-

Table 4.2 *Index of residential gas and electricity prices, UK (2000–2008)*

Year	Gas		Electricity	
	Price indices	*Total effect*	*Price indices*	*Total effect*
2000	104.5	100	105.7	100
2008	243.4	233	189.4	179

Source: BERR (2009)

strated in Northern Ireland, where people are beginning to cut peat to provide a free source of fuel (McMullan, pers comm).

UK price controls

When the cause of a fuel price rise is international energy costs, then the problem is, to an extent, out of the government's control. However, greater vigilance by the government and the Office of the Gas and Electricity Markets (Ofgem) could have been exercised to make sure that all the price increases passed on to customers were, in fact, justified. With reference to all customers, not just households:

> World forces have increased energy costs, but the cost increases do not explain all of the price increases in the UK... Specifically, between 2003 and 2006 expenditure by gas and electricity customers increased by £8.2 billion (or 60 per cent). Higher fuel costs only accounted for a little over half of this – £4.5 billion... Other cost increases explain £1 billion to £1.5 billion of the increase. It seems that there has been a significant increase in margins along the supply chain, especially in electricity, of over £2.5 billion, accounting for as much as 30 per cent of the price increases. (FPAG, 2008, p7)

The relationship between world prices and, therefore, wholesale prices is that for gas they 'only constitute around half of the final price of gas to domestic customers, so a wholesale price rise of, say, 20 per cent could only be used to try and justify a 10 per cent increase in retail prices' (Rutledge and Wright, 2008, p22). Much of the media coverage implies that there is a 1:1 relationship.

There is a complex web of factors involved in the analysis of company costs and profits. The different components (e.g. generation and supply) are separate companies, albeit within one overarching conglomerate (e.g. British Gas is part of Centrica). It is perfectly appropriate for these separate companies to trade with each other through bilateral contracts (without the need to participate in the quoted markets). The overarching company policy will dictate the relative profitability of the generator and the supplier. For instance, with Centrica in 2007, upstream profits on gas production were low, so 'these

Table 4.3 *Annual cost to individual customers of utility programmes (2008/09)*

	Renewables Obligation (RO) – UK	Carbon Emissions Reduction Target (CERT) – Great Britain	EU Emissions Trading Scheme (EU ETS) – UK	Total
Electricity customers	£11	£19*	£31	£61
Gas customers	NA	£19	NA	£19
Total				£80

Note: * The Energy Efficiency Levy in Northern Ireland is £5 per electricity customer, not included.
NA = not applicable
Source: HC 293 (2008, para 68); HC 37 (2009, Q360, Ev 81); Campbell (pers comm)

were exceeded by a 500 per cent increase in profits from domestic customers as falling wholesale prices were not passed on to consumers' (Rutledge and Wright, 2008, near Table 11).

The six major UK energy companies (supplying 99 per cent of residential gas and electricity) are still, *de facto*, vertically integrated and able to profit from this relationship, as confirmed by the House of Commons select committee:

> While the 'Big 6' claim to be losing money in their domestic supply businesses ... there is evidence that they are making much greater margins on electricity generation. (HC 293, 2008, para 23)

Another cause of price increases comes from programmes required by government, but funded by the utilities, largely through passing the price on to consumers (Table 4.3). The situation is particularly unfair with the European Union Emissions Trading Scheme (EU ETS) as the costs are being passed on to customers, despite the utilities obtaining all of the phase 1 and most of the phase 2 trading allocations for free. All of these are climate change policies.

The total cost per residential customer of £80 is paid by all households, including the fuel poor, as part of their bill. These sums are increasing, particularly because of the enlargement of energy-efficiency programmes, such as the Carbon Emissions Reduction Target (CERT). In September 2008, the prime minister required an additional £910 million of energy-efficiency measures to be funded by the utilities, but in relation to these costs was only able to say that he hoped the prices would not be passed on to consumers (Wintour, 2008). The government is imposing policies on the utilities in order to contain government expenditure. It has no ability to ensure that these costs will not be passed on, even to the poorest householders, so they are undoubtedly making fuel poverty worse. The fuel poor are already paying £400 million a year (£80 × 5 million households). As a minimum, the government and Ofgem should ensure that the benefits of CERT go disproportionately, if not exclusively, to the fuel poor to compensate.

Meanwhile, the government's own coffers are receiving more money from the VAT levied at 5 per cent on rising fuel prices. With the £8.2 billion quoted by the Fuel Poverty Advisory Group (FPAG), this represents additional income of £410 million annually for the 2003 to 2006 period. Another source of income for the government comes from the progressive auctioning of the EU ETS allowances: the first auction in November 2008 raised £54 million (ENDS, 2008, p15). There will now be four a year. The money is going into the Treasury and has not been identified for energy-efficiency or fuel poverty policies, as it could have been, particularly if it is seen as part of the alternative to a windfall tax.

Competition

The expectation is that the six major companies will compete with each other and that this provides sufficient constraint on prices. Ofgem decided that there was enough competition and relinquished its ability to control consumer prices in April 2002 so that the companies have been subsequently free to make their own judgements on what the market will bear. An immediate effect was as follows:

> In 2002, the profit margin on domestic energy sales was raised by Centrica from 0.4 per cent to 4.2 per cent and ... according to the company's preliminary 2007 results its profit margin on domestic energy supply has now risen to 8.8 per cent. (Rutledge and Wright, 2008, p22 and Figure 6)

The extent to which six companies do provide a sufficiently competitive market is a moot point, but one that is increasingly being questioned, particularly as the companies gain experience of each other's strategies:

> It is clear, though, that in a retail market dominated by six big players, it is easy for those players to make informed judgements about the behaviour of their competitors. This can distort competition, without any active collusion occurring. The regulator therefore needs to remain very watchful. (HC 293, 2008, para 34)

The net effect is that the utilities are making substantial, unwarranted profits for their shareholders, sometimes at the expense of the fuel poor. These excess profits have been derived from various strategies, including overcharging through price rises and the EU ETS. The recognition of this situation has led to a discussion about the opportunity for a windfall tax:

> We are disappointed by the superficiality of Ofgem's current analysis. We recommend that the government now conducts and

publishes a rigorous analysis, estimating the value of any windfall profits which companies have gained, and the use to which they have been put, or are planned to be put. (HC 293, 2008, para 18)

However, the government appears to have decided against a windfall tax 'at this moment' (HC 37, 2009, Ev 81, Q362).

Another indicator of the way in which the companies can manipulate the market relates to announcements of price changes. Price rises, even when large, are frequently made with very little notice – for instance EDF Energy and British Gas announced increases of up to 35 per cent in prices 'with immediate effect' (Brignall, 2008; Milner, 2008). The opposite may be happening with price cuts. There have been few price reductions, but in June 2007, Scottish Power and EDF announced cuts of up to 11 per cent to take effect in seven weeks' time (Brignall, 2007). The size of the cuts is also difficult to justify. In February 2009, when oil prices were about a third of the 2008 peak, British Gas announced a 10 per cent drop in its gas price. The electricity price was not reduced until three months later (Osborne, 2009).

There is sufficient evidence to demonstrate that the utilities are increasing their own profits at the expense of households and, in particular, the fuel poor: 'apart from the anti-competitive *structure* of the UK's domestic gas and electricity markets, there is also evidence of actual anti-competitive *behaviour*' (Rutledge and Wright, 2008, p26).

Predicting fuel price rises

It would be expected that there is recognition in fuel poverty policy of the disastrous effects that rapid fuel price rises can have on the fuel poor, particularly since 2003. In relation to fuel poverty policy, a humane approach would have been to have taken a precautionary perspective and assumed that prices could rise above expectations, thus protecting the fuel poor whatever happened. This does not appear to have happened.

The government has long recognized that 'international oil and gas markets … are extremely hard to predict' (DTI, 2001, p18), but appears to have erred on the cautious, minimalist side. For instance, in 2001, the government considered a 'reasonable range' of residential price movements from 1999 up to 2010 would be from +15 per cent to –10 per cent for gas and +5 per cent to –2 per cent for electricity, both in real terms (DTI, 2001, p19). It has subsequently become clear that those estimates were far too optimistic as energy prices have risen considerably more than the top of the 'reasonable range': as shown in Table 4.1, fuel prices had already risen by over 60 per cent by 2008, let alone 2010.

Between 2000 and late 2008, the government's own predictions about likely high oil prices in 2020 have increased from a US$24.4 per barrel to US$95 per barrel both in 2007 prices (Hansard, 2008). This fourfold real increase has not been matched by comparable growth in assistance for the fuel poor.

Although the increases have been greater than envisaged in 2001, they have not come as a sudden surprise. The reality of existing household fuel price rises, and likely further increases, has been a matter of concern since at least 2003 and it has been particularly noted in the annual reports from both FPAG and the government that:

- 'The potential impact of these price increases on progress towards meeting the targets set out in *The UK Fuel Poverty Strategy* means that efforts will have to be focused on finding the most sustainable or "future proof" ways of tackling fuel poverty' (Defra, 2005, p45).
- 'The current situation on energy prices means that our fuel poverty targets are being placed under serious pressure. We are acutely aware that the impact of price rises over the last two years on the number of households in fuel poverty has yet to be fully realized' (Defra, 2006, p4).

In the summer of 2008, world oil prices peaked at US$145, whereas by early 2009 they were down to US$35 per barrel. This extreme variability does make predictions about the levels of fuel prices, and subsequent extent of fuel poverty very difficult. However, the price of household energy has not reflected the reduction in oil prices and remains high and continuing to escalate. The government believes that retail costs peaked in December 2008, a few months after the peak in wholesale prices (Hansard, 2009). Time will tell.

There are several reasons, independently of and in addition to world oil prices, why UK residential fuel prices are expected to stay high or even rise in future. This is beyond the £80 already being paid out (Table 4.3):

- 'There is growing evidence that the supply companies are now anticipating a surge in wholesale electricity prices over the next five years as a result of an expected rapid decline in the capacity margin of UK electricity generation' (Rutledge and Wright, 2008, pp26–27).
- The development of carbon capture and storage at new coal-fired generating plants is expected to add 2–3p/kWh to electricity bills (CCC, 2008, p48).
- There will also be the £100 billion (1–2% of GDP) cost of new low-carbon supply (e.g. nuclear and renewable energy, as electricity decarbonisation is a major part of the Climate Change Committee (CCC) programme (CCC, 2008, pxv).
- 'In most scenarios examined ... between now and the middle of the next decade ... we would expect to see an increase in electricity prices' (DTI, 2007, p132).
- In relation to climate change targets, 'the cost to current and future consumers of delivering the target (in addition to the impact on prices caused by the third phase of the EU ETS) will be significant' (Ofgem, 2008b, p17).

- The CCC is recommending that most energy-efficiency improvements are funded through the next Supplier Obligation (SO), rather than by government (CCC, 2008, pp229–30 and Figure 6.5 (Chapter 6)). This could be a substantial amount of expenditure that is passed on to energy consumers, rather than income taxpayers. A highly regressive policy, unless there is a strong bias towards the fuel poor in the compensating expenditure.
- The prime minister announced in September 2008 a further £910 million expenditure by the utilities. This is partly for CERT and partly for the new Community Energy Saving Programme (CESP) to start in September 2009.
- Introducing a feed-in tariff will cause prices to go up, perhaps substantially (Mitchell, 2008, p179), although it is not clear if this displaces some of the renewable obligation costs to consumers.

Not all of these are inevitable:

> ... electricity prices are higher than they need to be because policy is confused and contradictory ... the core of the problem is the haphazardly extravagant way in which we procure and reward generation. (McIldoon, 2008, p3)

'Future proofing' the fuel poor must now mean that they are to be protected from ever increasing fuel price rises. There should be no policy built on the expectation of decreasing fuel prices.

Fuel pricing and the fuel poor

There are no surveys of fuel-poor households – all the numbers presented by the government about the size of the problem are produced by a model, developed and revised by the Building Research Establishment (BRE) (Chapter 2). The BRE model of fuel poverty uses data on regional fuel prices for the same year as the house condition survey. These are not the costs incurred by households and the regional values may not be indicative of the actual charges paid. So the fuel poverty model may underestimate the real costs to the fuel poor.

What is the evidence for how the fuel poor are faring within these average increases? Are they doing better or worse than the average householder? The government has given Ofgem a:

> ... specific statutory obligation in relation to vulnerable customers [to] ensure that more vulnerable customers can and do access the lower prices and better services and products available to them. (Ofgem, 2008b, p20)

This is an important obligation, although it only looks at *accessing* existing opportunities, rather than accepting that there might need to be an improved range of options. There is a similar subtext with the conclusions from the Fuel Poverty Summit held by Ofgem in spring 2008:

> ... *energy suppliers committed to improving the targeting of their social measures to fuel poor customers and keep consumer advice groups better informed of the wide range of help available to customers struggling to afford their energy bills.* (Ofgem, 2008b, p22)

The implication is that there is no need for new measures. All that is needed is better targeting and more information to advisers. This is disappointing as:

> *Energy purchases are some of the most difficult for households to carry out efficiently – in other words, at lowest cost. In part, this is due to the intrinsic properties of energy (e.g. it is impossible to store, has no substitutes, demand cannot be postponed). However, the difficulty is also now due to the fact that consumers must compete in the market to buy their energy needs.* (Thomas, 2008, p263)

The problems that the fuel poor are having with the energy market can be demonstrated. There are several circumstances which result in the fuel poor paying extra, or receiving inadequate assistance, some of which result from clear company policy. The following are examined in more detail:

- prepayment meters – an expensive choice;
- disadvantageous utility policies – profits before justice;
- not switching – penalizing loyalty;
- social tariffs – a limited option.

Prepayment meters: An expensive choice

There are three main methods of paying for fuel: through a bank direct debit, standard credit, when cash or cheque is used to pay the amount in the bill, and prepayment meters (PPMs). Online payment is becoming the fourth option. With a PPM a household can budget carefully since all usage has to be prepaid. None of it is obtained on credit.

The utilities in Great Britain have always argued that the costs of providing and servicing a prepayment meter are higher than those for other payment methods – estimated to be £18 per annum in 2000 (SSE, 2000, p10). There was some validity in this initially, when the new token PPM was first brought in. But the increase in the numbers in use should have resulted in some economies of scale. A total of 5.9 million PPMs are in use, but it is not known in how many households, as some people have both fuels on PPMs. As a minimum, it is assumed to be 4 million households (i.e. just more than those with electricity

Table 4.4 *Anual cost of using electricity through a prepayment meter (2000–2008)*

	England and Wales	Scotland	Northern Ireland
2000	£272	£280	£314
2004	£267	£298	£325
2008	£425	£437	£384

Note: Assuming consumption of 3300kWh per year and including standing charge and VAT.
Source: DECC (2009b, Table 2.2.2)

only). PPMs have both higher standing charges (for the use of the equipment) and unit rates (Defra, 2006, p26).

All three payment methods are cheaper in Northern Ireland in 2008 than in the other UK countries, although previously the reverse was true. In Northern Ireland, the cost of a PPM (known as a keypad, for electricity mainly) is 4.9 per cent cheaper than the standard credit and 2.5 per cent below the direct debit. There is a logic in this situation, as well as social justice, in that the users of a PPM are providing the utility with the money before the energy has been used and there is, therefore, no opportunity for additional debt. Partly as a result of severe fuel poverty and partly because of the relative drop in price, twice as many people have electric PPMs in Northern Ireland than in Great Britain (England, Wales and Scotland) (29 to 13 per cent; DECC 2009a, 2009b, Table 2.4.2). The relative cheapness of the Northern Ireland keypad is a demonstration of what can be achieved by a rigorous, innovative regulator, who chooses to protect the fuel poor. This control has had a dramatic effect on relative prices (Table 4.4) so that costs in England, Wales and Scotland are now substantially higher.

The true costs of a PPM are difficult to establish and can be subject to considerable debate. Ofgem has summarized the component costs for the four main payment methods, as provided by five of the main suppliers (Figure 4.1). These show that direct debit is the cheapest, though usually the cost of paying online is lowest. The allocation of costs between the different payment methods is curious. For instance, as Ofgem concedes, there should be no allocation of bad debts to PPMs: the one thing that is impossible to do with a PPM is to run up a debt. The debt can only be accrued under one of the other methods and then transferred to a PPM for repayment. Therefore, PPMs should be credited with debt recovery, not debt creation. The higher competition costs shown for PPMs than for either direct debit or standard credit indicate that PPM customers change more frequently, which is probably untrue. Again, it is debatable that this should be an allowable cost. What is clear is the substantial premium being paid by users with PPMs for both gas and electricity – £120 a year. Across all PPM owners this could be a total of over £500 million. The additional costs of a PPM in Great Britain are hard to justify, particularly in comparison with the lower cost of the Northern Ireland keypad.

This PPM premium has been known about for several years:

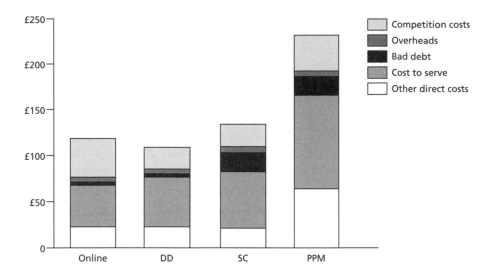

Notes: DD = direct debit; SC = standard credit; PPM = prepayment meter. Combines gas and electricity.
Source: Ofgem (2008a, p89)

Figure 4.1 *Suppliers' costs of residential payment methods, per customer, Great Britain (2005–2007)*

- In 2000, the PPM was already 5 to 7 per cent higher than standard credit (DTI, 2001, p130).
- In its first report, the FPAG recommended that the cost of a PPM should be reduced (FPAG, 2003, p3).
- In 2004 it was at a level of £63 if both fuels were obtained via a PPM instead of through direct debit (HC 878, 2004, p4).

The FPAG has been clear: 'customers with prepayment meters and those paying by cash/cheque are subsidizing those paying by direct debit and online' (FPAG, 2008, p9). Similarly, energywatch has stated: 'The government has not taken action to address the iniquitous tariffs paid by standard credit and prepayment customers' (HC 1099, 2008, p14). It has taken considerable public pressure and concern to get Ofgem to investigate the issue in 2008.

In March 2009, Ofgem decided 'to propose a prohibition of unjustified price differences'. This is despite the existing requirement in EU directives that any difference in terms and conditions for different payment methods should reflect the costs to the supplier of the different payment systems (Ofgem, 2009b). Again, it is difficult to know how much this Ofgem initiative will be beneficial as it is a 'proposal' and relates to 'unjustified' price differences. The latter will be highly subjective, as the figure demonstrates.

In practice, for the six main utilities in Great Britain, the average differential between PPM and direct debit charges, for both gas and electricity combined, has increased by more than 50 per cent between early 2005 and early 2008 (i.e. from £80 to £125) (Ofgem, 2008a, p85). The select committee believed this was slightly higher (£144) by mid 2008 and that an even greater profit was being made out of standard credit customers (HC 293, 2008, paras 84–85). As a result of public pressure, the government and Ofgem are now focusing on the disparity, so the differential started to reduce slightly from September 2008. This does not obscure the fact that growth in the differential, if not the differential itself, should not have occurred in the first place.

The relationship between the different suppliers is as important as the range within each supplier: the Scottish and Southern Electricity (SSE) direct debit tariff is below British Gas's social tariff. Switching is important; but comparisons are difficult and often temporary. An electricity PPM customer using 6600kWh and living in the northern region of England could be asked to pay £590 per annum by EDF Energy or £850 per annum by npower (Ofgem, 2007a, p28). It is not surprising that people find it difficult to get the cheapest tariff. The whole process is an absolute maze of shifting numbers.

For many households, the use of a PPM is a definite choice, even when they know that this is an expensive payment method. Other households are given a PPM as an alternative to disconnection, when in debt. The problems of living within a tight budget mean that the financial control that comes with a PPM is wanted because it prevents (further) debt. The existing arrangements with ordinary meters mean that household budgeting is difficult and requires great restraint. It thus seems particularly unjust to penalize the careful poor for trying to avoid debt by making the cost of the PPM both high and increasingly so.

Ownership of a PPM is not synonymous with being fuel poor (Figure 4.2). This figure demonstrate the dilemma of fuel poverty again: whichever category is examined, the fuel poor are often a relatively small proportion. Looking at the areas of overlap between the three circles, but using data for England in 2006 (BERR, 2008, Table 23, 30–33):

- 13 per cent of the vulnerable customers are fuel poor;
- 15 per cent of the vulnerable customers are using a PPM;
- 15 per cent of electricity and 13 per cent of gas PPM customers are fuel poor.

Whichever group is targeted by policy will include a majority who are not fuel poor. This is true of a wide range of categories (Tables 2.9, 4.6, 6.11 in Chapters 2, 4 and 6 respectively) and is not a reason for saying that PPMs are unimportant. They are one of the solutions, like many other factors. The follow-on from this situation is that any form of subsidy on PPMs would be paid by the 75 per cent of the fuel poor who have some other payment method (standard credit or direct debit). That is one of Ofgem's concerns (Maxalister, 2008). However, at the moment, PPM users are providing a subsidy to some other group of customers or shareholders and that is not satisfactory either.

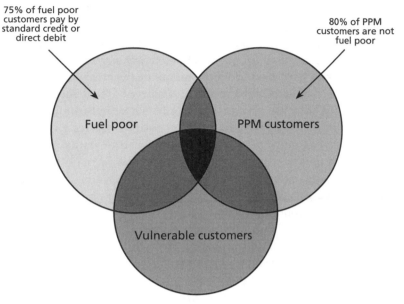

Source: Ofgem (2007a, p34)

Figure 4.2 *Fuel poverty, vulnerability and prepayment meter ownership*

Disadvantageous utility policies: Profits before justice

PPM customers have recently begun to switch suppliers more actively, mainly in response to doorstep selling: 'Of those PPM consumers [who] switch as a result of direct sales, over 48 per cent of gas consumers and 46 per cent of electricity consumers are switching to more expensive deals' (Ofgem 2008a, p109). This is a clear indication of the suppliers' preparedness to put profits before the needs of the fuel poor. In 2007, 20 per cent of PPM users switched supplier (Ofgem, 2008b, p24). Energywatch estimated that the combined effect of higher average costs for PPMs together with half of those switching paying higher prices means that customers are overcharged between £300 million and £400 million a year (HC 293, 2008, para 85). There are additional profits being made from the higher tariffs charged to standard credit customers.

There is no semblance of a consumer-friendly policy in these findings. People need to have the confidence that advice from their utility is honest and accurate. Otherwise, householders will not accept advice on energy efficiency or believe in the rationale behind utility investment programmes. The companies need to understand that trust has to be earned, and it isn't being.

Not switching: Penalizing loyalty

In our liberalized market, the expectation is that consumers will keep their energy bills to a minimum by switching from expensive to less-expensive suppliers of that fuel. Ofgem's recent study confirmed that some of the disadvantaged are those customers who have never switched and who are paying a significant premium as a result. Customers who have remained with the original supplier in their area (the old electricity boards, known as the incumbents) experience higher costs than people who have switched away from them, in the area, or people who have switched to them, out of the area. This penalty is also experienced by households who are not in receipt of a dual-fuel discount – for instance, because they are on electricity only. There are about 15.8 million accounts held by these 'loyal' customers, who are collectively paying around £585 million a year more than the average, and an even larger amount in comparison with the cheapest alternative (Ofgem, 2008a, p112). This is equivalent to £37 per customer per annum per fuel.

One of the reasons for not switching is that the household does not have access to broadband and/or lives in a rural area where there is less likelihood of a company representative knocking on the door. These explain the low level of switching in Wales, particularly among pensioners (Roberts, pers comm). Ofgem is aware of this method of differential pricing:

> *On an average basis over the past three years, around three-quarters of the gross profits of the Big 6, and all of their net profits, arise from their in-area electricity customers, which represent 48 per cent of their customer accounts.* (Ofgem, 2008a, p9)

It does seem an extraordinary way for the utilities to reward loyalty, by leaving prices high and for so many people. It may be a natural consequence of a liberalized market, but it certainly is not helpful for many of the fuel poor. Again, the relationship between non-switchers and the fuel poor is not known, but it could be substantial. It is assumed that people who have not switched are some of the least self-confident in society, who do not actively try and change their situation, for fear it might get worse. This is probably the same group as those who do not claim the benefits they are entitled to, the 'I'm not complaining' group.

Social tariffs: Limited policies

The utilities, both gas and electricity, are required to consider the problems of their disadvantaged customers and one way in which they are demonstrating that concern is through the introduction of social tariffs.

A social tariff is a relatively new concept and involves offering the most disadvantaged customers a lower cost than they would otherwise have been paying. The definition of a social tariff is not yet consistent; but the ideal is that 'Social tariffs should offer a better deal than the cheapest market price available from the supplier and should not depend on how consumers pay their bill' (Fuel Poverty Charter, 2008). The tariff would only be offered to certain households and the definition of these selected households has yet to be clarified.

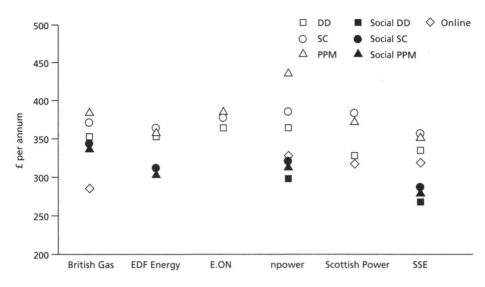

Notes: DD = direct debit; SC = standard credit; PPM = prepayment meter; SSE = Scottish and Southern Electricity.
Source: Ofgem (2008c, p15)

Figure 4.3 *Electricity bills, by tariff and supplier, Great Britain (2007–2008)*

Therefore, there is no understanding of the relationship between those eligible for social tariffs and the fuel poor, either in theory or in practice.

For April 2007 to March 2008, there was nearly a 60 per cent range between the cheapest and most expensive methods of purchasing 3300kWh of electricity or 20,500kWh of gas. The range was from £280 to £440 for electricity (Figure 4.3) and £400 to £640 for gas (Ofgem, 2008c, p16). Thus, a household on the two most expensive tariffs (£1080) could save £400 per annum by switching to the two cheapest social tariffs. These are very large differences for a standard product: there is no difference in the quality or characteristics of the electricity and gas delivered to the home.

The amount of help that the social tariff provides to the individual householder partly depends on the supplier. For some companies, the range between direct debit and PPM was fairly narrow: £40 for British Gas, whereas for npower it was £100. Any social tariff will, almost by definition, involve a cross-subsidy from other consumers since it is unlikely to be cost reflective.

The provision of social tariffs costs the companies £57 million per annum in 2007/08 and benefited about 800,000 customer accounts (Ofgem 2009b). This implies that the average benefit was £71 per annum per account. It is not clear how many households this means, as most people have two accounts, one for gas and the other for electricity. The number is, however, only a small proportion of the 5 million households in fuel poverty, perhaps as low as 8 per cent.

The suppliers have undertaken to increase expenditure on social tariffs, probably doubling the amount (a figure of £225 million over three years has been agreed, but this includes money for hardship funds as well); but it is not clear how the benefits will be distributed. It is extremely unlikely that all of the fuel poor will be eligible. Social tariffs do exist with at least five of the major suppliers; but the companies are probably aiming to contain their costs by limiting access to this tariff.

The social tariffs are, therefore, a useful contribution for a minority of disadvantaged households – there is no precision about who will be eligible (e.g. elderly only, or those on benefits), nor how the utility will identify these customers. The social tariffs do not compensate for the other increases that have been imposed on low-income households. For instance, the £71 reduction through social tariffs is less than the £80 surcharge from government policies (Table 4.3).

It is unclear as to how the social tariff will be allowed to vary between suppliers and across regions. If it is successful, it would eliminate any opportunity for competition between companies over their social tariffs. Whether successful or not, there is a risk of a lot of diversionary political activity being focused on social tariffs, when they will have only a limited benefit to a small proportion of the fuel poor, a view apparently shared by the minister for fuel poverty at the Department of Energy and Climate Change (DECC): 'I do not think social tariffs are the answer' (HC 37, 2009, Ev 78, Q343).

Other company policies and fuel poverty

The companies all operate their own policies on several other issues, such as attitudes to installing PPMs or disconnection, which have impacts on the fuel poor. It is clear that these are largely independent of Ofgem – this may be because Ofgem does not try to influence them or because it has no powers. The net effect is to create further problems for the fuel poor. For instance:

- Rates of disconnection are only partially linked to debt levels and are mainly determined by company policy. This was confirmed in 2005, when the Sohn Review concluded that there were 'significant variations in approach by suppliers' (Thomas, 2008, p248).
- Rising fuel debt is not helped by the infrequency with which the companies read the meter and send accurate bills: five of the six companies read the meter twice a year, whereas SSE only read it once (and only bill every six months). This confirms the good sense of those households who want to stay on a PPM.

Avoiding debt is particularly difficult and important at a time of rising fuel prices. Those on fixed (low) incomes (especially benefit claimants and pensioners) are unlikely to be able to increase their spending on fuel to compensate, or perhaps at all. In the short term, their only options are to reduce their fuel consumption or to go into debt.

Do the fuel poor have the cheapest options?

It is not unreasonable to expect that the poorest households should have access to the cheapest products, whether this is bread, clothing or energy. However, it is clear that this is not happening with fuel and the fuel poor cannot be confident that they have, or could find, the lowest price fuel for their circumstances. Establishing which is the cheapest energy supplier is not a simple task for anyone, and the companies do not make it easy, especially for the fuel poor.

The relationship, in reality, between fuel prices, tariffs, payment methods and fuel poverty is difficult to disentangle. There are certain sectors of the population who do have to pay more for their fuel including (Ofgem, 2008a):

- those on PPMs;
- people who have not switched suppliers;
- people who have erroneously switched to a more expensive fuel;
- people who are off-gas and cannot access the dual-fuel rebates;
- people who are still with the original supplier in an area (the incumbent) and have not benefited from competition;
- electricity-only customers because there is a higher premium on this fuel than on gas.

In total, Ofgem has (2008a, p113):

> ... *identified that suppliers benefit in total by around £1 billion per annum from premiums charged to certain groups of customers... This premium is borne disproportionately by vulnerable consumers and those without access to the gas grid.*

The £1 billion could be a conservative estimate and it could be as high as £1.6 billion (Table 4.5). Over half of this can be interpreted as the disadvantaged subsidizing the better-off households because the utilities have been able to create cross-subsidies. These are in addition to the amounts paid by all house-holders on the costs of government-imposed policies, such as the Renewables Obligation (RO), EU ETS and CERT.

The expenditure on fuel by the 5 million households in fuel poverty in 2007 totalled roughly £3.3 billion (Table 3.1 in Chapter 3). If all of the £1.6 billion surcharge had been paid by them (which it was not), it would represent half of that expenditure, which should not have been levied against these disadvantaged households and is being used to subsidize better-off households or shareholders. This is an unbelievably large penalty. The offsetting social tariffs can be seen as a minor contribution and even if they were doubled or trebled, this would still be true. And it is these additional costs, borne by the vulnerable, that are likely to be increased as a result of the new initiatives and supply requirements listed above.

Table 4.5 *Fuel cost penalties paid and benefits received by the fuel poor and vulnerable, Great Britain (million) (2008)*

Via	Penalties	Benefits
Prepayment meter (PPM)	£300–£400	
Ignorance, non-switchers, loyal customers	£585	
PPM switched in error	£54	
Social tariffs, 2008		£57
Unnecessarily high price increases (FPAG), 2006	£167	
RO, CERT, EU ETS – fuel poor only	£400	
Total	£1606	£57

Source: Text

In other words, the liberalized market is working and the better-off are benefiting handsomely from it, as they have for some time (Boardman and Fawcett, 2002). The options for the government and Ofgem, within this liberalized market, are limited and depend upon greater regulation, not less.

The suppliers have responded to pressure from the government and Ofgem with more than £300 million being taken off the premiums paid by customers, including PPM users (Hansard, 2009). Only a small proportion of this will be going to the fuel poor; but it demonstrates both how much the utilities were profiting and how easily they can reduce costs when they feel that it is required or are put under political pressure.

Ofgem has introduced some new licence conditions, but these are focused on 'information' and empowering 'consumers to engage effectively in the market' (Ofgem, 2009a). Ofgem largely retains its faith in the market, but acknowledges the need to protect the vulnerable by 'prohibiting undue discrimination' for a limited period. In the face of the £1 billion levy on the most disadvantaged customers, as proved by Ofgem's own research, this response is close to doing nothing. Obviously, there are constraints for Ofgem working in and with a liberalized market:

> It seems hopelessly unrealistic to expect profit-led private companies to voluntarily offer concessionary terms, which must be paid for out of profits or passed on to potentially price-sensitive consumers. (Thomas, 2008, p265)

The onus is, therefore, on government to intervene, having recognized the problems, and to propose some appropriate solutions. Now is an appropriate time to reassess the way in which the privatized liberalized market could be made to assist the fuel poor and socially disadvantaged, and, if additional regulation proves too difficult, to consider a radical restructuring of the energy supply industry.

Role of fuel prices in fuel poverty

There is no doubt that changes in fuel prices have a strong effect on the numbers in fuel poverty. There are several contributory reasons for this:

- All customers of the same utility experience the same price rise on the same day – the prices have to be paid.
- The price rises can be both unexpected and large. Within this timescale, responses by the household (e.g. greater energy-efficiency improvements) would not be possible. So there is no opportunity to offset the increase and to maintain the same standard of living and the same expenditure. Hardship is inevitable.
- The fuel poor are particularly sensitive to fuel prices because the proportion of their income spent on fuel is roughly double that of other households.
- Every price increase pushes the 10 per cent of income line up the distribution curve and affects ever more households (Figure 3.1) – each successive increase has a larger impact.
- For benefit-recipients, the substantial time lag between a price rise and linked additional income can be as much as 18 months ('Benefit rates over time' in Chapter 3).
- Fuel costs are flexible, not fixed amounts, as with rent or some mobile phones, so it is easier to cut back and go below the required level of expenditure for comfort and health.

The net effect is that 'Small consumers ... are paying too much for their power' (Thomas, 2006, p583).

The characteristics of the fuel poor, in relation to sources of energy, are part of a trio of tables to help establish the effect of the two different definitions of fuel poverty: full and basic income (Table 4.6 together with Tables 2.9 and 6.11 in Chapters 2 and 6 respectively). Whichever definition is used, the fuel poor are more likely to be on standard credit or a PPM, the two most expensive tariffs. They are less likely to be using gas, the cheapest fuel, and more likely to have no central heating, which implies a colder home. By removing housing costs, there is an increase in the proportion of hosueholds using PPMs (because more rental properties are included) and those with no central heating.

Utility funding for energy efficiency

The suppliers of gas and electricity – and, shortly, the generators of electricity – are required to invest in residential energy-efficiency improvements. The details of what they achieve are given in Chapter 6. The expenditure is added to household bills (Table 4.3) so that it is particularly regressive for low-income households, who already spend twice the proportion of their weekly budget on

Table 4.6 *Characteristics of fuel pricing and the fuel poor, England (2006)*

	Characteristic	Percentage of fuel poor (full income)	Percentage of fuel poor (basic income)	National average (%)	Sources from BERR 2008
1	Standard credit – gas*	44	42	30	Tables 32, 68
2	Standard credit – electricity	43	41	31	Tables 30, 66
3	Not on gas	23	22	13	Tables 32, 68
4	Prepayment meter – electricity	18	27	14	Tables 30, 66
5	Prepayment meter – gas*	15	25	12	Tables 32, 68
6	No central heating	12	29	4	Tables 42, 78
7	Gas central heating**	75	75	86	Tables 42, 78

Notes: * Of those on gas. ** Of those with central heating.
Source: BERR (2008)

fuel, in comparison with better-off households. This is meant to be compensated for, at the moment, by a requirement to ensure that the vulnerable, known as the Priority Group, receive additional benefit. During 2008 to 2011, under CERT, this is 40 per cent of the carbon savings. As the poor have no capital, the utility has to pay a higher proportion of the cost of these measures, if not fund them entirely, so the 40 per cent carbon saving requires about 50 per cent of the expenditure or more. Because of poor targeting (Table 3.6), the proportion of expenditure going to the fuel poor is less than they contribute, making the policy highly regressive (FPAG, 2008, p16). Some utilities have stated, that in future, there should be a split between the carbon savings and measures to be undertaken in the homes of the vulnerable (HC 88-II, 2007, Ev 464). If this subdivision of targets were to occur, there would be an even greater risk of utility-funded programmes exacerbating fuel poverty. The converse is more appropriate: the benefits of utility programmes should be disproportionately aimed at the fuel poor so that, over time, the poorest households are compensated for this excess contribution. This is what happens in Northern Ireland where the £5 per customer Energy Efficiency Levy is spent solely on the fuel poor or community groups. None goes to better-off households.

New policies

Cost of utility programmes

CERT continues until 2011; after that it will become the SO, but the shape of this is still under discussion. It could be an increased CERT or something completely different, such as a limit on the carbon emissions from the average household. This would have the benefit of moving from a theoretical calculation (with Energy Efficicy Commitment (EEC) and CERT) to one based on actual consumption, and would be a great step forward.

The CCC believes that the additional costs of obligations on the suppliers to mitigate climate change will put 1.7 million households into fuel poverty

(CCC, 2008, p395). As demonstrated above, the cost of various utility programmes and government policies, implemented through the utilities, is already substantial and potentially could be very large – considerably in excess of any benefits from social tariffs for a few households.

In an ideal world, all of the funding for fuel poverty programmes would come out of taxation since few of the fuel poor pay income tax (and pay less of other taxes such as VAT). This taxation could include contributions from the utilities: Ofgem says that 'auctioning EU Emissions Trading allowances would provide a revenue stream that could be recycled into fuel poverty programmes' (Ofgem, 2007b, p13). The aim must be to ensure that no funding stream puts up residential fuel prices and causes additional fuel poverty.

Smart meters

The installation of smart meters (for both electricity and gas) could provide benefits for the fuel poor by removing the fear of unexpected large bills, based on estimates. The other real benefit comes from clear display units, which are initially independent of, but eventually linked to, the smart meter. These should provide information on how much energy is being consumed and how much has been spent since the last payment. This educative tool was to have been provided, for free, to all households from April 2008 (DTI, 2007, p11) but the policy was not implemented. The government is consulting on whether all homes should have a smart meter by 2020 (Vaughan, 2009). This is despite the ongoing Energy Demand Research Project, which is assessing the impact of new billing methods, informative displays, advice and smart meters.

To protect the fuel poor and ensure that smart metering really does provide benefits for them will require tougher regulation than Ofgem has recently demonstrated. For instance, smart metering could assist the fuel poor by eradicating the surcharge for PPMs, as with the keypad in Northern Ireland. This could also happen independently of any move to smart meters.

Reverse block tariffs

Most tariffs do one of two things: charge the same unit rate for the energy delivered to the home, regardless of quantity; or charge an initial rate that then reduces for consumption above a certain level. While the former is neutral, the latter is definitely harmful for the environment as it encourages excess consumption. It is also more beneficial to better-off households since they spend more (in absolute terms) than poorer people. An alternative proposal is to reverse the process and have the cheapest price for the first units and then increase the cost above a certain level, known as a reverse or reverse block tariff. This proposal is being promoted, among others, by ex-Northern Ireland Regulator Douglas McIldoon.

In Northern Ireland, the average electricity consumption per household is 4200kWh, with a long tail of demand created by high users. McIldoon has proposed, as one permutation, that the 28 per cent of householders using less

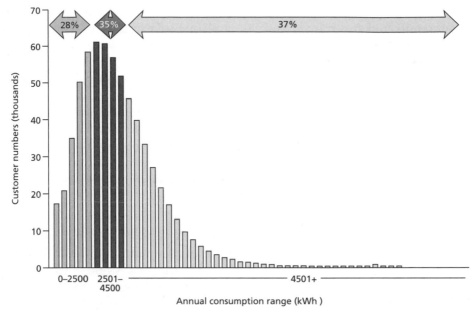

Note: All standard tariff domestic customers, including keypad users. Top arrows refer to the proportion of households in each group.
Source: McIldoon (2008, p35; data from NIEES)

Figure 4.4 *Possible reverse tariff for electricity, Northern Ireland*

than 2500kWh pa (the first five bars in Figure 4.4) would pay a reduced rate. The next group of householders (35 per cent) using up to 4500kWh per annum would end up paying about the same as at present, as a result of a lower rate for the first 2500kWh offset by a higher rate for the next 2000kWh. The 37 per cent of households in the long tail would be paying a higher amount than at present. As a result, consumers 'are paying less for consumption that is essential for civilized existence and more for electricity that is optional' (McIldoon, 2008, p34).

The benefit of a reverse tariff is that it ensures small users, such as the average fuel-poor household, will pay less, while providing more incentive to large users to reduce their consumption. An added benefit is that the cost of government programmes, such as CERT or the RO, could be loaded onto the long tail, the highest prices, and further reduce the impact on the poorest households. The main disadvantage of a reverse tariff occurs for poor households who are high users because they only use electricity. For these households, one compensatory mechanism would be to make sure that they are targeted by renewable schemes, such as solar thermal or photovoltaics, to ensure that they are offsetting their electricity consumption as much as possible and, potentially, keeping in the lower cost band.

The challenge of a reverse tariff is providing it in the current regulatory structure. It is therefore important that it has been suggested by the exregulator of Northern Ireland, as the regulatory system is the same for Northern Ireland as it is for Ofgem in Great Britain. A similar system already exists in Northern Ireland as prompt payers are given a 4 per cent discount on their first units (up to 6500kWh) and pay 4 per cent more for the later ones (McIldoon, pers comm). This would be an example of what the major charities are asking for:

> Require Ofgem to make sure energy suppliers introduce tariffs that encourage investment in energy efficiency and renewable technologies by rewarding low consumption, while protecting vulnerable consumers such as older and disabled people from high fuel costs. (Fuel Poverty Charter, 2008)

What seems certain is that 'Fuel poverty cannot be defeated through the structure of the electricity market in the near future and additional policy instruments are required' (McIldoon, 2008, p4).

Conclusions

The legal obligation to eradicate fuel poverty by 2016 was always a challenge for government and has been made considerably more difficult with the price rises since 2003. The challenge has been exacerbated by the policies of the utilities in maintaining high or inflating prices for the fuel poor and vulnerable. Ofgem, the regulator, has determined that the utilities are making £1 billion (net) a year out of discriminatory policies, which particularly hurt:

- the vulnerable;
- customers using the 5 million PPMs;
- half of those with a PPM who have switched to a more expensive tariff;
- those who have never switched and are still with the same supplier (i.e. the incumbent).

The real total may be closer to £1.6 billion if the additional cost of government policies (e.g. the RO, EU ETS and CERT) and unexplained general increases are included. The 5 million fuel-poor households were probably spending a total of £3.3 billion on fuel between them, so if all this money could be returned to them, it would represent a 50 per cent reduction.

The objective should be to have absolute confidence that the fuel poor are able to obtain the least expensive tariffs. This is completely the opposite of the current situation and will require considerable direction by the government and intervention in the market by Ofgem if it is to be reversed.

With the same powers, the Northern Ireland regulator has taken a strong social justice approach and, together with the main suppliers, ensured that the cost of the PPM and the standard credit are below other payment methods, that there are no disconnections or standing charges. In fact, the regulator delayed liberalization as long as possible. It may be that Ofgem is belatedly recognizing that it has the powers and could intervene.

Social tariffs are a useful fig leaf for the utilities, providing a focus for political activity without radically altering the underlying situation. Social tariffs are of limited benefit in comparison as they are worth about £70 per annum for 0.8 million households.

All fuel price increases have a dramatic effect on the numbers in fuel poverty. This effect is increasing as prices rises because more households are affected – the 10 per cent line is creeping up the distribution (Figure 3.1 in Chapter 3). Another reason is that the UK has such an energy-inefficient housing stock. In these homes, the effect of a fuel price rise is felt quickly and keenly. In really energy-efficient properties, a fuel price rise has a negligible effect.

In addition to redressing these unacceptable fuel price penalties, other policies to assist the fuel poor could include:

- reversing tariffs so that the cost per unit increases with consumption as this would be one way of supporting the poorest, low-consuming households;
- making sure that all the utility-funded energy-efficiency investments occur in the homes of the fuel poor, as in Northern Ireland, where 80 per cent of the energy-efficiency levy goes to the fuel poor, and the remaining 20 per cent to community groups – this is the complete opposite of what several of the utilities are proposing.
- imposing a cap of £80 (the present level of expenditure, Table 4.3) on the amount the fuel poor can be expected to contribute to government and utility policies.

Fuel pricing policies are important because the money directly affects household energy bills. Policies to increase incomes have to be ten times as large to obtain the same benefit, as only 10 per cent is spent on fuel.

There are certain groups in society who are self-effacing and reluctant to push themselves forward. Other groups may be so overwhelmed with the problems of existing – for instance, because of poverty – that they have no time or inclination to consider the potential benefits of switching. They do not switch fuel suppliers and so do not take advantage of a liberalized energy market; in addition, many of them are the fuel poor. They are also the people who are not targeted by the utilities as preferred customers: they do not consume much energy, need a lot of persuasion to consider switching or cannot be identified. There are almost no policies to help them. They include the 'I'm not complaining' group. Worse still, the companies sometimes discriminate against them – perhaps by default, perhaps because of a wish to make additional profits from an unobtrusive group. Thus, the liberalized energy market is failing many of the most disadvantaged householders:

On prices, generally, the complacency for a long period of time of government, largely supported by Ofgem, in the face of apparently higher prices than necessary from some of the energy companies, has been startling. (FPAG, 2008, p34)

These unnecessary costs are clearly increasing fuel poverty – the utilities' own policies, sanctioned by Ofgem's passivity, are forcing people into fuel poverty. There is a long way to go before the role of fuel prices, as a cause of fuel poverty, is minimized.

References

BERR (Department for Business, Enterprise and Regulatory Reform) (2008) *Fuel Poverty Statistics: Detailed Tables 2006*, Annex to Fuel Poverty Strategy Report, 2008, URN 08/P33 BERR, Tables 23, 30–33, www.berr.gov.uk/files/file48038.pdf

BERR (2009) *Retail Price Index: Fuel Consumption*, Table 2.1.1, 'Quarterly energy trends', BERR, http://www.berr.gov.uk/files/file50355.pdf

Boardman, B. and Fawcett, T. (2002) *Competition for the Poor: Liberalisation of Electricity Supply and Fuel Poverty: Lessons from Great Britain for Northern Ireland*, Environmental Change Institute, University of Oxford, Oxford, UK

Brignall, M. (2007) 'New calls for inquiry into energy firms', *The Guardian*, 1 May

Brignall, M. (2008) 'British Gas provokes fury with biggest ever price rise', *The Guardian*, 31 July, p1

Campbell, R., Head of Campaigns, Policy, Research and Information, National Energy Action, Newcastle, pers comm

CCC (Climate Change Committee) (2008) *Building a Low-Carbon Economy: The UK's Contribution to Tackling Climate Change*, First report, CCC, December, www.theccc.org.uk/pdf/TSO-ClimateChange.pdf

DECC (Department of Energy and Climate Change) (2009a) *Energy Trends*, DECC, March, www.berr.gov.uk/files/file50354.pdf

DECC (2009b) *Quarterly Energy Prices*, DECC, March, www.berr.gov.uk/files/file50355.pdf

Defra (Department for Environment, Food and Rural Affairs) (2003) *UK Fuel Poverty Strategy: 1st Annual Progress Report*, Defra, London

Defra (2005) *UK Fuel Poverty Strategy: 3rd Annual Progress Report*, Defra, London

Defra (2006) *UK Fuel Poverty Strategy: 4th Annual Progress Report*, Defra, London

DTI (Department of Trade and Industry) (2001) *UK Fuel Poverty Strategy*, DTI, London, www.berr.gov.uk/files/file16495.pdf

DTI (2007) *Meeting the Energy Challenge*, White Paper on Energy, CM 7124, www.berr.gov.uk/files/file32551.pdf

DWP (Department for Work and Pensions) (2007) *A Reduction in the Number of Households in Fuel Poverty – Indicator 38*, www.dwp.gov.uk/ofa/indicators/indicator-38.asp

ENDS (2008) 'UK's Carbon Allowance auction raises £54m', 407, December, p15

Eurostat (2009) *International Price Comparisons for Small Gas and Electricity Users*, http://stats.berr.gov.uk/energystats/qep561.xls

FPAG (Fuel Poverty Advisory Group) (2003), *Fuel Poverty Advisory Group for England: First Annual Report – 2002/3*, Department of Trade and Industry, London, February

FPAG (2008) *Sixth Annual Report 2007*, FPAG, London, April, www.berr.gov.uk/files/file45365.pdf

Fuel Poverty Charter (2008) Supported by a coalition of Age Concern; Association for Conservation of Energy; Barnado's; Centre for Sustainable Energy; Child Poverty Action Group; Disability Alliance; energywatch; Friends of the Earth; Help the Aged; National Energy Action; National Right To Fuel Campaign; WWF, www.foe.co.uk/resource/press_releases/Fuel_Poverty_Charter_08092008.html

Hansard (2008) HC Written Answers (Session 2007–2008), vol 478, col 811, 1 July

Hansard (2009) HC Deb (Session 2008–2009), vol 489, 20 March, Joan Ruddock, Minister, column 1199–1200

HC 878 (2004) *Ofgem: Social Action Plan and Household Energy Efficiency*, Report by the Comptroller and Auditor General, Session 2003–2004, House of Commons, UK, July

HC 88-II (2007) *Climate Change: the "Citizen's Agenda"*, Eighth Report of Session 2006–2007, Environment, Food and Rural Affairs Committee, House of Commons, vol II Oral and Written Evidence

HC 293 (2008) *Energy Prices, Fuel Poverty and Ofgem*, 11th Report, BERR Select Committee, House of Commons, Session 2007–2008, www.publications.parliament.uk/pa/cm200708/cmselect/cmberr/293/29302.htm

HC 1099 (2008) *Energy Efficiency and Fuel Poverty*, Fifth special report of session 2007–2008, Environment, Food and Rural Affairs Committee, House of Commons, UK

HC 37 (2009) *Energy Efficiency and Fuel Poverty*, Third report of session 2008–2009, Environment, Food and Rural Affairs Select Committee, Stationery Office, London

Macalister, T. (2008) '"Energy anorak" at the centre of a storm', *The Guardian*, 14 March, p35, www.guardian.co.uk/business/2008/mar/14/utilities.householdbills

McIldoon, D. (2008) *Northern Ireland Electricity Consumers: Orphans in the Energy Storm*, Report for NIAUR, Belfast

McIldoon, D., Former Director General of Electricity Supply (Northern Ireland), pers comm

McMullan, J., Chair FPAG, NI and CEO Bryson Charitable Group, pers comm

Milner, M. (2008) 'Households hit by big energy price rise', *The Guardian*, 26 July, p8

Mitchell, C. (2008) *The Political Economy of Sustainable Energy*, Palgrave Macmillan, Basingstoke, UK

Ofgem (Office of the Gas and Electricity Markets) (2007a) *Domestic Retail Market Report*, Ofgem, June, www.ofgem.gov.uk/Markets/RetMkts/Compet/Documents1/DRMR%20March%202007doc%20v9%20-%20FINAL.pdf

Ofgem (2007b) *Social Action Strategy*, Ofgem, www.ofgem.gov.uk/Sustainability/SocAction/Documents1/sapstrategbroA5June07.pdf

Ofgem (2008a) *Energy Supply Probe: Initial Findings Report*, Consultation, Ofgem, www.ofgem.gov.uk/Markets/RetMkts/ensuppro/Documents1/Energy%20Supply%20Probe%20-%20Initial%20Findings%20Report.pdf

Ofgem (2008b) *Sustainable Development Report*, Ofgem, London, December www.ofgem.gov.uk/Sustainability/Documents1/SDR%202008%20-%20Master%20-%20FINAL.pdf

Ofgem (2008c) *Monitoring Suppliers' Social Spend*, Ofgem (171/08), www.ofgem.gov.uk/Sustainability/SocAction/Suppliers/CSR/Documents1/Monitoring%20Suppliers%20Social%20Spend%20171.08.pdf

Ofgem (2009a) *Energy Supply Probe: Proposed Retail Market Remedies*, Consultation, Ofgem, April, www.ofgem.gov.uk/Markets/RetMkts/ensuppro/ Documents1/Energy%20Supply%20Probe%20-%20proposed%20retail% 20market%20remedies.pdf

Ofgem (2009b) *Fuel Poverty Action Programme Update: Improving the Identification and Targeting of Existing Help to Fuel Poor Consumers*, Ofgem, London, March

Osborne, H. (2009) 'British Gas says electricity price cut will prune bills by £132 a year', *The Guardian*, 8 May

Roberts, R., Chair, FPAG Wales, pers comm

Rutledge, I. and Wright, P. (2008) Written evidence to the BERR House of Commons Select Committee: 11th Report on *Energy Prices, Fuel Poverty and Ofgem*, HC 293-II, Session 2007–2008, www.publications.parliament.uk/pa/cm200708/cmselect/ cmberr/293/293we86.htm

Thomas, S. (2006) 'The British model in Britain: Failing slowly', *Energy Policy*, vol 34, pp583–600

Thomas, S. (2008) 'Energy' in S. Thomas (ed) *Poor Choices: The Limits of Competitive Markets in the Provision of Essential Services to Low-Income Consumers*, Energywatch, www.psiru.org/reports/PoorChoices.pdf

Vaughan, A. (2009) 'Boxing Clever: Every UK household may get smart meter for gas and electricity', *The Guardian*, 11 May

Wintour, P (2008) 'Producers may pass on cost of energy package to consumers', *The Guardian*, 12 September

5

Energy Use and Emissions

The burning of fossil fuel is the primary source of carbon dioxide, the main greenhouse gas, creating a strong relationship between the quantity of energy use and the resultant carbon dioxide emissions. As a result, most climate change policy is about either decarbonizing the sources of energy, particularly electricity or demand reduction, so less is consumed. Where the latter is the focus, there are good synergies with the reduction of fuel poverty. Increasingly, as there is a move towards very low-energy homes, there is also a need to ensure that fuel-poor households have access to micro-generation technologies, particularly where these will save them money or even earn them income. There is a strong focus on the residential sector in climate change policies because it is a substantial source of emissions, is relatively well understood and could, therefore, be a relatively quick source of savings. The question for this chapter to examine is the ways in which there can be good synergies between policies on fuel poverty and those on climate change and the extent to which awkward conflicts can be avoided.

So far, it has been shown that the fuel poor are being strongly disadvantaged by the present utility policies, resulting in higher than necessary fuel costs. The government and the Office of Gas and Electrcity Markets (Ofgem), between them, have to recognize that intervention in the market is now necessary for the fuel poor.

Greenhouse gases and UK trends

Although carbon dioxide emissions are the main cause of climate change, there are five other gases that contribute to the basket of six gases usually discussed. Of these, methane (CH_4) is linked to household emissions since it is natural gas and can leak from the gas network. These five other greenhouse gases contribute less than 10 per cent of the residential emissions: over 90 per cent is in the form of carbon dioxide. The global warming impact of the six different gases is combined by relating them all to the effect of carbon dioxide and is expressed as CO_{2e} (i.e. carbon dioxide equivalent), as in Table 5.1.

Table 5.1 *Annual greenhouse gas (GHG) and carbon dioxide emissions: Total and residential, UK (1990–2020)*

	GHG (million tonnes of CO_{2e})	Total (million tonnes of CO_2)	Carbon dioxide Residential (million tonnes of CO_2)	Residential change
1990	773	593	156	
2000	675	551	145	
2001	678	562	151	+4.6%
2002	656	545	146	–3.4%
2003	661	556	152	+2.0%
2004	659	556	153	+1.2%
2005	653	553	149	–2.6%
2006	648	551	148	–0.7%
2007	637	543	142	–4.1%
2008	624	532	141**	0.7%
2008–12 Average	600			
2020	449–514*			
2000:2008	–7.6%	–3.4%	–2.8%	

Notes: * Depending on whether the target is an 'interim' budget or the tougher 'intended' budget if negotiations in Copenhagen, December 2009, are successful. ** Estimated.
Source: DECC (2009a, annex A) for 1990–2008, first two columns; Defra (2009) for third column; CCC (2008, ppxix, xxi) for 2008+ (penultimate line and one above)

Between 1990 (the base year for the first commitment under the Kyoto Protocol) and 2008, total UK greenhosue gas emissions fell by nearly 20 per cent (from 773 to 624 $MtCO_{2e}$), but carbon dioxide emissions by only half that amount and residential carbon dioxide emissions by slightly less. In all cases, this is below the trajectory for a 60 per cent reduction in emissions between 1990 and 2050 (Boardman, 2007, p11) and even further away from the trajectory for an 80 per cent cut. The carbon emissions from the residential sector represent around 26 per cent of all UK carbon dioxide emissions, but more in the devolved administrations – for instance, they are 34 per cent in Scotland. Carbon dioxide emissions from the home are vital to climate change policies.

Most of the government's targets are in greenhouse gases and this is being used as the metric in the Climate Change Act statistics. The UK has various obligations and commitments in terms of energy use, carbon dioxide and greenhouse gas emission levels. These include (in relation to 1990):

- 12.5 per cent reduction in greenhouse gases by 2008 to 2012 under the Kyoto Protocol. The UK has already achieved 19 per cent because of reductions from the other five greenhouse gases, rather than carbon dioxide.
- 80 per cent reduction in greenhouse gases by 2050, under the 2008 Climate Change Act.
- The Climate Change (Scotland) Bill commits Scotland to a 42 per cent target by 2020, which is equivalent to the UK's intended target.

- Wales is implementing a 3 per cent per annum cut in greenhouse gases, without including any carbon offsetting. This is specifically designed to combine with tackling fuel poverty (WAG, 2009, pp17, 59).

The Climate Change Committee (CCC) advises the government on compliance with the 2008 Climate Change Act and has proposed targets for the first three five-year budgets of 2008 to 2012, 2013 to 2017 and 2018 to 2022. The latter is represented by the 2020 total in Table 5.1. The CCC has suggested two major approaches for reductions by 2020: an interim target, which exists until the next international agreement is achieved, perhaps at Copenhagen in December 2009, and a more ambitious (intended) one that will then come into force. By 2020, these represent 34 per cent and 42 per cent reductions in greenhouse gas emissions, respectively, over 1990. By 2050, to achieve the overall 80 per cent reduction in greenhouse gas means that UK residential carbon emissions have to be effectively zero (Turner, 2009).

Carbon intensity of fuels

The fuels used in the home emit, at some stage of the process, very different quantities of carbon for a unit of delivered energy (Table 5.2). A process of de-carbonizing requires fuel switching and, therefore, new equipment. The fuel switching may be at the electricity generating station (gas-fired stations replace coal-burning ones) or in the home (installing gas instead of oil central heating). Electricity and gas are the two main fuels used in the home, with electricity being 2.7 times more polluting (in carbon terms) at the meter coming into the house. The effect of converting the fuel inside the home then has to be taken into account. Most electricity is used at 100 per cent efficiency and even when some of the output is heat, as from a light bulb, it is still within the home and potentially useful (e.g. during the heating season). Gas, however, has conversion losses in the home since a proportion of the energy is exhausted up the flue to the outside: the amount that is useful energy varies from 90 per cent or more with an efficient boiler to 65 per cent efficient with an old boiler. The carbon emissions per unit of useful energy are specific to the building and its equip-

Table 5.2 *Carbon intensity of domestic fuels, delivered energy, UK (2006)*

Fuel	gCO_2/kWh
Electricity from the grid	562
Electricity from combined heat and power (CHP)	304
Anthracite/all solid fuel	313
Heating oil	282
Paraffin/kerosene	258
Liquid petroleum gas (LPG)	225
Mains gas	206
Renewable energy	0

Source: Defra (2008a)

Table 5.3 *Carbon intensity of delivered electricity, UK (2000–2050)*

	gCO_2/kWh
2000	518
2004	543
2006	562
2010	500
2020	310
2030	80
2040–2050	40

Source: MTP (2009) for 2000, 2004; CCC (2008, pxxv) for 2006 onwards

ment; but even on this basis electricity is often more than twice as polluting as gas.

Grid electricity is the only one of the fuels to change substantially in carbon intensity over time because of the effect of the varying mix of fossil fuels and power stations being used to generate and supply electricity. In the last few years, as gas has risen in price and coal has become relatively cheaper, the amount of coal being used has increased. The result has been dirtier electricity in 2006 than in 2000 (Table 5.3). Over the longer term, there has been a consistent downward trend, as electricity was more than four times as polluting than gas in 1990 (Boardman, 1991, p90). This is the trend that is expected to recur.

Projecting the carbon intensity of electricity into the future is extremely difficult since it requires assumptions about the relative prices of the different fossil fuels, the speed with which traditional coal stations and nuclear power are phased out, the speed with which new capacity is brought in and in what way this new electricity is generated. Most of these assumptions are also affected by the quantity of electricity that is being used in the whole economy. The CCC has recommended a strong policy of decarbonizing the electricity supply, with relatively minor reductions before 2015; after that there have to be some really dramatic changes.

As the carbon intensity of natural gas does not vary over time, by 2025, electricity per unit of delivered energy will have the same level of emissions (about 200g CO_2/kWh). That is when the debate about the priority for different heating fuels becomes interesting. Before that point, the use of electricity should be limited, especially where an alternative such as gas is available.

Although the figure for grid electricity varies, the conversion factor used in various policies is often standardized to avoid rankings and results changing on an annual basis. For instance, the figure for all electricity in the Standard Assessment Procedure (SAP) (Chapter 6) is 422g CO_2/kWh (i.e. quite a bit lower than is being achieved at present). This means that recommendations (e.g. on the Energy Performance Certificate (EPC), Chapter 6) underestimate the benefits of switching to gas or saving electricity. This is one reason for the confusion about the carbon benefits, or not, of heat pumps. The use of heat pumps before 2025 may not result in lower carbon emissions where gas is available, or only if they prove to be extremely efficient in practice (with a co-efficient of performance of 4 or more).

Residential carbon emissions

The different mix of fuels used in the home and in methods of generating electricity means that per capita emissions from the use of energy in the home vary across the four countries (Table 5.4). Northern Ireland has the highest level and as the household contains more people in Northern Ireland, this will mean a further widening of the disparity.

Table 5.4 *Residential per capita carbon emissions, by country (2006)*

	Per capita carbon dioxide emissions (tonnes of CO_2 per resident)
England	2.5
Wales	2.6
Scotland	2.8
Northern Ireland	3.5
UK	2.5

Source: Defra (2008b, p7)

The least energy-efficient homes are the most expensive to heat and this usually means that they do not use gas. All of the alternative fuels – electricity, oil and solid fuel – are more carbon intensive, as well as being more expensive. If the 22 million homes in England in 2006 are divided by their energy efficiency into deciles, each decile represents 2.2 million homes. The energy efficiency can be measured by the SAP (explained on p126), with a high SAP score being an energy-efficient property (Figure 5.1):

- The 2.2 million least efficient homes have an average SAP of 19 and emit 12.7 tonnes of carbon dioxide per annum each.
- The 2.2 million most efficient homes have an average SAP of 71 and emit 2.9 tonnes of carbon dioxide per annum each.

This is not an accurate prediction of the quantity of emissions, solely of the relative magnitude under consistent conditions, for most of the energy used (Table 6.2 in Chapter 6). If it were full energy consumption, the carbon dioxide line would be somewhat higher, with a fairly uniform uplift. If it were actual carbon emissions, the line would be at a different angle as the poorest people cannot afford to use this much energy. Because the data are based on the SAP and identical standards of energy service (e.g. temperature in the home), it is possible to confirm that, at a theoretical level, improving the SAP rating reduces the amount of carbon dioxide emitted.

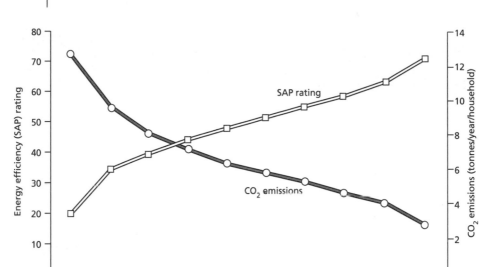

Source: DCLG (2008b, p135)

Figure 5.1 *Average carbon dioxide emissions and energy efficiency (Standard Assessment Procedure) rating, by energy-efficiency decile, England (2006)*

The group with the largest carbon emissions are the oldest properties. The pre-1919 building stock is responsible for 29 per cent of the carbon dioxide emissions, although they are only 22 per cent of the stock (DCLG, 2008a, p13) – as shown in Figure 5.2. The pre-1919 stock accounted for almost half (48 per

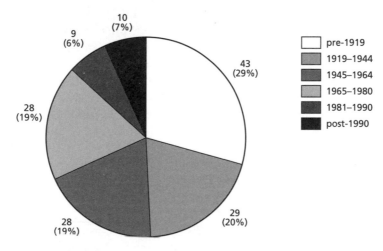

Source: DCLG (2008b, p144)

Figure 5.2 *Carbon dioxide emissions by dwelling age (million tonnes of CO_2), England (2006)*

cent) of all homes with emissions greater than 10 tonnes per year (DCLG, 2008b, p143). Wales also has a high proportion of older housing.

The task, at the present time, is to use less electricity as this is the most carbon-intensive domestic fuel. When electricity comes from cleaner sources of power, such as renewables, this will change and there could be a switch back towards electricity; but this is unlikely before 2020 or 2030. Whether this becomes an appropriate policy for households partly depends on the extent to which electricity is required elsewhere in the system (e.g. for transport).

Comparative fuel prices

Electricity is always the most expensive fuel to use in the home because it has to be generated and over half of the energy that goes into a conventional power station is wasted up the cooling towers. From 2000 to 2008, electricity was always four times the price of gas (Table 5.5). This echoes the relationship between these two main fuels in terms of their carbon intensity for the same reason. All of the carbon in the original primary energy used in the power station is allocated to the electricity that is generated. The most carbon-intense fuels are also those that are the most expensive. Therefore, in relation to the energy efficiency of the dwelling – and its SAP rating – reducing the cost improves the SAP rating and reduces the carbon emissions.

There is one caveat to this: Economy 7 and other off-peak electricity tariffs are only 20 per cent less polluting than on-peak electricity, but a lot cheaper (nearly the price of gas). So one of the ways in which fuel poverty policy and climate change policy diverge is over the use of off-peak tariffs, as these help the fuel poor, but not the environment

Other fuels, such as oil, liquid petroleum gas (LPG) and kerosene are also more expensive than gas, sometimes being twice the price. They are commonly used for heating in areas where there is no gas supply. The cost of providing space and water heating to the same level of service ranges from £795 per annum for a gas-fired boiler to £1789 per annum for LPG (Lynch, 2009, p6). Changing nothing else but the heating system and going from old electric storage heaters to a new condensing gas boiler would improve the SAP by 25 to 30 points (based on Wilkinson and Pickles, 2005).

Table 5.5 *Residential fuel prices, delivered energy, UK (2008 prices) (2000–2008)*

	Gas (pence/kWh)	Electricity (pence/kWh)	Heating oil (pence/kWh)	Coal (pence/kWh)
2000	2.1	9.6	2.7	2.4
2004	2.2	8.6	2.4	2.7
2008	3.0	12.3	4.3	2.7

Source: DECC (2008, Tables 3–6)

Table 5.6 *Expenditure on fuel (£ per week per household) (2006/07)*

	England	Wales	Scotland	Northern Ireland	UK
Electricity	7.8	8.2	8.9	9.2	7.9
Gas	7.5	7.5	7.5	1.5	7.4
Other	0.8	1.7	1	12.3	1.1
Total fuel expenditure	16.1	17.4	17.5	23	16.5
Total weekly expenditure	380.2	341.2	359.7	398.1	376.8
Fuel as percentage	4.2	5.1	4.9	5.8	4.4

Source: ONS (2008, Table A37)

The effect of the availability of fuels shows in the levels of expenditure on the different fuels for the countries of the UK. Northern Ireland has the most limited choice; so, despite a higher weekly expenditure, households in Northern Ireland have to pay the highest proportion of their budget on fuel (Table 5.6). This is largely due to the lack of access to natural gas and the reliance on oil for home heating. The cost of electricity in Northern Ireland is, relative to Great Britain, coming down, partly because of the extensive use of the keypad, one of the cheapest tariffs (Table 4.4 in Chapter 4). The reduction in the cost of electricity has not been sufficient to eradicate the cost penalties for Northern Ireland households because of their dependence on oil and coal (i.e. 'other' fuels). One group of households with high energy costs are those without access to gas, often in rural areas, where oil and LPG are two of the most common alternatives.

The relative importance of gas and electricity, the main residential fuels, depends on whether energy, money or carbon is being considered. Electricity is 48 per cent of the average household's expenditure, but 22 per cent of its energy use (Table 5.7). With carbon close to expenditure levels, the new carbon economy is, therefore, resulting in a greater emphasis on saving electricity and this means more consideration of lights and appliances. The normal approach is to focus on the main use of energy, which is gas for heating, so policy has almost exclusively focused on insulation. Unfortunately, the use of SAP tends to encourage this conventional perspective, rather than a coherent carbon and pricing approach, as it only covers 85 per cent of energy use (Table 6.2).

Table 5.7 *Comparisons between gas and electricity impacts, per household*

	Energy use (Great Britain, 2006)	Energy expenditure (UK 2006–2007)	Carbon emissions (Great Britain, 2006)
Gas	71%	45%	49%
Electricity	22%	48%	43%

Source: Utley and Shorrock (2008, p95) for column 1; Table 5.6, this volume, for column 2; Utley and Shorrock (2008, p96) for column 3

Consumption and expenditure

Residential carbon emissions declined by just 2.8 per cent between 2000 and 2008 (Table 5.1), when fuel prices rose by over 80 per cent (Table 4.1 in Chapter 4). How has the effect of price changes affected household energy consumption?

Table 5.8 *Residential gas and electricity consumption, UK (2000–2008)*

	Gas (TWh)	Electricity (TWh)	Households (millions)	Electricity per household (kWh)
2000	369.9	111.8	24.3	4600
2004	396.4 (+7%)	115.5 (+3%)	25.2	4583
2008	363.3 (–8%)	117.8 (+2%)	26.3	4479
2000:2008	–1%	+5%	+8%	–3%

Note: Not weather corrected
Source: DUKES (2009), Table 1.1.5 for gas and electricity consumption; household numbers from Table 2.4

Between 2000 and 2008, total residential consumption (across all households) of gas fell by 1 per cent and for electricity it went up by 5 per cent (Table 5.8). Within this period, when prices were falling (2000 to 2004), consumption rose for both fuels: 7 per cent for gas and 3 per cent for electricity. Since 2004, when prices have been rising, gas consumption decreased by 8 per cent, but electricity still increased by 2 per cent. The price of gas has risen more than electricity (Table 4.2 in Chapter 4).

These figures are for the whole country, during which period the numbers of households increased by 8 per cent. So, on average, each household is using less of both fuels. For electricity, this is easy to work out as the numbers of households and users are approximately the same: the average household has reduced electricity use from 4600kWh per annum to 4479kWh (3 per cent less). With gas it is more complex as the number of consumers of the fuel is a difficult statistic to obtain, so that trends per using household are rare. British Gas has provided some information on energy consumption by their customers. Between 2001 and 2008, gas consumption per household for British Gas users dropped by 17 per cent, whereas electricity consumption went down slightly by 3 per cent (British Gas Annual Reports). This mirrors national electricity consumption, so the 17 per cent drop in gas usage per connected household is also probably an appropriate national average.

A larger reduction in gas use might indicate that policies on insulating the building fabric and improving the efficiency of boilers have been effective. There have been few policies (e.g. some in Carbon Emissions Reduction Target (CERT)) to reduce electricity use in lights and appliances.

Energy consumption by the fuel poor, over time

Earlier chapters have shown the high proportion of the budget spent on fuel by poorer households (Table 3.1 in Chapter 3). The split between the different

Table 5.9 *Energy use by fuel and income group, UK (percentage of fuel expenditure) (1999/2000–2007/08)*

		30% of households with lowest incomes	70% other
1999/2000	Gas	41	43
	Electricity	52	51
	Other	7	7
2007/2008	Gas	43	45
	Electricity	51	48
	Other	5	7

Source: extracted from National Statistics (2000), Table 1.3 for 1999/2000; ONS (2008), Tables A6, A7 for 2007/08 data

fuels does not vary much, either over time or by income group (Table 5.9). There is a slightly higher proportion of gas use among better-off households in both the years cited; but the 30 per cent of households with the lowest incomes are gradually catching up: their consumption in 2007/2008 was in similar proportions to that of better-off households in 1999/2000. In both years, the better-off households spent at least 30 per cent more than the poorer ones. The slow rate of change demonstrates the longevity of many of the energy-related systems in the home.

While the proportions do not vary, the expenditure over time has changed in response to rising fuel prices. For a household on a tight budget, any increase in prices creates a dilemma: are there any purchases that can be sacrificed to provide the extra money required to maintain energy consumption? Over the period of 2000 to 2008, the Fuel Price Index (FPI) increased by four times as much as expenditure on fuel by the poorest 30 per cent of households (Table 5.10). This is too short a timescale for there to have been massive improvements in the efficiency with which the energy is used. Energy is clearly a basic necessity and householders strive to maintain their levels of consumption. However, when energy prices rise:

- the average household has cut back on energy consumption over this period and, in the absence of greater energy efficiency, this means that they are purchasing a lower level of energy services;
- the average poor household has cut back even more;
- it is not true to say that demand for energy is inelastic (i.e. it will follow price). This is not possible when price rises are rapid and substantial, particularly for the poorest households;
- the decline in energy consumption will be reflected in lower carbon emissions;
- there has been an increase in hardship and deprivation, so, not surprisingly, fuel poverty has doubled (Table 2.3 in Chapter 2).

The growth in relative and, probably, absolute fuel poverty can be further confirmed by the relationship between expenditure by the two income groups

Table 5.10 *Change in expenditure on fuel and the Fuel Price Index (FPI), UK (2000–2008)*

Change in expenditure on fuel			FPI
30% of households with lowest incomes	Other 70%	Average	
+28%	+50%	+45%	+105% (+62% in real terms)

Source: data derived from Tables 3.1 and 4.1 in Chapters 3 and 4 respectively

over time. Continuing to use the 30 per cent of households with the lowest incomes as a proxy for the fuel poor, richer households have increased their expenditure on gas and electricity, between 1999/2000 and 2007/08, by one third more than the poorer households (Table 5.11). During 1999/2000, richer households spent 41 per cent more than poorer households on gas and 31 per cent more on electricity. Eight years later, the gap had grown to 57 per cent and 42 per cent, respectively. Hence, the effect of the fuel price rises has been to exacerbate the relative poverty of these poorer households, including the fuel poor.

Other explanatory factors, such as the weather, apply to all groups alike. This is too great a change to be caused by improved energy efficiency: as shown in Chapter 6, the rate of improvement is about 1 per cent per annum. There has been a slight differential in this rate of improvement, with the social housing sector improving faster than the private one; but this does not match neatly onto income groups. Another potential explanation is that the households in the different income groups are of different sizes; but there has been no sudden change in this statistic. Both Tables 5.10 and 5.11 imply a worsening of fuel poverty as a result of substantial fuel price increases.

There is also a substantial range of fuel expenditure within an income group (Ekins and Dresner, 2004, p6). Working from household fuel expenditure back to energy consumption, it was demonstrated that the range of energy use within an income decile was greater than the range of consumption between bands: the specifics of the household dominate. Some of the poorest households would be spending more on fuel than some of the richest households.

Table 5.11 *Ratio of expenditure by different income groups, UK (1999/2000–2007/08)*

	30% of households with lowest incomes	Other 70% relative to 30%
1999/2000, gas	1	1.41
2007/08, gas	1	1.57
1999/2000, electricity	1	1.31
2007/08, electricity	1	1.42

Source: extracted from National Statistics (2000), Table 1.3 for 1999/2000; ONS (2008), Tables A6, A7 for 2007/08 data

What is fuel used for?

On average in 2006, 58 per cent of energy was used for space heating, 25 per cent for water heating and 17 per cent for all other uses, including lighting and cooking (this latter category is predominantly electricity, whereas the previous two are usually gas) (Utley and Shorrock, 2008, p91). There is a gradual shift occurring, with less energy being used for space heating and more for lights and appliances. This trend both reflects the increased efficiency of the building fabric and boiler and the growth in household equipment. The latter trend has been occurring for some time (Figure 5.3).

There is virtually no information on the breakdown of these use categories by income group. Low-income groups do own fewer light bulbs per house and have less equipment, partly because they have smaller homes. The 22 per cent of households with the lowest incomes in Great Britain in 2007 have average ownership of televisions (98 per cent), whereas ownership of washing machines is slightly below average (88 instead of 96 per cent) and home computers about half the average level of ownership (37 instead of 70 per cent) (GHS, 2007, Table 4.21). Single pensioners are the least likely to own a computer (23 per cent; GHS, 2007, Table 4.22).

Offsetting these lower levels of ownership is the likelihood of poorer households owning equipment that uses a lot of electricity. For instance, with cold appliances:

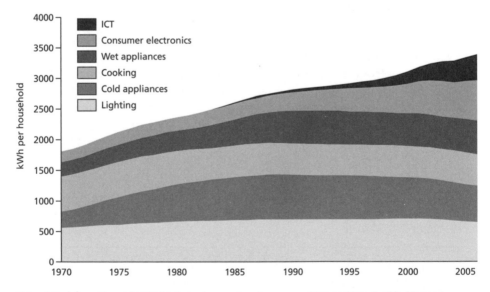

Notes: ICT = information and computer technology; wet appliances – washing machines, tumble driers and dishwashers; cold appliances = all refrigeration.
Source: CCC (2008, p218, citing BERR, 2008, p46)

Figure 5.3 *Electricity consumption per household in domestic appliances (1970–2006)*

> *... many low-income households suffer a substantial penalty through owning old and faulty cold appliances. This adds a new dimension to discussions on fuel poverty, though the underlying reason is the same: with both housing and appliances, the poor have to incur high running costs because of their inability to obtain capital to invest in more efficient equipment.* (Boardman et al, 1997, p66)

Too little research has been undertaken in this area; but, despite lower levels of appliance ownership, electricity consumption in lights and appliances in lower-income households is likely to be higher, per unit of energy service, than in better-off ones. As Table 5.9 shows, for both groups, about half of all expenditure is on electricity, but the detailed breakdown of this into electricity for the different uses is not available.

The fuel poverty model (Chapter 2) assumes that certain uses are determined either by dwelling size (e.g. lighting) or by the number of people (e.g. hot water and washing machines). The data are based on actual consumption because of the lack of defined 'need' in these areas.

The reduction in demand for cold appliances (refrigeration), shown in Figure 5.3, has resulted from European Union (EU) policies on, first, labelling the energy efficiency of the product and then the introduction of mandatory minimum standards in 1999 – a market transformation approach to policy (Boardman, 2004). Mandatory minimum standards, when nothing below these can be sold throughout the EU, are an effective way of reducing energy use. These are of most benefit to better-off households, who buy new appliances, but much less benefit to the fuel poor. Less than 50 per cent of low-income households bought their cold appliances as new, the majority purchased second-hand machines and these were often faulty (Boardman et al, 1997, p67). While old data, there is no particular reason to assume that the situation has changed.

Fridgesavers was a unique policy that was devised to solve this problem and make sure that the poorest households were able to acquire energy-efficient appliances. The scheme got energy-efficient fridges into low-income homes. The applicant had to be in receipt of an income-related benefit and their fridge had to be old, but working. It was replaced with a new energy-efficient fridge for only £25 (the price of a second-hand appliance) or a fridge-freezer for £50 (Changeworks, 2009). A total of 250,000 low-income households throughout the UK benefited from this programme. No other policy has replicated this scrappage scheme, but could and probably should do. The replacement of category G existing boilers within the CERT is the nearest present equivalent.

There has been a focus on low-income households in the delivery of low-energy light bulbs through the CERT Priority Group (Chapter 6).

Who uses which fuels?

The average UK household uses gas for heating and hot water and electricity for lights and appliances, with cooking being a mixture of the two fuels. The real problems occur when households do not have the use of these two fuels. Then there is often higher expenditure and raised carbon emissions and a greater risk of fuel poverty. All-electric homes are predominantly poor, while gas use is the same across all income groups. Oil-using homes are most likely to be better-off households.

Coal is only used in a small number of homes (1 per cent; Utley and Shorrock, 2008, p39) and oil-fired central heating is only slightly more extensive (4 per cent of centrally heated homes) and is being installed in some fuel-poor homes through Warm Front. As the price of oil is still high, relative to other fuels, and has to be paid for in bulk, this is not an appropriate policy for the fuel poor.

In both Scotland and Northern Ireland there has been a strong policy push to install central heating in fuel-poor homes or to improve the standard of the existing boilers.

Off-gas

All households in the UK are on electricity (bar a minute proportion); but quite a few are not joined to the gas network. About half of these are because they live in a rural area and the grid has not been extended to their village or home. The other half live in urban areas where the gas network is present, but not in their property. For instance, some tower blocks have to be all electric because a gas explosion could result in the building collapsing, as at Ronan Point. These tower blocks could have a gas-fired community combined heat and power (CHP) scheme installed to serve the whole block as in Aberdeen, but could not have individual gas boilers in each flat. This is what has been demonstrated so successfully in Aberdeen (King, 2009). In addition, a few households are no longer on gas because they have been disconnected.

The number of households off the gas grid is quoted to be 4.3 million customers in Great Britain by Ofgem (2008, p112); this represents 17 per cent of households. In reality, there are 4.3 million households in Great Britain who do not use gas for any form of heating (Utley and Shorrock, 2008, p87). That is not quite the same as saying they have no gas. These 4.3 million households pay at least an additional £240 million per annum because they cannot benefit from discounts on electricity as part of a dual-fuel scheme (Ofgem, 2008, p112).

Not being attached to the gas grid, particularly where the building has solid walls, is a major cause of hard-to-heat properties. Ofgem has incentivized bringing mains gas to communities, which will lead to about 20,000 new connections in about 400 communities. It is not clear how many of these will be fuel poor, nor what the timescale is (HC 37, 2009, Ev 87, Q405).

All electric

A large subset of households without gas uses solely electricity; for this reason, these households have above average carbon emissions. There were nearly 3 million of these homes in the UK in 2006 – 2.5 million in Great Britain and an estimated 0.4 million in Northern Ireland. The category is growing as new flats are often all electric. About 85 per cent (2.1 million) will be using cheaper off-peak electricity for heating so that their expenditure is partly under control. The other 15 per cent have electric non-central heating (Utley and Shorrock, 2008, p87; Wingfield, pers comm), which could be using expensive ordinary tariffs. What is needed is a policy that ensures that homes with Economy 7 or other off-peak tariffs are super-insulated in order to minimize their carbon emissions.

There are 0.375 million homes in Great Britain using on-peak electricity for heating and they are almost certainly in fuel poverty. In Wales, 40 per cent of all-electric homes are in fuel poverty. All-electric homes are predominantly in the lowest three income deciles.

Another source of all-electric homes is the trend towards installing more heat pumps (ground or air sourced). These use electricity to pump water through a series of pipes that extract heat from the ground or the air and transfer it to the inside of the home. This means that demand for electricity is increasing, before decarbonization has occurred, which is detrimental to the UK's carbon emissions.

In the immediate future (i.e. up to 2025), gas-powered CHP is a more appropriate installation than a heat pump, where gas is available, whether at the community level or in the individual home. In these systems, the space and water heating are from a boiler, but the wasted heat is used to generate electricity. Thus, the electricity is very low carbon or even carbon free (Table 5.2), depending on the assumptions made.

Low- and zero-carbon technologies

As well as improving the efficiency of the fabric with insulation and installing a modern boiler, there is now the opportunity to transform the home into a mini-power station by generating some of its own electricity or heat. There are several competing or overlapping definitions in this area. A renewable source (of energy) is defined in the Utilities Act 2000 (chapter 27) as 'sources of energy other than fossil fuel or nuclear fuel'. Micro-generation usually means small-scale renewable or low-carbon on-site generation. Heat pumps and CHP are normally included, whereas district CHP and large wind is not. It is highly debatable whether heat pumps should be considered a form of micro-generation; so, in order to minimize the confusion, the phrase 'low- and zero-carbon technologies' is used when referring to the full collection of technologies (Table 5.12).

Each of these technologies has different characteristics, which makes them more or less suitable in a specific situation. Low- and zero-carbon technologies can be accommodated into a building in a variety of ways, regardless of whether

Table 5.12 *Low- and zero-carbon technologies*

	Heating only	Heating and electricity	Electricity only
Low carbon	Heat pumps (ground and air)	Combined heat and power (CHP)	–
Zero carbon	Solar thermal; biomass boiler or stove	CHP from energy using waste or biomass	Solar photovoltaic, micro-wind or micro-hydro

Source: adapted from Boardman et al (2005, p63)

it is an existing or a new home. The changing sophistication of the technologies, the varying levels of demand for the technology (sometimes worldwide) and the resultant costs and property-specific considerations all make the choice of technology, and the quantity and appropriate date of installation highly variable. Some comments are given as general guidance on where to use them and present ownership levels (Boardman, 2007, pp59–61). The policy challenge is to ensure that the fuel poor and other low-income households are able to have low-carbon technologies – for instance, CHP and solar thermal.

In *The UK Fuel Poverty Strategy* it was stated that:

> ... *pilot schemes on renewable energy sources and micro-CHP are about to be set up to explore how these technologies can be used to help the fuel poor, particularly in areas without access to mains gas.* (DTI, 2001, p4)

Only limited progress appears to have been made since publication of the strategy. Installations of micro-renewables or CHP rarely occur through CERT in the Priority Group because they usually require a client contribution (Ofgem, 2009). The fuel poor, with no savings, cannot find this money. There are no programmes designed to get low-carbon technologies into the homes of the fuel poor – the only policies are of greater benefit to better-off households, thus widening the energy efficiency and carbon gap between the income groups. For instance, the Low Carbon Buildings Programme has provided grants of a proportion of the costs to householders installing, mainly, solar thermal in their homes (DECC, 2009b). It is unlikely that more than a handful have gone to the fuel poor, largely because of their lack of capital.

The CCC has looked at the technical potential and found that there could be 61 million installations of low- and zero-carbon technologies (including ground source heat pumps) by about 2020 and that CHP or district heating could be extensive. However, few of these are likely to happen with current policies and attitudes. For the realistic potential 'the bulk of the emissions reductions in the residential sector is driven by biomass and solar water heating' (CCC, 2008, p235). The wider take-up of low- and zero-carbon technologies is being actively debated, but normally without reference to the fuel poor (Walker, 2008).

One local authority which has facilitated the installation of low- and zero-carbon technologies is Kirklees. Home-owners are able to borrow up to £10,000 interest free through the Re-Charge scheme. The loan is secured on the property and repaid when it is sold, and the council pays the interest meanwhile. The council has made £3 million available over three years and 10 per cent has been ring-fenced for the fuel poor (HC 37, 2009, Ev 97).

The government has a tough target of providing 15 per cent of UK energy from renewable sources by 2020 as our contribution to European policy. This is binding, which means that there are financial penalties for non-achievement. Enabling the fuel poor to have access to low- and zero-carbon technologies would be a sensible contribution to this target, but no such policies presently exist.

Future policies

The CCC considers that their proposals to meet the UK's carbon reduction budgets will put an extra 1.7 million households into fuel poverty by 2022, largely as a result of higher fuel prices – 1.1 million from gas and 0.6 million from electricity price increases (CCC, 2008, p395). The CCC considers that most of the investment in energy efficiency and the cost of decarbonizing the energy system will be the responsibility of the utilities. Hence, fuel prices for householders, including the fuel poor, will increase substantially. The CCC's view is that 'fuel poverty impacts should be mitigated, and our analysis suggests that this could be achieved at manageable cost' (CCC, 2008, pxxviii). It assesses this cost to be in the order of £500 million annually, presumably above existing expenditure, as these are additional fuel-poor numbers (CCC, 2008, p395). Not all of the money would be spent on energy-efficiency improvements as higher incomes and a greater use of social tariffs would be needed. Their definition of a social tariff appears to be the same as a reverse block tariff, rather than the usual definition (Chapter 4).

New low-carbon policies will have to remain as the government's primary responsibility, rather than shared with Ofgem. The government's 'refusal to amend Ofgem's primary purpose to take proper account of today's low-carbon imperatives remains deeply disappointing' (SDC, 2009, p22).

Ofgem is required to take notice of 'future' customers; but more than seven years after this being added to its primary duties, it still has not explicitly stated what this means (Mitchell, 2008, p59). Considering this responsibility, it is particularly surprising that Ofgem does not have children included in its category of vulnerable households (see p24), although they are, without doubt, the future and in need of protection.

Energy efficiency is crucial in the debate about climate change and the fuel poor because of the way in which it transforms a series of negative situations into a virtuous collection (Table 5.13). Too much emphasis has been placed, in the past, on moving the better-off households, with high energy use to a low-energy use scenario (green). It is now important to find ways of moving the

Table 5.13 *Relationships between energy services and energy efficiency*

	Low income	Better off	Green
Energy use	Low	High	Low
Efficiency	Low	Medium	High
Energy services	Low	High	High
Carbon emissions/intensity	High	Medium	Low

Source: Author

low-income household direct to a green one, without waiting for the higher incomes that allow the higher consumption of a better-off household.

Feed-in tariffs

With the limited grants available for micro-generation technologies, the payback period for householders who install them can be very long (Bergman et al, 2009, p27). To overcome this, a new government initiative is the proposal to pay householders for the amount of electricity or heat that they produce from renewable sources. This was included in the 2008 Energy Act, and the government is committed to introducing a proposal for a renewable energy tariff before the end of 2009. It is expected to be operative in April 2010, possibly for both electricity and heat. If the latter, this would presumably include solar thermal and, perhaps, biomass-fired heating. The expectation is that the feed-in tariff will be for all the electricity and heat that is generated, not just that which is exported (as in Germany). This is a much more generous approach and recognizes that all energy from renewable sources, whether used in the home or not, contributes to the annual total and the government's renewable energy target of 15 per cent by 2020. This could be an important form of income for the fuel poor if (and it is a big if) there are policies to ensure that they have access to all the capital required to install the low- and zero-carbon technologies in the first place.

Personal carbon allowances

One proposal that combines the needs of the fuel poor with climate change mitigation is the introduction of personal carbon allowances. These are progressive if they cover energy use in the home, personal transport and flights – less than one transaction a week. The poorest people are less likely to fly, or even own a car, so that they are more likely to have an asset (part of their carbon allowance) to sell, which provides some income (Roberts and Thumim, 2006; Fawcett et al, 2007). This makes personal carbon allowances a redistributive policy, with a strong degree of certainty – the government will achieve the desired cut in emissions because more allowances will not be issued. The government has declined to consider the policy because:

> *The findings of the research indicate that, while personal carbon*
> *trading remains a potentially important way to engage individu-*

als, and there are no insurmountable technical obstacles to its introduction, it would nonetheless seem that it is an idea currently ahead of its time in terms of its public acceptability and the technology to bring down the costs. (Defra, 2008c, p4, para 1.7)

Conclusions

The strong correlation between levels of carbon emissions and prices for the different fuels means that most climate change policies are good for fuel poverty and most policies to improve the energy efficiency of low-income homes are good for climate change.

The main potential area of conflict between fuel poverty and climate change policies arises over Economy 7 or Economy 10. These off-peak electricity tariffs, used mainly at night, are cheaper than the standard tariffs, but nearly as polluting. They are, therefore, good for fuel poverty, but bad for the environment. The ideal policy approach is one that recognizes this dichotomy and accepts that some households (mainly the fuel poor) should continue to use Economy 7, but that, in order to minimize the carbon emissions, the properties should be super-insulated. This was the original Electricity Council recommendation when the tariff was first introduced, before 1970 (Boardman, 1991, p15).

A related problem is the growing use of heat pumps, whether air source or ground source (the former is for small properties and the latter requires a fairly large garden). This is more general than fuel poverty policy. Heat pumps are, at present levels of the carbon content of electricity and their efficiencies in practice, just as polluting as using a gas-fired system. So heat pumps should only be installed where there is no access to the gas grid and biomass-fired systems are impractical. This is likely to remain true until about 2025, when the carbon content of electricity is expected to have reduced so that gas and electricity are carbon equivalent.

One of the major solutions to fuel poverty is to ensure that the householders have the maximum income possible through a major campaign to increase the take-up of benefits. This could achieve quick results, so people have more money with which to keep warm in their leaky homes. This, in turn, implies more energy consumption and carbon dioxide emissions in the short term and, therefore, bigger adjustments by the non-fuel poor. An equitable approach to climate change would indicate that a strong focus on the energy efficiency of the homes of the fuel poor would prevent some of these extra emissions.

In one particular area, climate change policy could be harmful for the fuel poor – if it results in higher fuel prices for the fuel poor whether through a carbon tax, utility funding for demand reduction or new supply. As shown in Chapter 4, the poor are already facing substantial unjustified price hikes:

> *If the price signal for carbon was what we wanted to use in order to create the conditions for a low-carbon economy, then the market is doing our job for us. But it is doing it in a way that is deeply regressive, inequitable and certain to increase fuel poverty.*
> (Harman, 2008, p29)

The worsening fuel poverty must constrain the policy options for climate change alleviation. All-electric homes and homes with no gas create special problems for the fuel poor and for climate change policies as they are typically expensive to run and highly polluting. There are excellent synergies when high levels of insulation are installed and if reverse tariffs are introduced. These properties should become a priority for the installation of low- and zero-carbon technologies – for instance, solar thermal for hot water.

The most polluting homes are those without gas and older properties and should be the areas to tackle first, from a carbon perspective. The older the property, the greater the likelihood of it having a high theoretical level of energy consumption and carbon emissions. Half of the most polluting homes were built before 1919. As the SAP only covers space and water heating (and some lighting), additional policies are needed to reflect the use of the remaining electricity in lights and appliances. These statements are true of the whole housing stock.

There is a need to ensure that fuel-poor households can be truly low carbon, not only by insulating the property, but also by providing low-carbon options (e.g. solar thermal, solar photovoltaics and combined heat and power) to the fuel poor. These could also provide a source of income, depending on the design of the feed-in tariff that the government is proposing to introduce in 2010. The introduction of a feed-in tariff that is not supported by a capital investment programme in low-carbon technologies in low-income homes would only widen the relative fuel poverty gap.

Policies that focus on getting energy-efficient appliances into low-income homes are necessary and appropriate. At the moment, few low-income house-holds benefit from the minimum performance standards being introduced for new equipment, as over half of them may buy second-hand appliances and those that buy new are focused on low capital cost items. Programmes, such as Fridgesavers, should be implemented to assist the fuel poor. These are scrap-page schemes targeting the least efficient, but working equipment and a new CERT initiative on category G boilers is a good precedent. It needs to be extended to other pieces of equipment. The trickle-down effect of waiting for efficient appliances to become second hand and thus of benefit to the fuel poor is definitely inadequate.

One proposal that combines the needs of the fuel poor with climate change is the introduction of personal carbon allowances. These are progressive if they cover energy use in the home, personal transport and flights. The poorest people are less likely to fly, or even own a car, so that they are more likely to have an asset (part of their carbon allowance) to sell, which provides some income.

The dramatic rise in fuel prices since 2003 is resulting in greater relative deprivation in low-income homes: they are less able to respond and maintain consumption levels than better-off households.

There are strong policy synergies between the need to reduce fuel poverty and the need to reduce carbon emissions. The real challenge is to make sure that both sets of policies focus on both sets of priorities, at the same time. There is a risk, as exemplified by the CCC report (CCC, 2008), of seeing fuel poverty as a peripheral side issue that can be tackled by social and fuel pricing policy. This is incorrect and has failed for the last 30 years. The obligations to the present generation must not be obscured by our commitment to future generations and they do not have to be.

References

Bergman, N., Hawkes, A., Brett, D., Baker, P., Barton, J., Blanchard, R., Brandon, N. P., Infield, D., Jardine, C., Kelly, N., Leach, M., Matian, M., Peacock, A., Staffell, I., Sudtharalingam, S. and Woodman, B. (2009) 'UK microgeneration. Part 1: Policy and behavioural aspects', *Energy*, vol 162, February, pp23–36

BERR (Department for Business, Enterprise and Regulatory Reform) (2008) *Energy Consumption in the UK*, BERR, London

Boardman, B. (1991) *Fuel Poverty: From Cold Homes to Affordable Warmth*, Belhaven Press, London

Boardman, B. (2004) 'Achieving energy efficiency through product policy: The UK experience', *Environmental Science and Policy*, vol 7, pp165–176

Boardman, B. (2007) *Home Truths: A Low-Carbon Strategy to Reduce UK Housing Emissions by 80% by 2050*, Research report for the Co-operative Bank and Friends of the Earth, London, www.foe.co.uk/resource/reports/home_truths.pdf

Boardman, B., Lane, K., Hinnells, M., Banks, N., Milne, G., Goodwin, A. and Fawcett, T. (1997) *Transforming the UK Cold Market*, DECADE project, ECI, University of Oxford, Oxford, UK

Boardman, B., Darby, S., Killip, G., Hinnells, M., Jardine, C.N., Palmer, J. and Sinden, G. (2005) *40% House*, Environmental Change Institute, University of Oxford, Oxford, UK

British Gas Annual Reports: www.centrica.co.uk/files/reports/2008ar/index.asp, and similar for other years

CCC (Climate Change Committee) (2008) *Building a Low-Carbon Economy: The UK's Contribution to Tackling Climate Change*, First report, Committee on Climate Change, December, www.theccc.org.uk/pdf/TSO-ClimateChange.pdf

Changeworks (2009) *Fridgesavers*, www.changeworks.org.uk/content.php?linkid=307

DCLG (Department for Communities and Local Government) (2008a) *English House Condition Survey 2006: Headline Report*, DCLG, London

DCLG (2008b) *English House Condition Survey 2006: Annual Report*, DCLG, London

DECC (Department of Energy and Climate Change) (2008) *Greenhouse Gas Policy Evaluation and Appraisal in Government Departments*, www.decc.gov.uk/en/content/cms/statistics/analysts_group/analysts_group.aspx

DECC (2009a) *UK Climate Change Sustainable Development Indicator: 2008 Greenhouse Gas Emissions, Provisional Figures, Annex A*, March, www.decc.gov.uk/en/content/cms/statistics/climate_change/climate_change.aspx

DECC (2009b) *Low Carbon Building Programme – application statistics*, DECC, www.lowcarbonbuildings.org.uk

Defra (2008a), *Guidelines to Defra's GHG Conversion Factors*, April, www.defra.gov.uk/environment/business/reporting/pdf/ ghg-cf-guidelines-annexes2008.pdf

Defra (2008b) *Local Authority CO_2 Emissions Estimates 2006 – Statistical Summary*, Defra, September, www.defra.gov.uk/environment/statistics/globatmos/download/ regionalrpt/local-regionalco2statssumm06.pdf

Defra (2008c) *Synthesis Report on the Findings from Defra's Pre-Feasibility Study into Personal Carbon Trading*, Defra, April, www.defra.gov.uk/environment/ climatechange/uk/individual/carbontrading/pdf/pct-synthesis-%20report.pdf

Defra (2009) *Key Facts about Climate Change: Carbon Dioxide Emissions by End User: 1990–2007, UK*, www.defra.gov.uk/environment/statistics/globatmos/gakf07.htm

DTI (Department of Trade and Industry) (2001) *The UK Fuel Poverty Strategy*, DTI, London, November, www.berr.gov.uk/files/file16495.pdf

DUKES (2009) *Digest of UK Energy Statistics – Long Term Trends, Energy*, www.decc.gov.uk/en/content/cms/statistics/publications/dukes/dukes.aspx

Ekins, P. and Dresner, S. (2004) *Green Taxes and Charges: Reducing Their Impact on Low-Income Households*, Joseph Rowntree Foundation, York

Fawcett, T., Bottrill, C., Boardman, B. and Lye, G. (2007) *Trialling Personal Carbon Allowances*, UK Energy Research Centre and Esmée Fairbairn, London

GHS (2007) *General Household Survey 2007*, www.statistics.gov.uk/downloads/ theme_compendia/GHS07/GeneralHouseholdSurvey2007.pdf

Harman, J. (2008) *The Green Crunch: Why We Need a New Economics for Britain's Environmental Challenge*, Fabian Society, London

HC 37 (2009) *Energy Efficiency and Fuel Poverty*, Third report of session 2008–2009, Environment, Food and Rural Affairs Select Committee, Stationery Office, London

King, M. (2009) 'New dawn for CHP?', *Energy Action*, NEA, Newcastle, No 107, April, pp16–17

Lynch, D. (2009) *Rural Fuel Poverty*, National Energy Action, Newcastle, UK

Mitchell, C. (2008) *The Political Economy of Sustainable Energy*, Palgrave Macmillan, Basingstoke, UK

MTP (2009) *Carbon Dioxide Emission Factors for UK Energy Use*, BNXS01, Market Transformation Programme, *www.mtprog.com/spm/download/document/id/785*

National Statistics (now Office of National Statistics) (2000) *Family Spending: A report on the 1999–2000 Family Expenditure Survey*. Denis Down (ed), The Stationery Office, London, www.statistics.gov.uk/downloads/theme_social/ FamSpend99-00v2.pdf

Ofgem (Office of the Gas and Electricity Markets) (2008) *Energy Supply Probe: Initial Findings Report*, Consultation, Ofgem, www.ofgem.gov.uk/Markets/RetMkts/ ensuppro/Documents1/Energy%20Supply%20Probe%20-%20Initial% 20Findings%20Report.pdf

Ofgem (2009) *Carbon Emissions Reduction Target – Update*, Ofgem, London, February

ONS (Office for National Statistics) (2008) *Family Spending: A report on the 2007 Expenditure and Food Survey*, Rachel Skentelbery (ed), Palgrave Macmillan, ONS,

www.statistics.gov.uk/downloads/theme_social/Family_Spending_2007/
FamilySpending2008_web.pdf

Roberts, S. and Thumim, J. (2006) *A Rough Guide to Individual Carbon Trading: The Ideas, the Issues and the Next Steps*, Centre for Sustainable Energy, Bristol, and Department for Environment, Food and Rural Affairs, London

SDC (Sustainable Development Commission) (2009) *A Sustainable New Deal*, SDC, London

Turner, A. (2009) *Building a Low Carbon Economy*, Powerpoint presentation to Friends of the Earth conference, 9 February, www.theccc.org.uk/other_docs/FoEScotland%209%20Feb%2009.pdf

Utley, J. I. and Shorrock, L. D. (2008) *Domestic Energy Fact File*, Building Research Establishment, Watford, UK

WAG (Welsh Assembly Government) (2009) *One Wales: One Planet. The Sustainable Development Scheme of the Welsh Assembly Government*, WAG, May, www.assemblywales.org/bus-home/bus-guide-docs-pub/bus-business-documents/bus-business-documents-doc-laid/gen-ld7521-e.pdf?langoption=3&ttl=GEN-LD7521%20-%20One%20Wales%3A%20One%20Planet%20-%20The%20Sustainable%20Development%20Scheme%20of%20the%20Welsh%20Assembly%20Government

Walker, G. (2008) 'Decentralised systems and fuel poverty: Are there any links or risks?', *Energy Policy*, vol 36, pp4514–4517

Wilkinson, B. and Pickles, D. (2005) 'SAP targets and affordability in social housing', *Energy Action*, NEA, July, pp18–19

Wingfield, D., Fuel Poverty Statistician, DECC, pers comm

6

Energy Efficiency of the Housing Stock

The fuel poor are definitely paying more than they should have to for fuel and are getting somewhat less income than they are entitled to. Both of these would be useful improvements and would offset, at least partially, some of their fuel poverty. Both incomes and fuel prices relate to the household's weekly income and expenditure and its ability to pay recurring running costs. The role of energy efficiency – whether in the boiler or as an attribute of the building fabric – and what people are actually paying for their energy services is the third of the main influences on fuel poverty. It has a different impact than incomes and fuel prices because of the role of investment in equipment: the boiler, the light bulb, the refrigerator and the loft insulation all require capital expenditure. This is sometimes a considerable sum of money; but it is a one-off or rare cost and the greater energy efficiency of this new piece of equipment means that the recurring energy costs are lower. Improved energy efficiency is the permanent non-reversible component of reducing fuel poverty. The fuel poor, like anyone in poverty, rarely have access to sources of capital, so this expenditure has to be funded through some other medium. The energy efficiency of the homes of the fuel poor indicate, in a very real sense, the extent to which society is concerned about fuel poverty.

Another real benefit of energy efficiency is that, when it results in a reduced demand for energy, the synergies between fuel poverty and climate change policy, examined in the last chapter, are achieved.

The UK has a good selection of statistics on the housing stock, particularly in England, although there are never enough. The way in which data on homes is broken down differs from the categories of social statistics, so there is information about the age of the property, but rarely about the homes of pensioners. This makes matching the housing and social profiles difficult – they are facing in different directions. The information on the worst housing and the homes of the poorest people cannot easily be brought together, even on paper.

From the outset the government has recognized that energy-efficiency improvements to households were central to delivery of the government's climate change and fuel poverty objectives. In 2001, *The Fuel Poverty Strategy* stated that:

> *The government believes that a substantial majority of the 2.2 million to 2.4 million vulnerable fuel-poor households will require assistance through energy-efficiency improvements.* (DTI, 2001, p37, para 4.30)

That recognition has been repeated, both by the government and its advisers:

> *The most sustainable way to eradicate fuel poverty is to 'fuel poverty' proof the housing stock, which means that a dwelling will be sufficiently energy efficient that regardless of who occupies the property, there is a low probability that they would be in fuel poverty.* (DTI, 2006, p31)

> *Government analysis suggests that there is a greater cost-effective potential to reduce energy consumption and greenhouse emissions by households than by transport, industry or other sectors of the economy.* (NAO, 2008, p44)

As a result, there has been more fuel poverty policy in relation to the energy efficiency of the home than on incomes or fuel prices.

As already demonstrated, attempts to target policy on the poorest people are failing dismally from a fuel poverty perspective, with only about 20 per cent of the money actually reaching the fuel poor (Table 3.6). This chapter assesses a different approach: would we be more successful at eradicating fuel poverty if we targeted the worst homes? In order to answer that question, it is necessary to establish who lives in the most energy-inefficient homes and whether these are the poorest people. And how much is being achieved by the various energy-efficiency programmes.

Measuring energy efficiency

The fuel poverty model, or methodology, is described in Chapter 2 (p28). This is largely independent of other methods of calculating energy efficiency and is used to support government statements on fuel poverty policy, progress and statistics (e.g. BERR, 2008a, 2008b).

For general (non-fuel poverty) policy, the Standard Assessment Procedure (SAP) is the government's official measure of the cost of achieving a specified level of energy services in the home (e.g. 21°C in living rooms, 18°C elsewhere, when occupied). SAP covers all space and water heating and the electricity used in fixed light fittings (i.e. about 85 per cent of all energy). The other uses of energy for cooking, moveable lighting, washing machines, fridges, etc. are excluded from SAP's energy use, costs and carbon emissions. This is because the SAP is designed to reflect the energy efficiency of the dwelling, irrespective of its size, geographical location and the income or behaviour of its occupants. It therefore reflects those energy-related activities that are specific to the building, rather than those that move with, and are dependent upon, the occupants. The SAP rating currently in use dates from 2005 (i.e. SAP05) and is on a scale of 1 to 100, with higher numbers being more energy efficient.

The SAP rating, for the uses that it covers, encompasses both the energy efficiency with which they are provided and their cost. To derive the SAP, the energy cost is divided by the floor area of the dwelling to give a relative figure (cost of energy per square metre). This means that any saving (whether energy, carbon or money) from an improvement in energy efficiency will depend on the floor area: the saving per square metre has to be multiplied back up by the actual size, in square metres, of the dwelling. All other things being equal, the energy used by a dwelling is proportional to its floor area (Chapman, pers comm). It is assumed that larger dwellings are occupied by more people, so not only is there more space to keep warm, there is also a greater need for hot water and lighting.

All SAP ratings are, therefore, based on a theoretical situation – that homes are warm, with good supplies of hot water and adequately lit, for the assumed number of occupants. Whatever the criticisms of the SAP (Banks, 2008), it is a system designed to provide a consistent ranking of homes: even if there were changes to the SAP procedure, they would not affect that this home, at this point in time, is more energy efficient than that one. Because of its theoretical basis, there is a limited relationship between the predictions of energy consumption under the SAP and what is happening in practice. This is most important when assessing the effect of energy-efficiency improvements as the energy, money and carbon savings will be less, sometimes substantially less, in practice. It is useful to be able to compare properties on a like-for-like basis; but the failure of energy savings to materialize can cause policy uncertainty and confusion.

The SAP is used in most official statistics of the energy efficiency of the housing stock throughout the UK, but a reduced Standard Assessment Procedure (RdSAP) is the basis of the calculations for the Energy Performance Certificates (EPCs). Any differences between SAP and RdSAP are not relevant here. The EPC is required for each dwelling when it is sold or rented and each property is labelled with a band, ranging from A to G, with A the best and G the worst (Table 6.1). The SAP of a property does not fluctuate (e.g. it does not go down as a result of higher prices or fabric deterioration); it can only improve from its baseline as a result of a capital investment in insulation or a new boiler. Below a SAP of 52.5, the scale is logarithmic, so that an increase at the lowest levels results in a bigger cost saving per point raised than an increase of the same size further up the scale. Above 52.5 the scale is linear, so all increases of a single SAP point result in the same benefit. This effect combines

Table 6.1 *Energy Performance Certificate (EPC) bands, SAP05 rating, running costs and fuel poor, England (2006)*

EPC	SAP05 ratings	Housing stock (millions)	Fuel-poor households (millions)	Theoretical*, partial fuel costs for 85m² house (£ per annum)
A	92+	0	⎫	80
B	81–91	0.05	⎬ 0.03	187
C	69–80	1.70	⎭	294
D	55–68	6.68	0.30	427
E	39–54	9.00	0.87	587
F	21–38	3.66	0.77	811
G	1–20	0.91	0.45	1216
Total		**22.00**	**2.42**	

Note: * Theoretical because they are based on equally warm homes. Partial because 15 per cent of energy use is not covered by the SAP.
Source: DCLG (2008a, p6) for column 2 household numbers; Defra (2008, p55, Chart 17) used to estimate column 3, fuel poor; Chapman (pers comm) for column 4 costs

with the bands being of unequal size to give more money saved moving from a G to an F than in changing from a D to an A.

The fuel costs in Table 6.1 are partial. To get to the full fuel cost in 2006, the standing charge for electricity (£40) has to be added, together with expenditure on electricity and gas for cooking and £300 for the remaining lights and appliances (taken to be 3000kWh at 10 pence/kWh; Table 5.5 in Chapter 5) (i.e. a total of £340). The amount will not vary with the energy efficiency of the property, but it will be related to the assumed number of people in the household and the size of the dwelling. The proportion of expenditure that is for lights and appliances will, therefore, vary considerably. When these costs are added in, for the same size property, there is a factor of roughly four between the energy costs of living in the most energy-inefficient home (£1216 + £340 = £1556) and a band A property (£80 + £340 = £420). The varying effect is true for energy consumption:

> ... *the power taken by lighting and domestic appliances makes a relatively small contribution to overall fuel usage among the least efficient dwellings (less than 20 per cent for those with SAP ratings below 20) [whereas] it can account for more than a half in very efficient dwellings.* (DOE, 1996, p246)

Taking the households in the most severe fuel poverty (the 19 per cent living in a band G property), their total theoretical expenditure of £1556 is what they needed to spend in 2006. In comparison, the 30 per cent of households on the lowest incomes only spent £660 (p49) in 2007, a mere 42 per cent: they were under-consuming by at least half. This indicates the depths of fuel poverty – and cold – for many households.

Table 6.2 *Balance between SAP and non-SAP fuel usage, expenditure and carbon, UK (2007/08)*

	Energy (kWh)	£	Carbon
SAP: Space and water heating, fixed lighting	85%	58%	68%
Non-SAP: Other lights, all appliances	15%	42%	32%

Note: For an average 85m² home, using a total of 19,760kWh over the whole year.
Source: uses data from Tables 3.1, 5.2, 5.5, 5.8 in Chapters 3 and 5

The above figures are a combination of theoretical assumptions about the amount of energy needed, particularly for heating, in SAP and actual use in lights and appliances. Using information already provided in the book and dealing solely with actual use, the split between what is and is not included in SAP varies according to which metric is being considered (Table 6.2). Too much of policy ignores what is omitted from SAP and not enough recognizes the importance of the cost of energy and its carbon intensity. As stated in Chapter 5, Table 6.2 confirms there are strong synergies between a policy focus on carbon (for climate change) and on money (for fuel poverty).

In reality, homes can be so energy inefficient that they have a negative SAP rating and are below the scale. The energy costs for them would be higher still. The range is also expanded by the effect of dwelling size if, for instance, the comparison is between a 45 square metre C-rated dwelling and a 120 square metre G-rated house; yet these could both be occupied by a low-income pensioner. The pensioner could either be living in the large, old family home that has not been improved, or have moved to a recently built, well-insulated small sheltered housing scheme. The income received by the pensioner from benefits would be the same in both cases (even housing and council tax benefit are related to housing costs, not housing condition). The energy efficiency of the home is not reflected in the state benefits or any financial support for the fuel poor. That is why a new energy-related benefit is suggested in Chapter 3.

There are problems for fuel poverty analysis in the way in which SAP and RdSAP accommodate changing fuel prices. Each version (e.g. SAP01, SAP05 and, shortly, SAP09) uses an average of the fuel prices in the three years prior to its release. These fuel prices are not subsequently changed until the next version. With each new version, the new costs are 'deflated' so that the SAP does not change, even if fuel prices have. The deflator between SAP01 and SAP05 was 0.9. This makes the use over time of SAP or RdSAP extremely problematic for fuel poverty purposes. It may be inappropriate to have a standard, as in the National Indicator (NI) 187 (Chapter 8), that relates fuel poverty to a SAP level: the numbers in fuel poverty are strongly affected by changing fuel prices, which are effectively neutralized in each SAP upgrade. The SAP is best at comparing households and fuels within one version, but less useful when the comparison is across versions. For instance, fuel poverty could be increasing, but the proportion of homes with a SAP less than 35 does not change between versions.

The fuel poverty model (Chapter 2) also makes an assumption over fuel prices that is disadvantageous for the fuel poor. It assumes that households pay the average price for their fuel and tariff in that region. But as shown in Chapter 4, there are substantial variations in the prices paid by the fuel poor, even within a region. For instance, the fuel costs in the fuel poverty model will underestimate the expenditure of those households which have stayed with their electricity and gas companies and not switched, as they are paying more than those which do switch. Any averaging across the region would negate this range, which Ofgem has shown is detrimental to the disadvantaged.

Energy efficiency of the home

However it is measured, the energy efficiency of the housing stock increases each year (Table 6.3) because of three factors:

- the addition to the stock of brand new homes with relatively high SAP ratings (e.g. SAP05 70+); this has been around 200,000 per annum;
- demolitions of old properties – demolition rates have been very low for the past decade or so, only removing about 20,000 properties a year (0.01 per cent of the housing stock), so that it will take well over 1000 years to replace the existing 25 million homes in the UK (Boardman et al, 2005, p87).
- any energy-efficiency improvements to existing properties, beyond those that are repairs or replacements;

The overall rate of improvement is slow: about 1 SAP point a year with about 30 per cent coming from the first two factors (Shorrock, pers comm). This confirms that the changes in the numbers of households in fuel poverty is little to do with any energy-efficiency improvements.

The stock is becoming more energy efficient, as confirmed by the decline in the rate of heat loss through the building fabric of the average Great Britain home by 9 per cent from 269W/°C in 2000 to 247W/°C in 2006 (Utley and Shorrock, 2008b, p85).

Table 6.3 *Average energy efficiency rating (SAP05), by country (2000–2007)*

	GB	England	Wales	Scotland	Northern Ireland
2000	45.5	45.5			45.5*
2004	49.6	47.4			
2006	52.1	48.8	50.0		52.4
2007		49.8		57.3	

Note: * 2001; the figures for Great Britain exclude Northern Ireland. There does not appear to be a UK-wide average.
Source: Utley and Shorrock (2008b, p94) for GB; DECC (2009a, Table 3.5) for England; extract from Welsh Assembly Government (2009a) for Wales; SHCS (2008, p16) for Scotland; NIHE (2007, p126) for Northern Ireland

Table 6.4 *Energy savings from energy-efficiency improvements, by initial indoor temperature*

Initial temperature (°C)	Percentage of the theoretical energy saving achieved
14	54
15	60
16	66
17	72
18	78
19	84
20	90

Source: Milne and Boardman (2000)

The extent to which an energy saving will be made as a result of an energy-efficiency improvement depends partly on the initial temperature in the property (Table 6.4): the colder the property, the greater proportion of the benefit that is taken as additional warmth, rather than energy savings. However, both will occur, even in the coldest homes, because these are occupied by the poorest people who both want the additional money and the extra warmth. With warmth there is a limit, as Table 6.4 indicates: once the household is adequately warm, almost all the benefit is taken as energy savings. The definition of adequately warm used to be thought of as 21°C; but it may be increasing, partly because people wear thinner clothes indoors. However, few homes have temperatures as low as 14°C in 2009, although, as shown in Chapter 7, it is not unknown. It is to be hoped that there is no large-scale return to these temperatures with rising fuel prices and greater fuel poverty, as potentially indicated in Chapter 5 by declining real expenditure.

The importance of the original temperature in the home is one of the reasons why the predicted energy savings are more than those that occur (Hong et al, 2006). Many households were under-consuming energy to start with – that is why they were cold. They cannot save what they were not using.

There are two particularly strong influences on the energy efficiency of the building fabric: the date of the original construction and the number of external surfaces. SAP is used in the following statistics as a convenient way of comparing across types of properties at a point in time. In this context it is a useful way to indicate where the fuel poor are likely to be found.

Age of dwelling

The influence of the date of construction is that methods and standards of building have changed considerably as a result of growing technical knowledge, fashion and regulations. The level of insulation in the oldest properties is always the worst, as building regulations did not require any insulation before 1976 (Boardman, 1991, p62) and subsequent improvements to that building have not compensated. Excluding the most recent construction (post-1964),

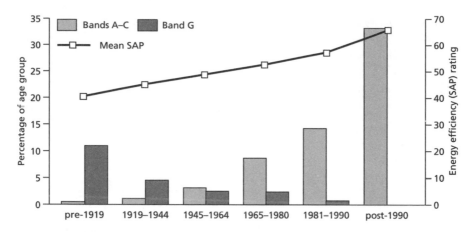

Source: DCLG (2008a, p142)

Figure 6.1 *Average and banded energy efficiency rating (SAP05) by dwelling age, England (2006)*

the improvements to the energy efficiency of the housing stock have been occurring most rapidly in properties originally built between 1944 and 1964 and the slowest rate of improvement has occurred in the pre-1919 homes (DCLG, 2008a, p143). Therefore, the gap between the standards in the pre-1919 properties and younger properties is growing. This is undoubtedly because of the greater costs and problems associated with improving homes that have solid walls and may be of townscape importance or architectural heritage. For instance, the proportion of homes with full double glazing is lowest in the pre-1919 group, indicating the uncertainties about replacing sash windows (DCLG, 2008a, p124), it then rises consistently across the age groups. By 2006, the effect of the age of the dwelling is that the average SAP05 rating varies from 42 for pre-1919 to 65 for post-1990 (Figure 6.1). There is a real energy-efficiency bonus from living in a newer home.

As shown in the previous chapter, the fuel cost and SAP variations are mirrored in the carbon emissions: the greatest emissions come from the least energy-efficient properties, under the same theoretical conditions.

External surfaces

Heat is lost to the cold outside air through the building fabric and ventilation, so the more external surfaces there are, the greater the rate of heat loss is likely to be. Hence, on average, the rate of heat loss in a flat was half that of a detached house in England in 2006 (Table 6.5). While flats are more energy efficient, in general, there are problems with adding insulation, for instance the cavities of all properties in the block have to be filled together, otherwise the insulation may just slip into the cavity of the flat below.

There is an additional energy bonus from living in a flat because flats are generally smaller in area than houses, so the total fuel bills will be lower. The

Table 6.5 *Type of dwelling by heat loss and fuel-poor numbers (2006)*

	Rate of heat loss, Great Britain (W/°C)	Fuel poor, England (%)
Detached	342	23
Semi-detached	264	33
Terrace	235	32
Bungalow	225	(figures included in detached above)
Flat	167	12
Average	247	100

Source: Utley and Shorrock (2008b, p20) for rate of heat loss in Great Britain; BERR (2008a, Table 39) for percentage of fuel poor

majority (64 per cent) of flats achieve a rating of D or better, with an average SAP05 rating of 57.1 (Figure 6.2), whereas nearly 70 per cent of houses have a rating of E or worse. There are two quite distinct distributions. The one caveat is that flats vary substantially: purpose-built flats are more energy efficient than converted ones (DCLG, 2008a, p139). Scotland has a lower average heat loss per home than England, partly because a high proportion (41 per cent) consists of flats or tenements (Utley and Shorrock, 2008a, p9).

Inevitably, there is a relationship between built form and housing density: more detached homes in rural areas and more flats and terraced houses in city centres. As a result, energy efficiency decreases in England from an average

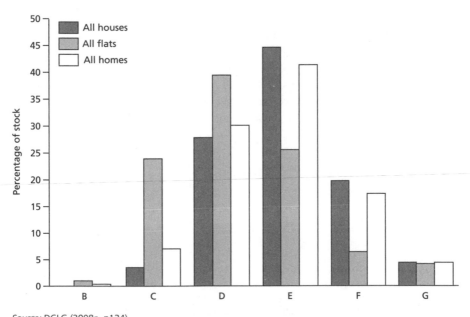

Source: DCLG (2008a, p134)

Figure 6.2 *Energy efficiency rating (SAP05) by house and flat, England (2006)*

SAP05 of 50 in urban and suburban areas to an average SAP05 of 30 in completely rural areas, outside of villages. In rural areas, the problems are compounded by the lack of gas and the need to buy expensive fuel (DCLG, 2008a, p145).

Which are the best homes?

The best homes are the newest homes for three reasons:

- The energy-efficiency standards of new homes continue to rise in England (Boardman, 2007, Chapter 4); these standards are defined by the building regulations, which are a devolved power in Scotland and Northern Ireland (BRE, 2005, p31) and will be shortly in Wales.
- An increasing proportion of new construction are flats: up from 17 per cent in 2000/01 to 45 per cent of all homes built in 2007/08 (DCLG, 2009a, Table 254).
- There is substantial downsizing in the types of homes being built, with the proportion of one- and two-bedroom properties increasing from one third to over half between 2000/01 and 2007/08 (Table 6.6). This is good for energy conservation and also, belatedly, is matching the demographic structure of the population. There has been a similar trend in Wales, where the proportion of one-bedroom new properties has doubled between 2000/01 to 2006/07 from 5 to 11 per cent, matched by a decline in new homes with more than four bedrooms from 34 to 28 per cent (ONS, 2008, p219).

The government has a target to build 3 million new homes by 2020. In order to achieve this, in 2007, the government raised its homebuilding target to 240,000 a year (ENDS, 2008, p55). 'But actual construction is currently far slower. Only 133,700 homes were built in the year to March 2009, a fifth less than the previous year and fewer still are expected to be completed this year' (Booth, 2009). Most of this decline has been in the private development of new homes for sale.

Table 6.6 *Size of new homes (2000/01–2007/08)*

	2000/01	2003/04	2006/07	2007/08
1 bedroom (%)	7	8	11	11
2 bedrooms (%)	27	33	42	44
3 bedrooms (%)	34	29	27	26
4+ bedrooms (%)	32	30	20	19
Total new homes England (millions)	0.133	0.144	0.168	0.167
Total new homes UK (millions)	0.175	0.190	0.218	0.214
New social housing in UK	13%	10%	12%	15%
New social housing in UK	22,880	18,230	26,910	28,840

Source: DCLG (2009a, Tables 209) for two total rows; DCLG (2009a, Table 254) for rest

The lack of new homes for tenants in the social sector has been recognized by the government: every year from 1983 to 2007 there was a net loss in the amount of social housing as more homes were sold through right-to-buy than were constructed (Beckett, 2009). The government's aim is for the construction of new social housing to increase to 50,000 per annum by 2012 and perhaps to elevate the rate to counteract the recession. Although the credit crunch has slowed the achievement of this target, the proportion of new construction that is for the social sector has increased from 9 per cent in 2003 to 18 per cent in 2008 (DCLG, 2009a, Table 244). The social housing that is built and funded through the Housing Corporation (now the Homes and Communities Agency) is of a high level of energy efficiency. It has been at level 3 on the Code for Sustainable Homes (CSH) since 2008 – two years ahead of the 2010 building regulations.

The main issue with new homes is to make sure that they are available for the fuel poor, specifically through rented social housing. The second issue is to ensure that they are built to the standard required by the building regulations and not to some lower standard because these regulations are not enforced properly (BRE, 2004).

In early 2009, new homes provided a real energy-efficiency bonus, both because the regulations were getting to a high standard and because many of the properties were small flats. However, very few new homes are for low-income households, let alone the fuel poor, except for some proportion of the new social-sector homes. The main solution to fuel poverty still lies in the conversion of the existing housing stock.

Which are the worst homes and how to treat them?

At the other end of the scale are the most energy-inefficient homes. The G band on the EPC consists of appalling properties that cost a fortune to keep warm and, if they are warm, are highly polluting. A wide-range of properties qualifies as G-rated. For instance, in a terraced, solid-walled house, with a pitched roof, single glazing, virtually no insulation (even on the hot water tank) and hot water heated by electricity, the heating system could be electric storage heaters, open fires, gas fires or even gas central heating and still have less than 20 SAP points (Banks, pers comm).

All the properties that are rated G and most, if not all, of those rated F are likely to be unhealthy, as defined by the Housing Health and Safety Rating System (HHSRS, Chapter 7). The local authorities should be taking action on these properties; but few are fulfilling their duties comprehensively. There are still 4.5 million households in England that have a SAP rating below 38 and are in the F and G bands (Table 6.1). These homes are seriously energy inefficient and about half are occupied by the fuel poor. The risk of being in an F or G category home is equally great for owner occupiers and privately rented (23 and 21 per cent of each group), and negligible for the social sector (7 per cent) (Whitehead, 2008, p84).

There are discussions about hard-to-heat, hard-to-treat and hard-to-reach properties, and there are many fuel poor in each category. Although a common expression, hard to treat is not really the right description, as the homes are treatable, but expensive. Hard-to-heat homes include those with solid walls and/or are not on the gas mains network (p114). Hard-to-reach properties are in rural areas as they are less accessible for and, therefore, less serviced by the various contractors providing energy-efficiency improvements to the fuel poor.

In rural areas, there is a considerable overlap between hard to heat and hard to reach. The net effect is that they are expensive to heat and less likely to be improved under one of the existing programmes. Low-income households in rural areas do have a higher risk of fuel poverty as they need to spend about 15 per cent more on fuel than households elsewhere. This is from a combination of being slightly larger and less energy efficient than other homes (Palmer et al, 2008, p28).

There are more hard-to-heat properties than just those in bands F and G:

> *BRE estimates that in England there are approximately 9.2 million homes that are defined as 'hard to treat' ... three-quarters of hard-to-treat homes are solid wall properties, equivalent to 6.6.million homes... The highest proportion is in London. The current rate of retrofit installation of solid wall insulation is ... 15,000 to 20,000 [per annum]'.* (EEPfH, 2008a, p6)

This imperceptible rate of improvement is not necessarily focused on the fuel poor. There are also a certain number of homes with cavity walls that cannot be insulated with cavity wall insulation (the gap in the wall is too narrow or too dirty, or the wall is too exposed to rain). Solid walls were no longer built from about 1930 onwards, so they are found in the older properties: nearly 90 per cent of pre-1919 properties are hard to treat (BRE, 2008b, p8). Solid wall insulation is one of the more expensive measures and, if done externally on properties with a heritage value, can be disfiguring. Just insulating the solid-walled back extension of a property would be effective as it is more than half the exterior wall surface of a terraced house and is not part of the streetscape. One third of the solid-walled homes in the UK (BRE, 2008b), and a higher proportion in Wales, have a rendered finish, so adding external insulation could be accommodated while matching the existing appearance.

The cost of insulating a solid-walled house is much contested; if a group of properties are done at the same time, it is about £6500 for external solid wall insulation and £3400 for internal, not including administrative and surveying costs, nor discussions with the residents (SDC, 2009, p8). Because many fuel poor households live in hard-to-heat properties, to make them fuel-poverty proof means that not only solid wall insulation is required, but also micro-renewables such as solar thermal, biomass-fired heating, a gas mains extension, or community combined heat and power (CHP). At the moment, work in this area has largely been confined to a relatively small number of pilot projects, mainly in social housing. There is, effectively, no market in the private sector.

It is worth emphasizing that the technologies to improve any home are known, available and proven. In some cases, they might become cheaper as they are used more widely or when delivered in bulk to an area. The problems of the worst homes are soluble. The extent to which they are deemed too expensive depends on the timescale taken for any calculation, the benefit allocated to increased warmth, comfort and health for the occupants, and the commitment to end fuel poverty.

One example of an available technology is the use of CHP to solve the problem of hard-to-heat tower blocks. Gas cannot be used in these properties for safety reasons, but a communal wet system, served by a boiler in the basement is acceptable. This was the solution adopted in Aberdeen (King, 2009, p16). Replacing the electric storage heaters both reduced the carbon emissions and provided affordable warmth. CHP could be an appropriate solution to the problem of solid-walled Victorian terraces in urban centres.

An energy-inefficient property is one that is expensive to heat: it only provides expensive warmth. That means that the fuel poor, living in the worst homes, are having to pay the most to keep warm: they get very little value for the money they spend on heating. This is the opposite of what is normally expected: that the poor should be able to buy the cheapest products (bread, food and clothing) so that they are able to live on their low incomes. Poor-quality housing provides the opposite of that situation. The fuel poor are concentrated in the homes with the lowest SAP ratings (Figure 6.3) and are having to buy the most expensive warmth.

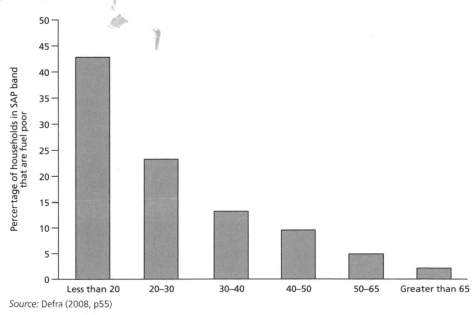

Source: Defra (2008, p55)

Figure 6.3 *Fuel poverty by SAP05 rating, England (2006)*

For households living in deprived areas, the risk of fuel poverty is only slightly increased because 'they tend to live in either smaller or more energy-efficient properties than their counterparts in other areas' (Palmer et al, 2008, p6), mainly social housing. This is important because of government programmes to tackle fuel poverty through an area-based approach, linked to multiple deprivation, as in the Community Energy Saving Programme (CESP) proposals discussed later in this chapter. 'If measures to combat fuel poverty are focused on areas of high deprivation, then they will only reach a small proportion of those in fuel poverty' (Palmer et al, 2008, p20). As discussed below, social housing has a higher average SAP rating than homes in the private sector, which contributes to the difference between the energy-efficiency of the homes of the poor and the fuel poor.

Tenure and energy efficiency

There is a degree of predictability about the types of properties lived in by the different tenure groups and, therefore, the level of energy efficiency. For instance, social-sector properties are largely post-1945 and over half are flats (Utley and Shorrock, 2006, p16), both good indicators of lower rates of heat loss. The addition of insulation also varies by tenure (Table 6.7). The overall trend has been towards more homes having the three measures that are defined as full insulation (Table 6.7) and less having none, gradually (Utley and Shorrock, 2008b, p28). The proportion with 'full insulation' will automatically rise because of the effect of new buildings; to decrease the numbers with no insulation requires intervention. By 2004, 28 per cent of privately rented homes had no insulation at all, against an average of 8 per cent, and only 6 per cent have full insulation, whereas the average is 16 per cent in 2004. This contributes to the sector having a high risk of fuel poverty.

There are twice as many properties without any insulation in Scotland as in England, but also the highest number with full insulation (in 2005) (Utley and Shorrock, 2006, pp 35, 78, 121).

Using a higher standard, social housing was substantially more energy efficient than the privately owned stock in 2006, with 20 per cent achieving

Table 6.7 *Level of insulation by tenure, Great Britain (2004)*

	No insulation (%)	Full insulation (%)
Owner occupied	4	17
Local authority	15	10
Registered social landlord	11	10
Privately rented	28	6
Average	8	16

Notes: No insulation means that there is no filled cavity, no insulation in the loft and not a single window that is double glazed. Full insulation is 100mm of loft insulation, a filled cavity and 80 per cent or more rooms double glazed. All three have to be present. A solid wall is treated as a filled cavity.
Source: Utley and Shorrock (2006, pp45–46, 116)

Table 6.8 *Energy Performance Certificate (EPC) bands and SAP05 rating by tenure, England (2001–2006)*

	2001			2006		
	Band G (%)	*Bands A–C (%)*	*Average SAP*	*Band G (%)*	*Bands A–C (%)*	*Average SAP*
Private sector		3	44.1	5	5	46.8
Social sector		12	51.9	2	20	57.4
All tenures	6.0	4.5	45.7	4.3	7	48.7

Notes: Private sector includes owner occupied and privately rented. Social sector includes registered social landlords and local authority housing.
Source: DCLG (2008a, pp24, 236)

band A to C ratings, four times the rate of the private sector (Table 6.8). There is a similar divergence with the worst properties, so the gap between the energy efficiency of the social and private sectors has increased from 8 to 11 SAP points since 2001. Much of the increase in the private sector will have come from new homes (few are for social housing), so this indicates that there has been a greater degree of intervention in the social sector, partially linked to the decent homes programme (below).

Since there is, on average, a link between income and tenure and those that are already spending in excess of 10 per cent of their income on fuel (Tables 2.11 and 2.12 in Chapter 2), there is a generalized relationship between income, tenure and energy efficiency. Lower income households are concentrated in the rented sector, particularly the social rented sector; but the majority of the fuel poor are in the private sector. Tenure is an important component of the fuel poverty debate.

Privately rented properties

One of the most difficult groups to influence is private landlords, who owned about 14 per cent of the UK housing stock in 2007, and the proportion is rising (DCLG, 2008b, p104). There was a wide spread of income groups within privately rented homes in England in 2006/07: there were about 250,000 households with annual incomes below £5000 and the same number with incomes above £50,000 (DCLG, 2009a, Table 809) – the privately rented sector combines two different distributions. Added to that, the income of the occupant is probably independent of the income of the property owner, who does at least possess a substantial capital asset – the property. The extent to which an affluent property owner should be subsidized in order to make sure that the low-income tenant has good-quality accommodation is an important under-discussed political debate.

Privately rented properties were inefficient at the point of construction: 45 per cent were built pre-1919 (Utley and Shorrock, 2008a, p86) and have had little added insulation (Table 6.7). As a result, nearly 16 per cent have a category 1 risk of excess cold under the HHSRS (described in Chapter 7, p181), which is the highest of any tenure group in England in 2006 (DCLG,

2008a, p78). Enforcing minimum standards, such as the HHSRS, would be appropriate, providing that it does not restrict the supply of housing. In this tenure group, the combination of very low incomes and energy-inefficient homes means that it has the highest risk of fuel poverty.

Social-rented homes

This tenure group typically lives in fairly modern (mainly built since 1945) properties, a large proportion of which are flats. The owners are either registered social landlords (RSLs, otherwise known as housing associations) or local authorities, with 7 and 11 per cent of the housing stock, respectively – proportions that have been fairly static since 2005. As demonstrated in Table 6.8, perhaps as a result of the decent homes programme, the rate of energy-efficiency improvements in social-rented properties has accelerated faster than in the private sector. Both local authorities and housing associations have made progress in improving the energy efficiency of their housing stock, although there is still a long way to go.

This tenure group has the lowest levels of income which combines with above average levels of energy efficiency to give a slightly below average risk of fuel poverty (16 per cent are fuel poor, when the sector is 18 per cent of all homes). This demonstrates the way in which greater energy efficiency can begin to offset a low income.

Owner occupiers

Owner occupation represented about 68 per cent of all homes in 2007, slightly below the peak of 70 per cent. Occupiers comprise two distinct groups. The first consists of those who own outright, having paid off the mortgage (31 per cent). This is predominantly older people – some are capital rich but income poor and in fuel poverty. The other subgroup are those with a mortgage (39 per cent) who are still in work and are younger: there is a rising problem in the number of households with mortgages who are becoming fuel poor. The two groups have very different income levels (Table 2.11 in Chapter 2), with many outright owners having low incomes: 40 per cent have less than £15,000 per annum. Fuel poverty among outright owners is probably at a similar level to that among privately rented households – both are likely to have low incomes and energy-inefficient properties.

Where do the poor live?

There is curious evidence about the energy efficiency of the homes of the poorest households. Those on the lowest 30 per cent of incomes had:

• Below average SAP01 ratings, with the 1998 level being SAP01 42.9 in comparison with the average of SAP01 44.9. Over 1991 to 1998, the gap had been closing (DTI, 2001, p139).

- Above average SAP05 ratings, with the 2007 level being SAP05 50 in comparison with the average of SAP05 48.8. The poorest homes had been above the average for the whole period of 1996 to 2006 (BERR, 2008b, p19).

The implication is, surprisingly, that the changes between SAP01 and SAP05 have been sufficient to reverse the relationship of these two groups. It also implies, initially, that the 30 per cent of households with the lowest incomes should not be in fuel poverty as they have reasonably efficient homes. But this would seem to contradict the relationship (Figure 2.1 in Chapter 2), of a strong correlation between poverty and fuel poverty. The more thoughtful conclusion appears to be that low-income households need to have the most energy-efficient properties if they are to avoid fuel poverty and a marginal improvement over the average is insufficient. To take a low-income household out of fuel poverty requires a really energy-efficient property: a level much greater than SAP05 50 is required to fuel poverty proof a home in 2006. It is, therefore, crucially important to differentiate between the homes of the poor and of the fuel poor. This demonstrates a further reason why any policy targeted mainly on low income will be missing many of the fuel poor: the criteria have to combine low-income with the energy-efficiency of the home occupied to improve targeting on the fuel poor. It is becoming clear that differentiating between where the poor and the fuel poor live is important and a way of clarifying the causes of fuel poverty. Looking at the poor first:

- They live in homes with a slightly above average level of energy efficiency.
- There is no correlation between areas of multiple deprivation and the risk of a category 1 hazard of excess cold under the HHSRS (DCLG, 2008a, p82, i.e. unhealthy houses, discussed in Chapter 7).
- Homes in the most deprived areas were more energy efficient and with a higher SAP05 rating than those in less deprived areas (DCLG, 2008a, p147). Again, the differences were small, but there, and reflect the predominance of social housing in deprived areas.
- With cavity wall insulation and loft insulation, the proportion of households owning them does not vary with income. With double glazing, there is a slight increase in ownership with income, until the top quintile, when it declines again, partly because these households live in older homes, often with architectural or townscape value (Table 6.9).
- Many of the poorest households (Table 2.11 in Chapter 2) live in the social sector and this has slightly above average levels of energy efficiency.

The lack of correlation between the presence of insulation and income level is interesting as it appears to represent a considerable shift since 1986 when there was a distinct gradient in ownership levels across the different socio-economic groups (SEGs) (Boardman, 1991, p86). It seems that the policy focus on decent homes in the social sector has delivered some of this change; fuel poverty is less

Table 6.9 *Ownership of main insulation measures, by income, England (percentage of homes with the measure) (2006)*

	Cavity wall insulation	Loft insulation 200mm+*	Full double glazing
Quintile 1: <£10,000	48.2	22.2	61.9
Quintile 2: £10,000–£15,000	45.6	19.9	64.1
Quintile 3: £15,000 £22,000	44.1	16.7	65.5
Quintile 4: £22,000–£33,000	41.2	15.5	66.0
Quintile 5: >£33,000	41.6	17.3	61.2
Average	44.2	18.2	63.7

Note: * Of all dwellings with loft space.
Source: BRE (2008a, Tables 1.8, 2.8, 3.8)

likely to occur just because of low income. The government is getting something right.

Where do the fuel poor live?

If you start with low income you do not find the most energy-inefficient homes or the worst fuel poverty; so what happens if you start with energy-inefficient homes: do you find low-income households?

The following data are from the 2006 *English House Condition Survey* (EHCS), when the total of fuel poor households was 2.4 million. By the end of 2008, it was thought to be 3.5 million in England and 5 million in the UK. This could alter the distribution and findings that follow, with more of the fuel poor being concentrated in the least energy-efficient homes. In 2006:

- Over half of the fuel poor were in the lowest two bands of the EPC (Table 6.1 and Figure 6.3), while only 17 per cent of the non-fuel poor live in these homes (Table 6.10).
- Most of the remaining fuel poor are in band E; there are tiny numbers of fuel poor in homes with a SAP05 >69.
- The fuel poor do live in the homes that cost more to heat and this is a quite different distribution than that of the non-fuel poor. The average for the fuel poor is SAP05 38 (in the logarithmic part of the scale), whereas the non-fuel poor average is 12 points higher.
- The 15 per cent of fuel-poor households in the most severe fuel poverty (those needing to spend >20 per cent of their income) had a property with an average SAP05 of 31. To have adequate warmth and other energy services, they would have needed to spend £1600 per annum out of an income of £5477 (BERR, 2008a, Table 7) in 2006 – an appalling 29 per cent, over eight times the average (Table 3.1). This is even worse than the theoretical calculation on p128. These households are on exceptionally low incomes of £100 per week.

Table 6.10 *Fuel poor and non-fuel poor, by Energy Performance Certificate (EPC) band, England (2006)*

EPC band (SAP05 ratings)	Fuel poor (%)	Non-fuel poor (%)	Total (%)
A (92–100)	–	–	–
B (81–91)	–	–	–
C (69–80)	–	9	8
D (55–68)	13	33	30
E (39–54)	36	42	41
F (21–38)	32	15	17
G (1–20)	19	2	4
Average SAP rating	38	50	49
Number of properties (millions)	2.42	19.58	22.00

Source: adapted from Table 6.1 in this chapter

The situation is still not cut and dried. Any policy that focused on the least energy-efficient homes (i.e. those in bands F and G would encompass 51 per cent of the fuel poor. But, not all the worst homes are occupied by the fuel poor, the fuel poor only represent 27 per cent of all the households with an F- or G-rated property (1.2 million out of 4.5 million) (Table 6.1). This is similar to the targeting problem with pensioners (Figure 3.3 in Chapter 3). In both cases, the target group represents half of the fuel poor; but around one quarter of the whole group are actually fuel poor. So, at one level, there do not seem to be any benefits in targeting the worst houses rather than the poorest people. However:

- With targeting the worst homes, the properties of the non-fuel poor are just as dreadful as those of the fuel poor (who pays for the improvements is a separate issue). Even with poor targeting, the net effects are all good.
- The other benefit of targeting the least efficient homes is that those in severe fuel poverty are concentrated in absolutely the worst homes, with the lowest SAP (Figure 2.3 in Chapter 2). The focus would be on the most deserving.
- The fuel poor in the least energy-efficient properties stay there for longer than the fuel poor in more energy-efficient properties. This again strengthens the case for dealing with the worst properties (Sefton, 2004, p394).
- When there is a high turnover of occupants, as in the privately rented sector, 'fuel poor households were mostly replaced by other fuel poor households' (Sefton, 2004, p393). Dealing with the property gets to the main cause of the problem.
- Some of the worst fuel poverty is thought to be found in the privately rented sector – long-term residents with extremely energy-inefficient properties. This is the home of the typical 'I'm not complaining' individual – someone who will not complain to the landlord for fear of possible repercussions. An inclusive approach would enable them to be found and not excluded from policy again.

- In all probability, these energy-inefficient properties have provided the conditions for fuel poverty over many years and will continue to do so. With increasing levels of fuel poverty, the expectation is that more of the occupants of the worst housing will become fuel poor.

One difficulty is that all pensioners are easy to find through the benefits system, whereas the worst homes cannot be found. That is the key to unlocking this approach (Chapter 9). The proposal in earlier chapters is to combine tackling the worst housing and helping the poorest people. This recognizes that fuel poverty results from the interaction of low income and energy-inefficient homes.

Some of the characteristics of the homes of the fuel poor link (directly or indirectly) to the energy efficiency of the property. In England in 2006, these combine three categories of factors (Table 6.11):

- those where the fuel poor are disproportionately likely to have the characteristic (categories 1 to 6); these are the main housing indicators of fuel poverty;
- one where the evidence varies substantially with the income definition (7);
- those where the fuel poor are disproportionately unlikely to have the characteristic (categories 8 to 9).

Table 6.11 includes the proportion of the fuel poor affected according to both the full income and the basic income definition in order to identify the effect of choosing one or the other. This is the third of a trio of tables looking at various characteristics of the fuel poor. The other two are Tables 2.9 (social) and 4.6 (fuel pricing and fuel poor) in this book.

Many of these characteristics overlap – for instance, some properties will be hard to heat, with a SAP below 38 and built before 1919. Similar priorities emerge in Scotland (SHCS, 2008, Table 20).

Table 6.11 *Housing characteristics of the fuel poor, England (2006)*

	Characteristic	Percentage of fuel poor (full income)	Percentage of fuel poor (basic income)	National average (%)	Sources from BERR 2008a
1	Hard to heat (solid wall, no gas)	56	54	39	Tables 48, 84
2	Under occupying	53	44	32	Tables 22, 58
3	SAP05 ≤38	48	41	22	Tables 41, 77
4	Property built before 1919	35	32	21	Tables 40, 76
5	In rural area	18	15	10	Tables 35, 71
6	Privately rented	16	19	11	Tables 13, 49
7	Social sector	16	30	18	Tables 13, 49
8	Home built since 1975	9	10	25	Tables 40, 76
9	Purpose-built flat	8	14	14	Tables 39, 75

Source: BERR (2008a)

The use of the basic income definition rather than full income means that the number of fuel-poor households in the social sector almost doubles and there is an appreciable increase in the number of privately rented fuel poor. This is to be expected because the basic income definition takes out most of the housing costs linked to rent – otherwise, fuel poverty is not concentrated in the social sector.

The proportion of homes that are in fuel poverty and under-occupied is increasing. Under-occupation, in general, is worst when the home is owned outright (the mortgage is paid off) and 58 per cent of these are under-occupied (DCLG, 2009b, p23). These, typically, are the old family home.

Existing policies

There has been substantial policy emphasis over the years on improving the energy efficiency of the homes of the fuel poor, usually for free. It has been shown in Chapter 3 that targeting of energy-efficiency programmes is poor, partly because of the mismatch between the definition of fuel poverty and eligibility for the various programmes: 42 per cent of fuel-poor households do not have any free energy-efficiency programmes for which they are eligible (Table 3.5). To compound the problem, the 58 per cent that are eligible for assistance can only receive around 20 per cent of the money in fuel poverty policies (Table 3.6). The bulk of the money is spent on the non-fuel poor. Here, the examination is of the extent to which the programmes are both targeted on the worst homes, with appropriate measures, and are removing households from fuel poverty.

The measures that are required to make existing properties energy efficient are known and are largely practicable even for hard-to-heat properties. Such technologies include solid wall insulation, micro-renewable technologies (such as solar water heating, photovoltaics/solar panels, heat pumps and wind turbines). Other technologies such as micro-combined heat and power (generating electricity in the home from the central heating boiler) are being field tested for the government.

Decent homes

A useful policy, funded by local government, is the Decent Homes Standard (DHS), which originally applied to all social housing and the homes of 'vulnerable households in privately owned housing, particularly those with children' (DCLG, 2004, p1). In this context, a vulnerable household is one in receipt of a principal means-tested or disability-related benefit (Hansard, 2008) (i.e. a narrower category of vulnerability than is used when defining fuel poverty). In reality, both central and local government have limited powers and money to require private home-owners to make their homes decent, so the programme principally deals with the social sector. In this way, the DHS complements Warm Front, as the latter is for the private sector. The DHS programme was not designed to tackle fuel poverty *per se*.

The DHS has a wide scope and providing a 'reasonable degree of thermal comfort' is only one of four parts. Hence, establishing expenditure related in any way to energy efficiency or fuel poverty has not proved possible with any accuracy. The definition of a decent home has varied, but since April 2006 a dwelling should be free of the risk of category 1 hazards, as defined by the HHSRS (Chapter 7). For fuel poverty, this effectively means the property should not be in bands F or G on the EPC in order to avoid the risk of excess cold.

The DHS is a trigger, not a benchmark, with a low intervention point – for instance, the absence of 50mm of loft insulation (the present standard in new homes is for 270mm). So, while the DHS has been effective at raising the energy efficiency of social housing, it is from a very low threshold:

> *The programme is widely seen as worthwhile for what it has achieved, but a missed opportunity because of what it never sought to achieve.* (HC 432-1, 2008, p14)

When intervention occurred, the recommended standard to be reached was a reasonable SAP01 65 (Defra, 2004, p4). The objective was for all social housing to be treated by 2010, and by 2010, it is anticipated that 3.6 million (95 per cent) of social housing will have been improved (DCLG, 2006, pp4, 6). The government has provided additional funds to complete the process (Treasury, 2008, p126). The average cost in 2005 of bringing a property up to a 'decent' standard under thermal comfort criteria was £2225 (DCLG, 2007, p15), so, it has not been expensive to bring dreadful properties up to a standard that makes them more affordable to keep warm. The DHS does seem to have been a factor in bringing the energy efficiency of social housing above the level of the average home, though the stated aim of achieving SAP05 65 has not been obtained.

There is no clarity about what is going to replace DHS when it ceases in 2010 (HC Library, 2009) or whether mandatory minimum standards should apply, as is being discussed in Wales and Scotland and recommended by the select committee:

> *... the government [should] include specific energy performance improvement standards in any social housing improvement programme that follows [the] Decent Homes [Standard] in 2010. In particular, we recommend ... a specific minimum, rather than average, Standard Assessment Procedure target for all social housing. We seek the government's view on the Local Government Association's suggestion that that minimum SAP rating should be 65.* (HC 432-1, 2008, p47)

In Scotland, the equivalent of the DHS is the Scottish Housing Quality Standard (SHQS), and social landlords must ensure that all their dwellings pass this standard by 2015, including being above the Tolerable Standard: for energy efficiency this means obtaining a SAP 50 (Scottish Executive, 2004, p5). A total of 68 per cent of all Scottish homes failed the SHQS in 2007, primarily because of energy inefficiency (SHCS, 2008, p35). This included 71 per cent of social housing.

Warm Front

Warm Front is the main government-funded energy-efficiency improvement programme for the fuel poor and is the name of the scheme in England; in Northern Ireland the equivalent is Warm Homes, in Scotland, Warm Deal, and in Wales it is the Home Energy Efficiency Scheme. Details of eligibility and measures offered are given in NAO (2009, p33). Most of the research has been about the English scheme; but there are likely to be substantial crossovers in experience to the programmes in the devolved administrations.

WF has been the government's flagship programme for dealing with fuel poverty since it was established in 2000 and is still being described by the government as its 'main programme for tackling fuel poverty in the private sector' in England (Hansard, 2009a). The programme provides assistance to vulnerable households on means-tested benefits through the installation of energy-efficiency measures and the provision of energy-efficiency advice and benefit-entitlement checks. The households have to self-refer for the scheme, but may be encouraged by visiting professionals, such as district nurses. The private housing sector (i.e. owner occupiers and privately rented) contains the vast majority of fuel-poor households (82 per cent; Table 2.11 in Chapter 2) and eligibility for Warm Front was described in Table 3.5 in Chapter 3. The details of the scheme have changed over the years, but the principles have remained the same.

The requirements placed on the Warm Front managing agent, Energy Action Grants Agency (Eaga), have been defined in terms of numbers of measures installed (outputs), rather than an obligation to bring a specified number of households out of fuel poverty (an outcome). For whatever reasons, of the over 2 million households who have been 'assisted' since the scheme started in 2000 (Hansard, 2009a), many receive minimal help (e.g. light bulbs, draught-proofing and hot water tank jackets). Between 2005 and 2008, 24 per cent of all homes treated by Warm Front only received two low-energy light bulbs (NAO, 2009, p14). At this level of assistance, the households will never be brought out of fuel poverty and this partly explains why predictions about the effect on the levels of fuel poverty have been surprisingly small (Chapter 1, p12).

For most fuel-poor households, having some measures installed under this programme is insufficient to lift them out of fuel poverty. For the period of April 2007 to March 2008, the average Warm Front property had a level of

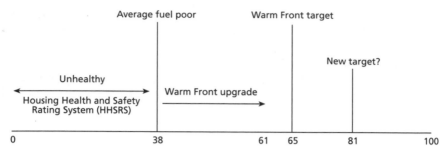

Note: The Housing Health and Safety Rating System (HHSRS) is described in Chapter 7; SAP05 81 is discussed later in this chapter.
Source: based on Eaga (2009)

Figure 6.4 *Warm Front and SAP05 ratings, England (2007/08)*

energy efficiency of 38 SAP points to start with (i.e. the average for fuel-poor homes) (Table 6.1). The Warm Front intervention resulted in the homes being lifted by an average 23 SAP points, to 61 SAP (Eaga, 2009). This was more than in previous years, largely because of an increased emphasis on heating systems (102,000 measures), with cavity wall insulation and loft insulation provided for nearly 90,000 homes. No solid wall insulation was delivered.

It is, therefore, possible to summarize the effectiveness of Warm Front (Figure 6.4). It takes homes that are of average energy efficiency (in terms of the fuel poor), improves them by an average of 23 SAP points, so that they still do not meet the target of SAP 65, set five years ago. Instead, what is needed is an upgrade of at least 60 points for a household in severe fuel poverty (say, from 20 to 81 SAP – discussed later). That would mean a strong focus on homes that are known to be unhealthy and failing the HHSRS.

The Scottish scheme of installing central heating has been effective at achieving increases in low-income homes (Scottish Government, 2009). Expenditure was £300 million between 2001 and 2008; but the success of the scheme has meant that it has been replaced by the Energy Assistance Package.

There are a number of other reasons why the Warm Front programme has had only a relatively limited impact upon fuel poverty to date and why it is barely contributing to the achievement of the 2010 and 2016 targets:

- It is not a condition of the programme that grant recipients are fuel poor. If the policies were sufficiently well funded to sweep up the fuel poor within a comprehensive approach, then that would not matter; but this is not the case. Only 25 per cent of the Warm Front expenditure goes on the fuel poor (Table 3.6 in Chapter 3).
- There is no requirement that the home is below a certain level of energy efficiency (i.e. no relationship with the SAP); so the worst homes are not necessarily being assisted.
- Although the scheme aims to achieve a particular level of energy efficiency (SAP05 65), there is no *requirement* to do so. The reason is that the

maximum grant level and the approved measures were insufficient to achieve SAP05 65, the level of efficiency that the government considered necessary (Defra, 2004, p18) to protect residents of a property from fuel poverty even before recent fuel price rises.

- Warm Front offers very few effective options for homes that are viewed as being hard to heat because the measures for addressing those homes will often cost more than the maximum grant available under the programme.
- With the more expensive measures (including central heating), the house-holder is often asked to 'top up' the grant to cover the full cost. As most fuel-poor households are unable to provide this money, they do not get the measures. The situation was getting worse, as in 2007/08, 25 per cent of all applications exceeded the grant maximum, in comparison with 15 per cent a year earlier (NAO, 2009, p17). The grant maxima have subsequently been raised.
- Another reason may well be that householders have to refer themselves for the scheme (NAO, 2009, p10). While there may be considerable publicity about the scheme, this still allows many of the less-assertive members of society to slip through the net, particularly as 'applicants are assessed on a "first come first served" basis' (NAO, 2009, p5).

Despite all of these problems with the targeting of Warm Front and the limited coverage of its measures, Warm Front does result in people having warmer homes (Chapter 7). The evidence on energy saving is more circumspect, under-lining the problems of trying to assess the real benefits of programmes framed in terms of the theoretical SAP rating. The government has increased the funding:

> ... to more than £950 million in the current spending round until March 2011, including an increase of £74 million announced in September and a further increase of £100 million in the pre-budget report. We are also providing £50 million to ensure that people receive the help that they need sooner rather than later. (Hansard, 2009a)

The maximum grant was raised in April 2009 to £3500, if the property is on the gas grid, and £6000 if not. These increases are designed to avoid the need for top-up expenditure by the householder. Warm Front is being expanded to include the installation of low-carbon heat and power technologies such as solar thermal water heating and air-source heat pumps. These technologies will initially be trialled in small-scale pilot programmes (DECC, 2009b). It remains to be seen if these higher grant levels will result in more homes being lifted out of fuel poverty, rather than just reducing the depth of fuel poverty in the house-hold.

There are further options for improving the scheme:

> *Only a small increase in the impact of the scheme would be achieved by excluding households not in receipt of a means-tested benefit or by excluding those living in homes that are already energy efficient (with a SAP of 60 or more). Combining these two measures would have a more substantial effect. [Another] option ... would be to install significant measures only in those dwellings that fail the thermal comfort criterion of the Decent Homes Standard or to introduce an average SAP improvement target.*
>
> *To make a more substantial difference, more radical changes are needed, such as the introduction of a much lower SAP threshold (at around 30) or a fuel poverty 'check' to ensure that grants are only offered to households identified as being fuel poor.* (Sefton, 2004, pvii)

One of the most useful alterations would be, as Tom Sefton (2004) suggests, to require outcomes from Warm Front (i.e. the homes treated have to be below average energy efficiency and to be lifted out of fuel poverty). The government did consider an approach like this, but largely rejected it. One of the reasons was the problem of identifying a low-SAP property before it has been surveyed and there was no single parameter that acted as an adequate surrogate (Defra, 2004, pp42–43). That was, however, before the introduction of EPCs. Now that these are available, it would be possible to build up profiles of the housing stock in each local authority so that low SAP homes are identifiable, without the need for surrogates (Boardman, 2007, p50). Fuel poverty eradication is the primary justification for this proposal so that the homes of the fuel poor can be found.

Sefton's (2004) comments chime with the gist of the evidence in this book: better targeting involves focusing on the worst housing, albeit while continuing to provide the measures at no cost to those on means-tested benefits.

Warm Zones

In recognition of the problems of identifying the fuel poor and that there are often concentrated pockets of deprivation, the Warm Zones policy was introduced in 2000 – the first area-based policy. This permits – and requires – a careful and detailed approach, involving all properties, regardless of tenure or income. A total of 14 Warm Zones have been set up, covering over 1 million households, although some are now closed. Kirklees is the biggest, with over 175,000 homes. The seven active Warm Zones in England were delivering £1 million of energy-saving measures and advice each month by the end of 2006 (EEPfH, 2007).

Funding is supported by the local authority, but usually comes mainly from the utilities, partly as new money, partly through channelling their energy-efficiency commitment (below) funds into the area. Well over one quarter of households in a Warm Zone can be in fuel poverty: it is estimated to be about

33 per cent in Newcastle Warm Zone and is highest in local authority and private-rented properties (Connor, pers comm). All households are offered a fully integrated service, with free or heavily subsidized insulation and heating measures, benefits assistance and energy-efficiency advice. It is only the total package that succeeds in lifting households out of fuel poverty because of the depths of deprivation – the energy-efficiency measures alone are rarely sufficient.

Even when only part way through their programme, some Warm Zones have been more successful at reducing fuel poverty than Warm Front, partly because they are tackling every property in a given area in a coherent manner. One of their problems has been the lack of money for measures for hard-to-heat homes:

> *The Warm Zones pilots removed approximately 7 per cent (7782) of households from fuel poverty. This varied from 2 per cent (Hull) to 23 per cent (Stockton). The target was 50 per cent [over the lifetime of the project]. Warm Zones also removed 10 per cent of the severely fuel poor from that category (although nearly all remained within marginal or moderate fuel poverty).* (CSE and NEA, 2005, p27)

A major reason for success is that they proactively visit every target home and do not wait for the occupant to self-refer, as with Warm Front. This is important because, in relation to the original home energy-efficiency scheme:

> *... there is little evidence ... that households in the least energy-efficient homes will self-select to this kind of scheme ... more active measures are needed ... to overcome potential barriers to participation.* (Sefton, 2004, p396)

The success of Warm Zones has led to three further proposals for area-based approaches. First, the proposal for low-carbon zones focused on the fuel poor, which replicates Warm Zones, but with a required target of SAP 80 (Boardman, 2007, p88). Second, the mayor of London is offering to support ten low-carbon zones; but these are a maximum of 1000 households and the focus is on carbon savings rather than fuel poverty. Third, the government has consulted on the CESP, which focuses on areas of multiple deprivation in a series of pilots from September 2009. These (pilots) target hard-to-heat homes, but may not be set an output target or required SAP level. The proposal is that CESP would be funded by the utilities.

The Energy Efficiency Commitment and the Carbon Emissions Reduction Target scheme

The Carbon Emissions Reduction Target (CERT), which commenced in April 2008, is the replacement policy for the Energy Efficiency Commitment (EEC) series of schemes that started in 2002. Under all of these schemes, the energy suppliers in Great Britain are required to fund a mix of measures to achieve a specified level of energy/carbon reductions among their customers. It covers all households (private and social). The scheme operates so that a proportion of the savings have to be in the homes of the Priority Group – that is, households in receipt of specified (mainly income-related) benefits (i.e. a similar class to those eligible for the Warm Front scheme, but including social housing tenants; Table 3.5 in Chapter 3). It is in respect of measures delivered to the Priority Group that CERT can be expected to make any contribution to fuel poverty eradication, because they are provided at no cost to the household.

The government's conclusions on the effectiveness of CERT as a fuel poverty measure are that 'energy supplier activity from 2002–2011 has the potential to remove over 100,000 households from fuel poverty in GB' (Defra, 2007, p19). The use of the word 'potential' is disconcerting; but even so, over a ten-year period the EEC/CERT scheme is only expected to lift a tiny proportion of households out of fuel poverty. This is at a time when an extra 1 million households were being put into fuel poverty, every year, largely because of rising fuel prices and the policies of the utilities (Chapter 4).

The measures offered by CERT for free are similar to those provided through Warm Front, and there is duplication – and competition – because all the households helped by Warm Front are also eligible for CERT Priority Group. This overlap is unfortunate, especially as 42 per cent of fuel-poor households are not eligible for either.

The expenditure on CERT (and its predecessors) does not come from the state, but from the utility companies. Ultimately, therefore, the money for this programme is paid for by a levy on all householders in their fuel bills, with a potential negative effect on fuel poverty. Both the gas and the electricity utilities contribute, and shortly the electricity generators will as well.

CERT is twice the size of the previous EEC (i.e. the amount of savings required from the scheme has doubled) and this means that the contribution from individual householders, through their fuel bills, will double. However, the proportion of savings that have to be achieved in the Priority Group has been cut from 50 to 40 per cent and the group itself is expanded (to include all those over 70), which means an increase from 8.8 million to 11.2 million eligible households (EEPfH, 2008c, p54). The Fuel Poverty Advisory Group (FPAG, 2008, p16) have been critical of the effect of this 'highly regressive' change and note that 'the increase in benefits for the Priority Group will ... be markedly less than the increase in prices paid by them'.

The other major criticisms of CERT are similar to the ones outlined for Warm Front:

- A mismatch exists between the Priority Group and the fuel poor.
- There is a failure to link the effect of the improvements undertaken in the homes of the Priority Group to any aspect of fuel poverty.
- The design of the scheme is in terms of outputs (i.e. measures), not outcomes (i.e. reductions in fuel poverty).
- In addition, there is a reliance on contributions from the householder as the supplier usually pays only 50 per cent under CERT (EEPfH, 2008b, p6). The free measures are for the Priority Group only.
- In Scotland, where cavities are 90mm rather than 60mm, the cost of filling them is greater, so the utilities are less likely to fill a cavity wall with insulation in Scotland than in England. There are no regional targets. This problem would be resolved if CERT installers received greater carbon credits for filling a Scottish cavity since it saves more energy.

CERT is continuing to emphasize the most obviously cost-effective measures, such as loft insulation and cavity wall insulation (Table 6.12). There has been a particularly strong focus on low-energy light bulbs, while these are still allowed. As incandescent bulbs are phased out, the compact fluorescent light bulbs (CFLs) will not be an allowable measure because that is all households can purchase in the shops anyway. The utilities gave away 120 million low-energy light bulbs during the nine months of April to December 2008 (not all of these to the Priority Group), and lighting represented 30 per cent of all savings, in theory. This amounts to five light bulbs for every household in Great Britain.

The Priority Group was less likely to receive appliances, solid wall insulation or heating because these are not fully subsidized by the utility, and the household or local authority would have to contribute to the cost; nor did they have any micro-generation installed (Ofgem, 2009, p3). There is a feeling that the CERT expenditure, on all groups, does not reflect the geographical population distribution, particularly in Scotland, partly because the properties are hard to reach. As fuel poverty affects a higher proportion of households in Scotland (Table 2.5 in Chapter 2), this means that the fuel poor there would be

Table 6.12 *Main Carbon Emission Reduction Target (CERT) measures (April–December 2008)*

	Type	*Number*
Insulation	Cavity wall	401,707
	Loft	405,179
	Solid wall	7161
Heating	Fuel switching	10,593
Lighting	Compact fluorescent light bulbs (CFLs)	120,665,853
Micro-generation	Heat pumps	440
	Solar water heating	186

Note: This is to all customers, not just the Priority Group.
Source: Ofgem (2009, p1)

subsidizing English households that receive assistance. With the Priority Group in Scotland, the problems of targeting have meant that there is a proposal to exclude all over 70s and only include those on the guaranteed element of pension credit (Scottish Fuel Poverty Forum, 2008, p21).

In Northern Ireland, the equivalent of CERT is the Energy Efficiency Levy. This is about £5 per customer, but the main recipients of the energy-efficiency measures are low-income households (80 per cent) and the rest is for community projects (20 per cent). None of the money is spent on measures in the homes of the better off. As the regulator in Northern Ireland (the Northern Ireland Authority for Utility Regulation, or NIAUR) has the same mandate as the regulator in Great Britain, it demonstrates what can be achieved when social justice is deemed to be important.

Summary of fuel poverty capital investment programmes

Since 2000, nearly £5 billion has been spent on the three main fuel poverty energy-efficiency capital programmes by a combination of central and local government and the utilities (Table 6.13). The annual rate of expenditure has increased, particularly for Warm Front and CERT. While £5 billion is a substantial amount of money, it is dwarfed by the £18 billion that has been given to all pensioners through the winter fuel payments (Table 3.4 in Chapter 3). The balance – or imbalance – between these two types of support for the

Table 6.13 *Expenditure on fuel poverty energy-efficiency programmes (£ millions) (2000–2011)*

	Central government				Utilities	Local	Total
	Warm Front (England)	Home Energy Efficiency Scheme (Wales)	Warm Deal and Central Heating Programmes (Scotland)	Warm Homes and Warm Homes Plus (NI)	EESOP/ EEC/ CERT PG only* (Great Britain)	government Decent Homes Standard** (England)	
2000/1	72				26	100	
2004/5	166			20	144	100	
2008/09	397	25	45.9	9	506	100	£1 billion
2000/01– 2008/09 inclusive	2021	93	378	109	1504	850	£5 billion
2008–2011	959				1900	150	

Note: * The Energy Efficiency Levy in Northern Ireland is not included – £4.5m in 2007/08 (DSDNI, 2007, p7). ** Thermal criteria only.
EESOP = Energy Efficiency Standards of Performance; EEC = Energy Efficiency Commitment; CERT = Carbon Emission Reduction Target; PG = Priority Group.
Source: various sources, including Campbell (pers comm); author for 2000–2008 totals; Hansard (2009b) and NAO (2009, p11) for Warm Front; Mackintosh (2008, p25) for Warm Deal; DSDNI (2007, p7, 26) for Warm Homes; Derived from DTI (2001, p149) for utilities 2000; FPAG (2008, p40) for utilities 2008/09; Based on FPAG (2006, p10) for Decent Homes 2000 and 2004; NAO (2008, p13) for Decent Homes 2008/09: DECC (2009c, p8) for utilities 2008–11 total; FPAG (2008, p14) for Decent Homes 2008–11 total

fuel poor is part of the dilemma for policy. Providing income support is popular and important, in the short term; but investing in energy-efficiency improvements is the only long-term solution.

Another policy dilemma is the extent to which these programmes should be funded by taxpayers, through the government, or by utilities, through energy bills. The important difference for the fuel poor is that they all have to contribute to the utility programmes (through their gas and electricity bills – Table 4.3 in Chapter 4). Only a small proportion of poorer households pays income tax and thus support government-funded schemes although their contribution to the Treasury through other taxes, such as value added tax (VAT), may be somewhat higher. The likelihood is that obtaining money from the poor through utility funding is more regressive. The government is requiring more expenditure by the utilities, and this method is seen as the future for policy by the Climate Change Committee (CCC). This is beneficial for the government at a time of financial stringency, but does hurt the fuel poor. The annual expenditure by the utilities on the CERT Priority Group is now bigger than the various Warm Front schemes.

Despite substantial capital investment, the level of fuel poverty is rising, so, by implication, the level is still inadequate. The government's policies are not ambitious enough. The real benefit of expenditure on energy-efficiency improvements for the fuel poor is that it both reduces a social evil and contributes to an environmental benefit, permanently. Energy-efficiency improvements are not reversible in the way in which changes to fuel prices and incomes are. Hence, the FPAG has stated 'the only sustainable way to end fuel poverty is through energy efficiency (and now also micro-generation)' (FPAG, 2008, p21).

The main contributory factors for this mismatch between expenditure and need have been rehearsed above, but in summary are:

- No programme has a target framed in terms of reducing the numbers of fuel poor.
- Any mention of house-specific targets have been couched as an aim, not a requirement.
- There is no obligation to target the least energy-efficient homes.
- There are insufficient measures to deal with hard-to-heat properties.
- Eligibility is based solely on social characteristics and not the energy inefficiency of the home.

As a result, the number of homes brought out of fuel poverty permanently as a result of energy-efficiency improvements since 2000 has been insignificant (Chapter 1, p12): there are still only 30,000 fuel-poor households in a home that is in band C or above in England in 2006 (i.e. greater than SAP 69).

The design of all three programmes means that many who are not fuel poor are eligible for help. The proportion of fuel poor assisted by all three

Table 6.14 *Proportion of assistance that the fuel poor are eligible for, England (2005–2006)*

	2005	2006	Increase
Warm Front	16%	25.5%	59%
Energy Efficiency Commitment Priority Group (EEC PG)	14.4%	21.5%	49%
Winter fuel payments	11.6%	18.7%	61%
All fuel poor (millions)	1.529	2.432	59%
Fuel Price Index (FPI)	137.8	171.8	25%

Source: RFRR (2007, Tables 11, 19, 21) for 2005; BERR (2008a, Tables 15, 28, 29) for 2006

programmes – Warm Front, the EEC Priority Group and the winter fuel payments – increased from up to 16 per cent in 2005 to up to 26 per cent in 2006 (Table 6.14). The growth in coverage reflected the rise in the total number of fuel poor as all the increases were in the range of 50 to 60 per cent. Thus, as the number in fuel poverty increases, so does the effectiveness of the intervention programmes: more of the recipients are fuel poor. Even so, at least three-quarters of the households being helped by these three major fuel poverty programmes were not in fuel poverty. There is still ineffective targeting and too little of the benefit is going to the fuel poor.

Interestingly, the growth in the numbers in fuel poverty has been at more than twice the rate of the rise in fuel prices: 59 instead of 25 per cent. It is not clear why; but as energy efficiency cannot decrease, it appears to confirm that absolute incomes have dropped, as shown in Chapter 3. Between 2005 and 2006, each 1 per cent increase in fuel prices resulted in an extra 36,000 households becoming fuel poor in England. By February 2009, the Fuel Price Index (FPI) was 244.1, an increase of 42 per cent over 2006. On a *pro rata* basis, an extra 1.5 million households will have become fuel poor – that is almost 4 million households in England by early 2009 in comparison with the government's projection to 3.5 million (Table 2.3). This higher figure matches the implications of Figure 3.1 in Chapter 3 and shows that fuel poverty may be growing faster in England than the government has acknowledged.

New policies

The prime minister launched a £1 billion package of measures on 11 September 2008 called the Home Energy Saving Package. Of this, £910 million is to come from the utilities through CERT and the new CESP over three years from September 2009. The prime minister stated that he did not think it was necessary for the costs to be passed on to consumers; but no firm undertaking appeared to be in place (Wintour, 2008), risking a regressive impact.

CESP is a proposed area-based approach, focusing on areas of multiple deprivations, to test packages of measures for hard-to-heat properties. It is out to consultation, but should cover 90,000 homes in 100 communities, with

£3900 per property from the utilities. The location in deprived areas means that the main focus will be on low-income social housing, not the most energy-inefficient properties. The proposals in CESP are unlikely to tackle the privately rented properties or off-gas properties, which tend to be in rural areas (SDC, 2009, p5). It may form the pilot for the next round of Supplier Obligation (SO), after CERT, so it is good if the government believes that area-based approaches and a comprehensive approach per property are the way forward. However, the programme is not likely to tackle fuel poverty as effectively as could have been done, for instance, through a low-carbon zone approach (Boardman, 2007, pp88–89).

There is debate about the form that the next SO should take, after CERT finishes in April 2011. It could require the utilities to reduce the average carbon emissions per household through a measured, not modelled, approach. There are alternative calls for the reform of:

> ... *the Carbon Emission Reduction Target to make way for a council-led area-based national insulation programme to provide basic insulation ... [such an] approach will deliver scale economies driving down costs to provide a much needed boost to semi-skilled employment, alleviate fuel poverty and reduce household energy bills.* (LGA, 2009, p5)

By 2050, the CCC wants there to be zero-carbon emissions from housing stock. It has assumed that the majority of this will be funded through a continuation of CERT and a new SO (Figure 6.5). In 2008/09, before the recent extension to CERT, the cost to householders was about £19 per annum per fuel (Table 4.3 in Chapter 4; i.e. £38 per annum for most households). The size of the programme predicted by the CCC implies that this will be at least four times as large by 2020 (i.e. about £160 per annum). This would be a significant burden for low-income households and the programmes would have to focus on the disadvantaged, in compensation. A preferable approach would be to cap expenditure by the fuel poor at present levels (Chapter 4).

In the April 2009 budget, the chancellor announced a £25 million package to encourage the deployment of community heating infrastructure across the UK over the next two years. Other funding includes '£100 million of new investment in measures to reduce the fuel bills faced by vulnerable people in social housing, particularly cavity wall insulation' (HM Government, 2009, pp39, 41). On a more ambitious scale, Secretary of State for Energy and Climate Change Ed Miliband has said: 'We need to move from incremental steps forward on household energy efficiency to a comprehensive national plan – the Great British refurb' (Jha, 2009). This is designed to make homes low carbon, including:

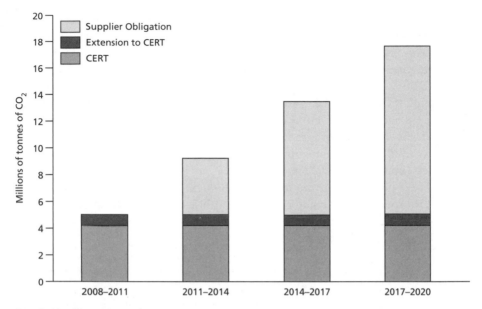

Note: Residential customers only
Source: CCC (2008, p230)

Figure 6.5 *Emission reduction paths from Supplier Obligation policies*

- By 2015, every home will have its loft and cavity wall insulated.
- By 2020, 7 million homes will have had whole house refurbishment, including low- and zero-carbon technologies.
- By 2030, the installation of cost-effective energy-efficiency measures in all homes.

This would, indeed, be the beginning of a major national programme; but little detail has been provided (as of June 2009). The Miliband plan did not mention the fuel poor. Miliband did, however, invoke the Stern Report and cited the need to spend now in order to save later. The aim is to cut residential carbon emissions by one third by 2020 (Jowit, 2009) and some of the proposals are designed to create new jobs (LGA, 2009).

In Scotland, the Energy Assistance Package was brought in from April 2009 to replace the Central Heating and Warm Deal programmes, and funding for this and the Home Insulation Scheme in 2009/10 is £60 million (Matthews, pers comm). This is a holistic package designed to maximize incomes, reduce fuel bills and improve the energy efficiency of homes. Importantly, it recognizes that extra help may be needed for those most vulnerable to fuel poverty (Scottish Government, 2009).

In Wales, there is a proposal to provide investment in energy-efficiency measures solely to those on a means-tested benefit who live in a home that has a low SAP rating (e.g. band E or below on the EPC). Both of these developments would improve the targeting of the HEES. The proposal would also couple the work to a house-specific cost-effectiveness approach (Welsh Assembly Government, 2009b).

Conclusions

The only long-term solution to fuel poverty is to improve the energy efficiency of people's homes. Around £5 billion has been invested since 2000 in improved energy efficiency in the homes of the fuel poor and the annual rate of expenditure has increased to £1 billion across the UK. This is still insufficient to prevent growing fuel poverty, largely because only about one quarter actually goes to the fuel poor, despite it all being labelled 'fuel poverty policy'. Better targeting of this money is the first priority and requires a radical re-thinking of policy.

A new focus on improving the energy efficiency of the homes of the fuel poor would start by identifying the worst houses and treating these, so that the occupants are no longer in fuel poverty. This is a new approach for three reasons. The fuel poverty programmes, at the moment:

- are not targeted on the worst homes;
- mainly focus on installing a number of measures – they do not have to bring the household out of fuel poverty;
- do not provide 100 per cent grants for 42 per cent of the fuel poor.

Targeting the least efficient homes (F and G bands on the EPC) would help 50 per cent of the fuel poor. While this is no better than is achieved by the winter fuel payment – which targets the 50 per cent of the fuel poor who are pensioners – it would have the advantage of being a permanent investment (or at least very long term). A single, adequate capital investment could ensure that in most fuel price situations the occupants of the house (current and future) will be able to afford adequate warmth and energy services, even if on a low income. The households in the most severe fuel poverty suffer from the combination of the worst housing and some of the lowest incomes. All of the fuel poor need to spend 28 per cent above the average on fuel, but have just over a third (£9300) of the average income (BERR, 2008, Table 7). Extreme poverty is an important component of severe fuel poverty. The gap is greater for non-vulnerable than it is for vulnerable households (BERR, 2008, Tables 9, 11).

The next question is to identify what level of energy efficiency would fuel poverty proof a home at the fuel price levels of early 2009. The calculations in Table 6.15 are somewhat convoluted, but do describe the necessary stages in the process of assessing this figure. The sums are approximate as there are several unknowns – for instance, whether the prices quoted include VAT or not.

In *Home Truths* (Boardman, 2007, p77) a SAP of 80 was proposed as the required standard to fuel poverty proof a home. This is now upgraded slightly

Table 6.15 *Calculations behind SAP05 81*

Source	Explanation	Process	Sum
Measuring energy efficiency, this chapter	The prices covered by a SAP rating exclude: • the electricity standing charge, assumed to be about £40 per annum; • the use of electricity in moveable lights, all appliances and cooking: assumed to be about 3000kWh at 10 pence/kWh (i.e. £300; gas for cooking would be cheaper).	(10 pence x 365 days) + (3000 x 10 pence)	£340
ONS (2007, p34)	The home has to provide affordable warmth for people on the lowest incomes. In 2006, the 10 per cent of households with the lowest incomes had an annual expenditure of £8000.		
Based on Retail Price Index in Table 4.1	Since then, assume, perhaps generously, that their income has increased by 3 per cent per annum to give a total in 2009 of £8840 per annum. In other words, they should be paying less than £880 for fuel and light if they are to avoid fuel poverty.		£880
1st row	From this £880 has to be deducted the money for the costs excluded from the SAP (i.e. the £340). This leaves the household with £540 for the costs covered by the SAP.	£880 – £340	£540
Measuring energy efficiency, this chapter	SAP05 prices for an average 85m² home were based on fuel prices for 2002–2004.		
Table 4.1 and Table 6.1	By February 2009, the Fuel Price Index had increased from about 115 to 244 (i.e. 112 per cent). Roughly assume that fuel prices have doubled. The cost of £540 has, therefore, to be related back to the costs at different SAP levels by doubling the costs shown in Table 6.1.		
From Table 6.1	The boundary between bands B and C was about £270; when doubled, this gives £540.		SAP05 81

Note: The £300 allowance for electricity for moveable lights and appliances is likely to be more than is needed for a pensioner and insufficient for a sizeable family, because it is an average.

to a SAP05 of 81, so that it is within band B, rather than the top of band C. Therefore, a home is fuel poverty proofed at the energy prices current in February 2009 and for households with an income of less than £8800 per annum in a 85 square metre home, if it has a SAP05 81 rating (i.e. it is a band A or B property). The total energy costs for the household would be <£880. A SAP05 81 has been endorsed by the major charities involved with fuel poverty: 'a major national programme to bring all properties up to a minimum energy efficiency standard of SAP 81 starting with the homes of the fuel poor' (Fuel Poverty Charter, 2008). It has also been approved of by the Environment Food and Rural Affairs (EFRA) select committee, which believes the creation of the Department of Energy and Climate Change (DECC) provides an opportunity to develop a 'road map' to 'set out how the energy efficiency of English housing stock can be improved to a specific level of energy efficiency, using SAP 81 where practicable, with a minimum level of SAP 65' (HC 37, 2009, p5). SAP05 81 would bring 83 per cent of households out of fuel poverty in England (Guertler and Preston, 2009); additional assistance would be needed for the remaining 17 per cent, mainly higher incomes.

All fuel poverty policies for the existing housing stock need to be focused on achieving a standard of SAP05 81, or better, as quickly as possible. This includes:

- a second DHS;
- Warm Front;
- CERT Priority Group;
- Warm Zones;
- the new CESP;
- the proposed low-carbon zones (Boardman, 2007, p88, and those being promoted by the mayor of London).

To be effective, they need, as the EFRA select committee have indicated, to be set in the context of a radical transformation of the whole housing stock – for instance, including address-specific databases of the energy efficiency of the housing stock and mandatory minimum energy-efficiency standards for all properties, linked to the bands on the EPC (Chapter 9).

Targeting the worst homes would recognize that:

- The oldest homes are, on average, the least efficient; but they are being improved more slowly than homes built since 1945.
- The benefits of moving a household from a G to an F are greater than the improvement achieved moving from D to A, in energy, money and carbon terms.
- The people in the most severe fuel poverty are living in the worst homes on exceptionally low incomes and probably spending between a third and a half of what they need on fuel.

At the moment, both Warm Front and CERT PG depend upon people self-referring themselves. They are designed to help those who are self-confident, aware of their rights and tolerant of building work and upheaval, at this stage in their lives. Not everyone fits into these categories, including the 'I'm not complaining' group.

An additional policy focus is needed with private landlords. The existing Landlord's Energy Saving Allowance (LESA) (Boardman, 2007, p56) is barely visible and should be both well publicized and extended.

Another group needing a special focus consists of those people living in rural areas. They are less likely to be helped by the existing schemes (it is expensive to reach them); but many have homes that are both solid walled and off the gas grid. Policies that use their rural location as an asset (e.g. with biomass or biogas systems) would be better for both carbon and fuel poverty policy than the present installation of oil-fired heating systems through Warm Front.

All of the required physical measures are reasonably practicable (as required in WHECA) in a technical sense. This includes the measures that are required to achieve a SAP of 65 (or even 81) in existing and hard-to-heat properties (including those with solid walls and those that are off the gas network). These technologies include solid wall insulation and heat pumps and micro-renewable technologies (such as solar water heating, photovoltaics and wind turbines). Other technologies, for instance micro-combined heat and power (generating electricity in the home from the central heating boiler) are being field tested for the government, some through the Technology Strategy Board's retrofit exemplars.

There has been too little honest description of the policies aimed at the fuel poor and, therefore, too little learning from experience. There has to be a better way to help the fuel poor than a set of policies that effectively exclude 42 per cent of the fuel poor and spend at least 75 per cent of the expenditure on the non-fuel poor. There have been opportunities for the government to improve the situation in the past, but they have not been taken. Better targeting helps to constrain the total budget required and results in more socially effective expenditure.

References

Banks, N., Researcher with Sustain, pers comm

Banks, N. (2008) *Implementation of Energy Performance Certificates in the Domestic Sector*, Working Paper, UK Energy Research Centre, London

Beckett, M. (2009) 'Gaining stock', *The Guardian*, 7 January, p3

BERR (Department for Business, Enterprise and Regulatory Reform) (2007) *Fuel Poverty, Detailed Tables 2005*, URN 07/P33, BERR, London

BERR (2008a) *Fuel Poverty Statistics, Detailed Tables 2006, Annex to Fuel Poverty Strategy Report, 2008*, URN 08/P33, BERR, London

BERR (2008b) *Fuel Poverty Statistics, Background Indicators, 2008, Annex to Fuel Poverty Strategy Report, 2008*, URN 08/P31, BERR, London

Boardman, B. (1991) *Fuel Poverty: From Cold Homes to Affordable Warmth*, Belhaven Press, London

Boardman, B. (2007) *Home Truths: A Low-Carbon Strategy to Reduce UK Housing Emissions by 80% by 2050*, Research report for the Co-operative Bank and Friends of the Earth, London, www.foe.co.uk/resource/reports/home_truths.pdf

Boardman, B., Darby, S., Killip, G., Hinnells, M., Jardine, C. N., Palmer, J. and Sinden, G. (2005) *40% House*, Environmental Change Institute, University of Oxford, Oxford, UK

Booth, R. (2009) 'Grow-your-own plan to reduce homes shortage', *The Guardian*, 1 June, p9

BRE (Building Research Establishment) (2004) *Assessment of Energy Efficiency Impact of Building Regulations Compliance*, Report for Energy Efficiency Partnership for Homes and the Energy Saving Trust, BRE, Watford, UK

BRE (2005) *The Government's Standard Assessment Procedure for Energy Rating of Dwellings – 2005 Edition*, BRE, on behalf of Defra, http://projects.bre.co.uk/SAP2005/pdf/SAP2005.pdf

BRE (2008a) *Energy Use in Homes 2006: A Series of Reports on Domestic Energy Use in England, Thermal Insulation*, BRE, http://projects.bre.co.uk/sap2005/pdf/SAP2005_9-82.pdf

BRE (2008b) *A Study of Hard to Treat Homes Using the English House Condition Survey – Part 1 and Part 2*, BRE, Watford, UK

CCC (Climate Change Committee) (2008) *Building a Low-Carbon Economy: The UK's Contribution to Tackling Climate Change*, First report, CCC, December

Chapman, J., Demos Associate, pers comm

Connor, D., Manager, Newcastle Warm Zone, pers comm

CSE and NEA (Centre for Sustainable Energy and National Energy Action) (2005) *Warm Zones Evaluation*, Centre for Sustainable Energy and National Energy Action, Submitted to Defra and DTI by the Energy Saving Trust, www.warmzones.co.uk/050301%20-%20Warm%20Zones%20Evaluation%20Final%20Report.pdf

DCLG (Department for Communities and Local Government) (2004) *What Is a Decent Home?*, Housing, DCLG, www.communities.gov.uk/housing/decenthomes/whatis/

DCLG (2006) *A Decent Home: Definition and Guidance for Implementation, June 2006 Update*, DCLG, London, www.communities.gov.uk/documents/housing/pdf/138355

DCLG (2007), *English House Condition Survey 2005 – Annual Report*, www.communities.gov.uk/publications/housing/englishhousesurveyannual

DCLG (2008a) *English House Condition Survey 2006: Annual Report*, DCLG, November, www.communities.gov.uk/documents/statistics/pdf/1072658.pdf

DCLG (2008b) *Housing Statistics*, DCLG, www.communities.gov.uk/documents/statistics/pdf/1095351.pdf

DCLG (2009a) *Permanent Buildings Completed, by House and Flat, Number of Bedrooms and Tenure*, Live tables, House-Building, DCLG, London

DCLG (2009b) *Survey of English Housing Preliminary Report: 2007–2008*, DCLG, London

DECC (Department of Energy and Climate Change) (2009a) Table 3.5 = Energy consumption in the UK, Domestic data tables, 2009 update, URN 09D/454, http://bis.ecgroup.net/Publications/EnergyClimateChangeDECC/EnergyStatistics.aspx

DECC (2009b) *New Improved Warm Front Scheme*, DECC press release, 23 April, www.decc.gov.uk/en/content/cms/news/pn049/pn049.aspx

DECC (2009c) *Carbon Emissions Reduction Target Amendments: Summary of Consulation Reponses and Government Response*, DECC, www.decc.gov.uk/en/content/cms/consultations/open/cert/cert.aspx

Defra (Department for Environment, Food and Rural Affairs) (2004) *Fuel Poverty in England: The Government's Plan for Action*, Defra, November, www.defra.gov.uk

Defra (2007) *The UK Fuel Poverty Strategy: 5th Annual Progress Report*, Defra, London, December

Defra (2008) *The UK Fuel Poverty Strategy: 6th Annual Progress Report*, Defra, London, October

DOE (Department of the Environment) (1996) *English House Condition Survey 1991: Energy Report*, DOE, London

DSDNI (2007) *Tackling Fuel Poverty: A Strategy for Northern Ireland*, Inter-departmental Group on Fuel Poverty, Annual Report 2007, www.dsdni.gov.uk/dsd_fuel_pov_1.pdf

DTI (Department of Trade and Industry) (2001) *The UK Fuel Poverty Strategy*, DTI, London, November, www.berr.gov.uk/files/file16495.pdf

DTI (2006) *Energy – Its Impact on the Environment and Society*, DTI, URN 06/441, July, www.berr.gov.uk/files/file32546.pdf

Eaga (2009) *The Warm Front Scheme Annual Report 2007/08*, Energy Action Grants Agency, Newcastle

EEPfH (2007) *Fuel Poverty in England – Schemes Receive Boost by Chancellor*, Energy Efficiency News, 19 December 2007

EEPfH (2008a) *The Insulation Industry – Working in Partnership with Government to Insulate the Existing UK Housing Stock by 2050*, Energy Efficiency Partnership for Homes, London, August

EEPfH (2008b) *Opportunities to Improve Hard to Heat Homes within CERT*, Energy Efficiency Partnership for Homes, London, December

EEPfH (2008c) *An Assessment of the Size of the UK Household Energy Market*, Element Energy for Energy Efficiency Partnership for Homes, November, www.eeph.org.uk/uploads/documents/partnership/Assessment%20of%20the%20UK%20household%20energy%20efficiency%20market_171108.pdf

ENDS (2008) 'Government told to revise housebuilding targets', Environmental Data Services, report 406, November, London

FPAG (Fuel Poverty Advisory Group) (2006) *Fuel Poverty Advisory Group for England: Fourth Annual Report – 2005*, Department of Trade and Industry, London, March

FPAG (2008) *Fuel Poverty Advisory Group for England: Sixth Annual Report – 2007*, Department for Business, Enterprise and Regulatory Reform, London, March

Fuel Poverty Charter (2008) Supported by a coalition of Age Concern; Association for the Conservation of Energy; Barnardo's; Centre for Sustainable Energy; Child Poverty Action Group; Disability Alliance; energywatch; Friends of the Earth; Help the Aged; National Energy Action; National Right To Fuel Campaign; WWF, www.foe.co.uk/resource/press_releases/Fuel_Poverty_Charter_08092008.html

Guertler, P. and Preston, I. (2009) *Raising the SAP: Tackling Fuel Poverty by Investing in Energy Efficiency*, Consumer Focus, London

Hansard (2008) HC, Written Answers (Session 2007–2008), vol 482, col 992, 11 November

Hansard (2009a), HC Deb (Session 2008–2009), vol 489, col 1202–3, 20 March, Joan Ruddock, Minister for Fuel Poverty, DECC

Hansard (2009b) HC Written Answers (Session 2008–2009), vol 494, col 754, 23 June

HC 432-1 (2008) *Existing Housing and Climate Change*, Seventh report, Session 2007–2008, Communities and Local Government Committee, House of Commons, London

HC 37 (2009) *Energy Efficiency and Fuel Poverty*, Third report of session 2008–2009, Environment, Food and Rural Affairs Select Committee, Stationery Office, London

HC Library (2009) *The Decent Homes Standard: Update*, House of Commons Library, www.parliament.uk/commons/lib/research/briefings/snsp-03178.pdf

HM Government (2009) *Investing in a Low Carbon Britain*, Building Britain's Future, Department of Energy and Climate Change, London, April

Hong, S. H., Oreszczyn, T., Ridley, I. and Warm Front Study Group (2006) 'The impact of energy efficient refurbishment on the space heating fuel consumption in English dwellings', *Energy and Buildings*, vol 38, pp1171–1181

Jha, A. (2009) 'Miliband announces green makeover for every home in Britain by 2030', *The Guardian* online, 12 February, www.guardian.co.uk/environment/2009/feb/12/carbon-emissions-miliband

Jowit, J. (2009) 'Radical eco-makeover plan to cover quarter of UK homes', *The Guardian*, 9 February

King, M. (2009) 'New dawn for CHP?', *Energy Action*, NEA, vol 107, pp16–17

LGA (Local Government Association) (2009) *Creating Green Jobs*, LGA, London

Mackintosh, K. (2008) 'Cold comfort', *Holyrood Magazine*, October

Matthews, P. (2009) Sustainable Development Commission, Scotland, pers comm

Milne, G. and Boardman, B. (2000) 'Making cold homes warmer: The effect of energy efficiency improvements in low-income homes', *Energy Policy*, vol 28, pp411–424

NAO (National Audit Office) (2008) *Programmes to Reduce Household Energy Consumption*, Report by the Comptroller and Auditor General, HC 1164, session 2007/8, NAO, London, November

NAO (2009) *The Warm Front Scheme*, Report by the Comptroller and Auditor General, HC 126, session 2008/9, NAO, London, February

NIHE (Northern Ireland Housing Executive) (2007), *Northern Ireland House Condition survey 2006 – Full report*, NIHE, www.nihe.gov.uk/housing_conditions_survey_2006.pdf

Ofgem (Office of the Gas and Electricity Markets) (2009) *CERT Update*, Ofgem, London, February

ONS (Office for National Statistics) (2007) *Family Spending: 2006 Edition*, E. Dunn and C. Gibbins (eds), Palgrave Macmillan, ONS, www.statistics.gov.uk/downloads/theme_social/Family_Spending_2005-6/FamilySpending2005-6.pdf

ONS (2008) *Annual Abstract of Statistics*, Ian Macrory (ed), Palgrave Macmillan, www.statistics.gov.uk/downloads/theme_compendia/AA2008/AA2008.pdf

Palmer, G., MacInnes, T. and Kenway, P. (2008) *Cold and Poor: An Analysis of the Link between Fuel Poverty and Low Income*, New Policy Institute, www.npi.org.uk/reports/fuel%20poverty.pdf

Scottish Executive (2004) *Scottish Housing Quality Standard (SHQS)*, www.scotland.gov.uk/Resource/Doc/47210/0030182.pdf

Scottish Fuel Poverty Forum (2008) *Towards 2016 – The Future of Fuel Poverty Policy in Scotland*, September, www.scotland.gov.uk/Resource/Doc/240939/0066903.pdf

Scottish Government (2009) *Energy Assistance Package*, www.scotland.gov.uk/Topics/Built-Environment/Housing/access/FP/eap

SDC (Sustainable Development Commission) (2009) *Response to the Community Energy Saving Programme Consultation*, SDC, London, May

Sefton, T. (2004) *Aiming High – An Evaluation of the Potential Contribution of Warm Front towards Meeting the Government's Fuel Poverty Target in England*, CASE report 28, Centre for Analysis of Social Exclusion, LSE, London

SHCS (2008) *Scottish House Condition Survey, Revised Key Findings 2007*, www.scotland.gov.uk/Resource/Doc/933/0079066.pdf

Shorrock, L., Building Research Establishment, pers comm

Treasury (2008) *Pre-Budget Report 2008: Facing Global Challenges: Supporting People Through Difficult Times*, www.hm-treasury.gov.uk/d/pbr08_chapter7_159.pdf

Utley, J. I. and Shorrock, L. D. (2006) *Domestic Energy Fact File (2006): Owner Occupied, Local Authority, Private Rented and Registered Social Landlord Homes*, Building Research Establishment, www.bre.co.uk/page.jsp?id=879

Utley, J. I. and Shorrock, L. D. (2008a) *Domestic Energy Fact File (2007): England, Scotland, Wales and Northern Ireland*, Building Research Establishment, www.bre.co.uk/page.jsp?id=879

Utley, J. I. and Shorrock, L. D. (2008b) *Domestic Energy Fact File 2008*, Building Research Establishment, www.bre.co.uk/page.jsp?id=879

Welsh Assembly Government (2009a) *Living in Wales 2004*, special extract, wales.gov.uk/topics/statistics/headlines/housing-2007/housing-2006/h dw200606142/?lang=en

Welsh Assembly Government (2009b) *National Energy Efficiency and Savings Plan Consultation*, March, http://wales.gov.uk/docs/desh/consultation/090316energysav-ingplanen.pdf

Whitehead, C. (2008) 'Housing' in S. Thomas (ed) *Poor Choices: The Limits of Competitive Markets in the Provision of Essential Services to Low-Income Consumers*, Earthwatch, www.psiru.org/reports/PoorChoices.pdf

Wintour, P (2008) 'Producers may pass on cost of energy package to consumers', *The Guardian*, 12 September

7

Warmth and Health: The Benefits of Action and the Penalties of Inaction

All of the statistics on income levels, fuel prices and rates of heat loss tend to disguise the human cost of fuel poverty, which is at its most severe when people are sick or die through cold-related ill health. The annual toll of excess winter deaths was one of the major reasons for initial concerns, dating from 1972 (Boardman, 1991, p23), though the focus then was on hypothermia. This, the most extreme form of cold-related death, is recognized as less of an issue now; but there remains a seasonal increase of deaths in winter. There is also an increasing awareness that many people become ill and need the services of the National Health Service (NHS), but fortunately do not die. These illnesses have financial as well as human impacts and will be the continuing and growing legacy of inaction on fuel poverty.

The link with fuel poverty is that if people are unable to achieve affordable warmth and are sitting in a cold home, then this is detrimental to their health. The aim is to keep people warm, fit and healthy. This was recognized in *The UK Fuel Poverty Strategy* (DTI, 2001) with its 238 references to health.

A wide range of studies has looked at different aspects of the evidence between cold-related ill health (morbidity) or death (mortality) and various other factors in people's lives, such as income levels, smoking and housing conditions. Some were extremely detailed; some took an epidemiological approach by looking at whole populations over several years. By definition, most of what is written about cold-related ill health and excess winter deaths is a description of fuel poverty. The medical evidence is one of the most meticulously researched areas of fuel poverty. All of the information in this chapter is from evidence, rather than modelled, and represents a small taster of the total body of work.

Curiously, and unfortunately, there is little evidence of the cost implications of this ill health and death to the NHS. It is possible, therefore, to look at who is the most vulnerable to the health implications of cold homes but not to assess what would be the cost savings for the NHS of greater action – or inaction – on fuel poverty.

Excess winter deaths

One of the accepted indicators of fuel poverty is the number of people who die in winter from cold-related illnesses, such as heart attacks, strokes and respiratory disease. It is one of the 16 indicators that the government uses to chart progress on fuel poverty (BERR, 2008). These are people who would not have died if it had stayed summer all year round. There is, for instance, no seasonal variation in deaths from cancer. The increase in excess winter deaths in the UK is a greater percentage than in other countries, even those with a harsher winter, such as Siberia or Canada. There are between 26,700 and 55,100 extra deaths a year in the UK: the number fluctuates mainly with the weather, but also if there is a flu outbreak, as in 1999/2000 (Table 7.1). When flu epidemics are removed, there is no obvious trend.

Excess winter deaths are measured as the increase in the months of December to March over the average of the four months before and the four months after this period. Thus, the winter of 2007/08 refers to December 2007 to March 2008, in comparison with the summer before and the summer after. Occasionally a cold snap in November (e.g. 1993) will result in substantial deaths that would be missed by this definition (Bowie and Jackson, 2002). In many areas, such as Northern Ireland, the risk of cold-related ill health extends well into the summer (Morris, pers comm). If a two-month winter period is taken, instead of the four months, then the peak is more than 40 per cent higher than the summer trough (Wilkinson et al, 2001, p3).

The increase in winter mortality is greatest for elderly people, at about 30 per cent for those over 75 years of age (Wilkinson et al, 2001, p8); but there is a winter peak for most age groups. Excess winter deaths in the UK are 'approximately double that of Scandinavian and other Northern European countries;

Table 7.1 *Excess winter deaths, by country (1999–2008)*

	England	Scotland	Wales	Northern Ireland	UK
1999/2000	45,650	5190	2880	1449	55,169
2000/01	23,290	2220	1640	589	27,739
2001/02	25,790	1840	1480	492	29,602
2002/03	22,620	2510	1400	534	27,064
2003/04	21,930	2840	1550	403	26,723
2004/05	29,740	2760	1930	554	34,984
2005/06	23,740	1780	1560	578	27,658
2006/07	22,380	2750	1400	713	27,243
2007/08	23,800	2180	1500	880	28,360

Source: Government Statistics (2009) for England and Wales; GRO (2008) for Scotland; DSD (2003, p47) and Morris (pers comm) for Northern Ireland

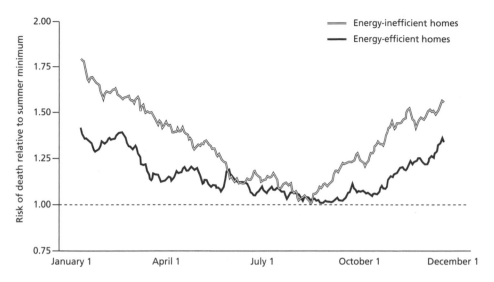

Source: Wilkinson et al (2001, p16)

Figure 7.1 *Seasonal fluctuations in mortality in cold and warm homes, UK (1991)*

however the rates in the Irish Republic, Spain, Portugal and Italy were comparable to, or higher than, those for the countries of the UK' (Bowie and Jackson, 2002, p5). It is not only the UK that has homes that are ill-equipped to cope with the cold.

When there are summer heat waves (as in 2003) and additional summer deaths, then this will result in lower levels of excess winter deaths in both the winter before and the winter after that summer. Thus, paradoxically, hot summers will imply that the problem of excess winter deaths is being solved, whereas in reality it is just being matched by a growing summer problem.

There is some residual controversy about whether people become ill as a result of cold within the home, or because they got cold outside the home and could not warm up enough when indoors. The evidence has accrued that the cause of death is getting cold in the home, rather than outside. Through a combination, at postcode level, of data about excess winter deaths, over the ten years of 1986 to 1996, and information about the energy efficiency of the properties in the area, it has been possible to demonstrate that winter deaths are higher in cold energy-inefficient homes than in warmer homes (Figure 7.1). There is no difference in the risk of death (i.e. between the two curves) during the summer months.

The study was a particularly comprehensive and thorough one; so, despite being fairly old data, it is worth looking at in some detail. The energy-efficiency data and measured temperatures came from the energy report of the *English House Condition Survey 1991* (DOE, 1996). Temperature measurements were discontinued after the *English House Condition Survey* (EHCS) of

1996 (DETR, 2000), so there are no national data since then that could be used for a similar analysis. The temperature in the home varied with:

- Tenure: housing association dwellings were the warmest and privately rented the coldest, each being 7 per cent of the sample.
- Dwelling age: dwellings built before 1900 were, on average, 2°C cooler than those constructed since 1980. There was a clear temperature gradient with dwelling age.
- Heating system: the 22 per cent of homes without central heating were 2°C cooler than those with central heating.
- Standard Assessment Procedure (SAP) rating: temperatures decline with energy inefficiency, with nearly 2°C difference between the top and bottom SAP quartiles.
- Receipt of benefits: homes were colder if more than 75 per cent of income was from benefits (38 per cent of households).
- Income: the half of the sample with the lowest incomes was colder.
- Dissatisfaction with the heating system – only 6 per cent were 'very unsatisfied', but they had the greatest risk of a cold home of any group.

The two most significant indicators of excess winter deaths were the age of the householder and the age of the property; indoor temperature and tenure were the next two most risky characteristics. Interestingly, there is little correlation between excess winter deaths and socio-economic group (SEG), nor did the lower SEG households have colder homes. One explanation of this somewhat surprising finding is the way in which households were allocated to a SEG. For instance, there was no separate group for retired people, although 40 per cent of the households were aged 60 or over. This indicates that retired people were allocated to the SEG that they had when working or, for widows who had not worked, that their husband had when working. The lack of relationship with SEG should not, therefore, be such a surprise and may not be a good test, especially as there is a link, albeit weak, between cold homes and low incomes. In addition, 'those with some of the least energy efficient and, hence, coldest homes include lone pensioners and other vulnerable groups' (Wilkinson et al, 2001, p20). The researchers concluded (Wilkinson et al, 2001, p18): 'the findings provide strong, although not conclusive, evidence that winter mortality and cold-related mortality are linked to sub-optimal home heating'. As a result of this evidence, Wilkinson et al (2001, p21), state: 'if the heating systems and energy efficiency of homes could be improved, substantial public health benefits should follow'. Because the Paul Wilkinson study was linked to the EHCS, there is no information on expenditure levels or pre-existing ill health.

Self-reported dissatisfaction with the heating system is a good indicator that the home is likely to be cold and the occupant's health at risk. In a European study, Belfast, in Northern Ireland, represented an extreme outlier in the relationship between average temperatures and coronary rates:

> *In this population the change in rates was much greater than expected... A possible explanation is a poorer standard of heating in Belfast than in the rest of Europe. The European household panel survey showed that the proportion of households in the United Kingdom and Ireland that reported being unable to keep their homes adequately warm was more than five times that in Germany.* (Barnett et al, 2005)

This was part of the evidence for the study group that the problem of excess winter deaths is associated with cold events in warm climates and that they are 'preventable'.

Similar studies have found links between excess winter deaths and the energy efficiency of the dwelling in Scotland:

> *EWDs [excess winter deaths] are relatively easy to measure and may be considered as the acute outcome of cold, damp housing. Mortality, however, is at the tip of an expensive morbidity 'iceberg'. House conditions play a decisive role, not only in determining at what age adults die, but, more importantly, they impact on occupant health and quality of life. Investment in energy-efficiency measures, such as central heating, insulation, double glazing and complementary ventilation strategies to ensure good indoor air quality, can drive major improvements in public health and reduce EWDs.* (Howieson and Hogan, 2005, p22)

The finding is replicated in Northern Ireland, as well. The variation in cold-related death rates can be explained as 'temperature [within the home] shortfall was the most common significant explanatory variable' (Morris, 2007, p13).

Excess winter morbidity

A cold-related death is a relatively easy, though sad, statistic to obtain. It is much more difficult to acquire data on the amount of cold-related ill health involving a visit to the doctor or hospital. It is common wisdom that when there is a cold spell, there will be an increase in the need for hospital beds. However, there are virtually no statistics on the numbers of patients involved or the cost to the health service, although NHS expenditure rises by 2 per cent in the coldest months of the year (Hansard, 1998).

Detailed evidence from the London Borough of Newham demonstrated a strong correlation between the risk of fuel poverty and the likelihood of an emergency admission to hospital for respiratory problems, among pensioners. This provides support 'in favour of additional public health-driven investment in domestic energy-efficiency measures to benefit the fuel poor and impact on cold-related health effects' (Rudge and Gilchrist, 2007, p856). For every 1°C drop in external temperature below 5°C, there are more visits to London clinics by seniors with asthma (12.4 per cent), other lower respiratory diseases (11 per cent), upper respiratory diseases (8.5 per cent), but not cardio-vascular problems (−2.2 per cent) (Hajat and Haines, 2002, p829). The Department of Health (DOH) believes that for every cold-related death there are eight non-fatal hospital admissions (DOH, 2009).

Children and health

Most of the focus is on elderly people as they show the greatest susceptibility to cold-related ill health; however, 'damp conditions are strongly linked to child-hood illness' (Gilbertson et al, 2006b, p12). Damp homes are caused by condensation forming on cold, poorly-insulated fabric. This results in mould, and occupants may develop allergic responses, such as asthma. A child who develops asthma because of living in a damp home is likely to have that asthma for many years (and perhaps for life), even when she or he moves into a warmer, more energy-efficient home. As a result, the ongoing human and health costs of this form of unhealthy housing are considerable. For several years there has been concern about the links between damp homes and respira-tory problems in children. There were real improvements in the health of children with asthma after central heating was installed in Cornish homes (Somerville et al, 2000). Asthma affects 1.1 million children in the UK, one of whom, nine-year-old Luke expressed his feelings on how his home was affect-ing his well-being (NEA, 2009):

> *I feel cold and sad*
> *I haven't got any heating*
> *My home is cold and damp*
> *Water runs down the wall*
> *And it makes my bed wet*
> *My fingers draw on the window*
> *It's like fog*
> *I try to pull the cover over me*
> *But it does not work.*

The horrific choice of heating or eating that is faced by fuel-poor households has potentially long-term harmful effects if young babies have reduced diets as well as a cold environment. According to the United Nations Children's Fund (UNICEF), if a child is malnourished before the age of two the damage is irreversible, both in terms of physical and mental development. While this patently refers most commonly to children in the developing world, there must be a risk of it occuring if British children are underfed in their first years. A group of children were found to be suffering in the US because the extra cost of heating in winter meant there was less money for food among poor house-holds. As a result, during cold spells, there was a 10 per cent drop in caloric

Table 7.2 *Children's physical and social response to inadequate heating*

Effect	Three years or more in a home with inadequate heating	All children in the group	Age of children
Respiratory problems (e.g. asthma)	15%	7%	All dependent children
Truanted	13%	3%	5–15 years
Expelled/excluded from school	10%	3%	5–18 years
In trouble with the police	7%	2%	8–18 years
No quiet place to do homework	10%	4%	11–15 years
Run away from home	12%	6%	11–15 years

Source: Barnes et al (2008, pp54–55)

intake among them and their parents, which was not found in richer households (Bhattacharya et al, 2003, p1153).

The National Centre for Social Research (NatCen) study considered the impacts of fuel poverty upon the young. When many other contributory factors were controlled for, the results suggested that living in homes that lacked affordable warmth was significantly associated with a variety of physical and social problems (Table 7.2). Among adolescents who had lived for more than three years in homes with inadequate heating, 28 per cent had four or more of these outcomes, compared with 4 per cent of children who had always lived in homes that had affordable warmth.

These negative social responses indicate a stressed child, unable to obtain privacy within the home and so he or she seeks it elsewhere, with the risks that this entails. While there have been few studies that link cold homes with children's well-being:

> ... the effects of fuel poverty for infants and children are primarily on physical health, which, in turn, might affect overall well-being and educational achievement. Amongst adolescents, by contrast, effects appear to be primarily on mental health.
> (Liddell, 2008, p9)

Families with children are disproportionately likely to state that they have difficulty keeping the home warm and in meeting the costs of doing so (Sefton and Chesshire, 2005, p47). The insidious implications for children of living in a cold home need to be factored into policy more strongly.

Summer heat waves

Summer heat waves are expected to occur more frequently as a result of climate change. Up to 2000 people died from heat-related causes in the UK in the summer of 2003 when temperatures were 2°C above average (White, 2004). In thirty years, this could be the average summer temperature in the south-east of England (UKCIP, 2009). The challenge is to make the housing stock better at both keeping warmth in during the winter and keeping heat out during the summer. Some energy-efficiency improvements achieve this – for instance, those that increase the thermal mass of the building – but not all. With a solid wall, external insulation incorporates the bricks into the useful thermal mass, whereas internal solid wall insulation reduces the thermal mass. There are also specific solutions to protect against the summer sun (e.g. shutters inside or outside the window, baffles/shading above the window; a design emphasis on buildings that have windows on both sides to generate a through airflow). The UK has not yet begun to introduce summer protection for the fuel poor and elderly; but the focus should, again, be on the dwelling. The introduction of air conditioning, particularly if it is powered by electricity, should be a very low priority and introduced only as a last resort. The greater use of electricity, particularly while it is such a carbon-intensive source of energy, will only exacerbate climate change.

Cold homes

The temperatures that should be achieved to give affordable warmth are 21°C in the living room and 18°C elsewhere, when these rooms are occupied. As the EHCS stopped measuring temperatures inside the home in 1996, there have been few recent measurements of how warm, or how cold, people's homes are. A study into the Warm Front scheme found that before intervention the average living room was 17.9°C, with 15.9°C in bedrooms. There was a long tail of low temperatures in the living room, right down to 2 per cent of households recording only 7°C. Even after improvements, several homes still recorded temperatures below 15°C and down to 12°C in the living room (Green and Gilbertson, 2008, p9). These are up to 9°C below the World Health Organization's (WHO's) recommendations.

There are few other measured temperature surveys. Information is provided by the Building Research Establishment (BRE), in the Domestic Energy Fact Files, as a result of deducing what could be happening to temperatures through making energy use in the home balance: this amount of energy appears to be used for heating; this is the rate at which heat is lost from the building; this is the efficiency of the central heating system, so this must be the temperature. The trend to higher temperatures is undoubtedly appropriate; but there must be some caution about the accuracy of the reported temperatures, particularly when subdivided (e.g. into those with or without central heating).

Similarly, there are relatively few studies that involve interviewing the fuel poor and establishing their views on warmth, or the lack of it. During 2000 to 2003, a sample of households was interviewed, both before and after energy-efficiency interventions. The reality of life for the fuel poor comes through. When asked if the home is cold:

> *Terrible. Sometimes we go to bed at 7 o'clock, and all our regular visitors know it's pointless coming after that time because they*

*know where we are. We find it easier to go upstairs to sit under-
neath the blankets to keep warm.* (Evelyn, middle-aged couple)
(Harrington et al, 2005, p263)

In a survey of five cities, the differences between the occupants of warm and
cold homes are as follows (Critchley et al, 2007, p153):

- The occupants of warm homes are likely to be the oldest, white British, in
  new properties, those with cavity walls, a SAP rating >65 or with a longstanding limiting illness.
- The occupants of cold homes are likely to be living alone, in areas of the
  greatest multiple deprivation, with draughts or condensation problems and
  to have poor psychosocial health (e.g. anxiety and depression). Distress
  was often correlated with a declared inability to control the heating system
  and, in a few cases, economic constraints.
- There is no significant relationship between cold homes and gender, educa-
  tional qualifications, tenure, the presence of children, household income or
  reported difficulty in paying the fuel bill.

This replicates the findings of the Wilkinson et al (2001) study in relation to
dwelling age and energy efficiency and the effect of the age of the occupants.
The change in the influence of tenure may be as a result of the ten or more
years' gap in the two data sets – social housing has become more efficient in the
interval. About one quarter of the sample had cold homes and in half of these
the respondents acknowledged the value of a warm home, but a dislike of a
stuffy one. This group did not appear to have difficulty in paying their heating
bills; nor did they appear to have mental health problems, so it can be deduced
that for just over 10 per cent of the sample, living in a cold home was
preferred. The other 10 per cent of the sample had cold homes as a result of
economic constraints or difficulty in controlling the heating system, and this
caused them distress (Critchley et al, 2007, p156).

There will be a trend towards the need for warmer homes as the population is ageing and more people are at home for most of the 24 hours. This trend
is increased with high levels of unemployment: the cost of keeping warm was
previously borne by the workplace, but now becomes the responsibility of the
householder. A similar trend that would push up the demand for heating
occurs when people start to work from home. In the first two examples, the
need for more heating occurs at a time when incomes are reducing.

Effect of energy-efficiency improvements

Better-quality, more energy-efficient housing is demonstrated to be important
in reducing fuel poverty and improving the physical and mental health of the
occupants. An assessment has been undertaken of the effects of Warm Front
interventions in England in low-income homes between 2001 and 2003,

known as the *Warm Front Study*. The focus was on households containing elderly people or children under 16. This detailed data-rich study has updated information that was previously only available from the 1991 and 1996 EHCSs. The strongest indicator of a cold home was a low SAP rating (SAP01 ≤41). Damp conditions and high relative humidity was more likely at lower SAP ratings and 'the risk of mould increased fastest at SAP01 ratings lower than 20' (Oreszczyn et al, 2006b, p132).

The improvements achieved appreciable gains in temperature, 'with heating system improvements having the greatest benefit' (Oreszczyn et al, 2006a, p251). Homes that just received insulation showed lower temperature gains. As bedroom temperatures rise, the chances of the occupants suffering depression and mental ill health decreases (Green and Gilbertson, 2008). The benefits of additional warmth and greater comfort were reported by over two-thirds of this sample and universally by those with limited mobility. Additional benefits came from the ability to afford more hot water, better food and more cooked food (partly because the kitchen is warmer and more comfortable to be in). Many benefited from the relief of a reliable heating system and the more relaxed home life now that most of the rooms can be used: 'I have no anxiety that the boiler's going to stop working... We're not grumpy because we can't get warm' (Gilbertson et al, 2006a, p952). 'About a quarter of respondents made an explicit link between mood and temperature' (Gilbertson et al, 2006a, p953).

The real benefits of increased temperature resulted in some mixed messages on energy consumption and fuel expenditure:

> *The combination of observed increase in thermal comfort with no decrease in the monitored normalized fuel consumption means that if all the sample dwellings were in fuel poverty prior to the WF [Warm Front] energy-efficiency measure, then the potential improvement in health is gained at the expense of increased heating cost, thereby moving them deeper into fuel poverty and compromising the government's fuel poverty strategy.* (Hong et al, 2006, p1180).

While it is true that energy use has not fallen, this is definitely not the same as saying the cost has risen. If fuel switching has been involved (and there is no detail on this beyond Gilbertson et al, 2006a, p949), then it is perfectly possible for the household to use more energy for less cost (e.g. where electricity has been displaced by gas). This is, in reality, what occurred: 'the findings actually show a decrease in fuel cost mainly from fuel switching (i.e. decreased reliance on portable electric units), despite an increase in fuel consumption and with little change in carbon emissions' (Hong, pers comm). Thus, the implications for fuel poverty are good, not bad.

Research in New Zealand found that:

Insulating existing houses led to a significantly warmer, drier indoor environment and resulted in improved self-rated health, self-reported wheezing, days off school and work, as well as a trend for fewer hospital admissions for respiratory conditions... Our study has shown that ... improving the thermal properties of older houses led to warmer houses and had demonstrable health benefits. Interventions of this kind, which focus on low-income communities and poorer-quality housing, have the potential to reduce health inequalities. Fitting insulation is a cost effective intervention for improving health and well-being and has a high degree of acceptance by the community, policy-makers and politicians. (Howden-Chapman et al, 2007)

In Wales, in order to remove households from fuel poverty, 'there needs to be considerable financial outlay (publicly and privately) to increase the level of income of pensioners in Wales, and to improve and modernize the heating and energy efficiency of the housing stock' (Burholt and Windle, 2006, p1206).

The Scottish Central Heating Programme 'significantly reduced condensation, dampness and cold in recipients' homes, long-term exposure to which is associated with poor health'. However, 'two years after installation, the programme had no clear impact on respondents' health or their use of health services or medication' (Platt et al, 2007, p1). This may be because there can be only a gradual return to better health, even when conditions improve, and two years is insufficient time – a conclusion of other studies. In a study of the effects of the Scottish programme to install central heating, the conclusion was that it was 'prudent to regard the direct impact of the central heating programme on health as limited' (Platt et al, 2007, p42).

The beneficial health effects of warmer homes have led several public health authorities to invest directly in energy-efficiency improvements themselves – for instance, in Cornwall (Somerville et al, 2000). There are a few other schemes like this (Press, 2003, pp10–11), where the local authority and health organizations have recognized the benefits of a combined focus. Sometimes, health officials, such as district nurses and midwives, are the people most likely to visit a home in fuel poverty and are able to link the household with available support, such as Warm Front and the Carbon Emissions Reduction Target (CERT).

In Northern Ireland, there is an 'investing in health' platform to ensure that funds are targeted at people with health risks from fuel poverty. The package includes energy-efficiency advice and support, benefit entitlement checks, and home safety and security measures. Fifteen councils have signed up for this and are partly supporting it with their own funds. However, there is still a concern that too strong a focus is on seniors. In 2007/08, the Warm Homes scheme only provided one tenth of the grants to homes with children (£1.4 million) in comparison with those received by pensioners (£14 million) (Liddell, 2009b).

Although increasing the ability of the household to keep warm, through energy-efficiency improvements, can reduce the ill-health effects of fuel poverty, there are two problems with any assessments of actual installations:

* It is not clear how long it would take for better health to demonstrate itself and the full effects may not be identifiable after, for instance, just one or two years.
* Many of the existing programmes (e.g. Warm Front) are poorly targeted, so the recipients do not necessarily represent those in fuel poverty, the most disadvantaged or the most vulnerable to cold homes.

Therefore, the savings to the National Health Service may be small in the first few years, although accumulating subsequently. The benefits to the occupants appear to be immediate, especially in relation to greater warmth. The converse is likely to be true: the underlying costs to the health service of cold-related ill health are growing insidiously as fuel poverty deepens. This is definitely a case where prevention, through prompt investment, will reduce long-term costs.

Warmth versus money

The cost of warmth in an energy-inefficient property is high: it is only energy-efficient homes that can provide cheap warmth, which would be affordable for a low-income household. There is evidence that people in the least efficient homes recognize the poor value that they are getting for their expenditure on heating, and so do not spend more than the basic minimum (Boardman, 1991, p178). When the home is improved and becomes more energy efficient, the cost of keeping warm falls. As a result, the household will spend more on heating as it is getting better value for the expenditure. This may have been what was happening in some Warm Front homes. What is confirmed by the Warm Front team and other studies is that the greatest increase in temperature occurs in those homes that were the coldest before. These households do not save much energy since they were not using much before anyway. This demonstrates the shock of using real data, with minimal savings, in comparison with the ambitious reductions shown by models: the savings cannot be made in something that was not being used.

Another factor in rising temperatures after an energy-efficiency improvement reflects the physics of heat loss. With an energy-efficiency improvement, some of the increase in warmth occurs naturally – the heat escapes more slowly so the average temperature rises – for instance at night, when the heating is switched off.

The effect of the interventions was more pronounced in colder dwellings with the temperature rising by 2°C or more, while in the warmest homes the temperature increase was about 1°C or less (Oreszczyn et al, 2006a, p249). This replicates the findings shown in Table 6.4 in Chapter 6 by Milne and Boardman (2000) and fits with common sense. The substantial proportion of the benefit that is taken as additional warmth in these cold homes does demonstrate the importance that people place on being warm. Warmth is not a discretionary expenditure.

There is another conclusion to be drawn from this evidence. Within energy economics there is a debate about the value of energy-efficiency improvements because the household has to spend the money saved on something. And almost inevitably that expenditure has some energy implications – part of the rebound effect (Sorrell, 2007). Thus, the argument is that these extra energy expenditures annul part of the benefits of the energy-efficiency improvements. In cold homes, the savings that are being taken up as additional warmth reduce the opportunity for a rebound into other energy expenditures. For households who are already warm, the energy-efficiency improvement releases money that could be spent on other energy-using activities, such as additional flights. Therefore, a focus on the coldest homes will limit the growth in discretionary energy consumption. Helping people obtain essential energy services, such as warmth, is good energy economics.

Mental and physical benefits – adults

There is a potential for both improved physical and mental health from energy-efficiency improvements. In relation to mental health, the *Warm Front Study* concluded that:

> ... *relief from financial pressures is associated with a reduction in anxiety and depression. Reducing fuel poverty is a major route to improving mental health... Prevalence of anxiety or depression ... fell from 300 to about 150 per 1000 occupants after Warm Front measures. This is a significant impact. For every 10,000 properties (with two adults) improved by Warm Front, about 3000 occupants will be relieved of anxiety or depression.* (Green and Gilbertson, 2008, pp14, 18)

Help the Aged has reported that one in four older people are so worried about the future that it is making them ill: the combined effect of poverty and loneliness (Boseley, 2008). Thus, improving the energy efficiency of their homes would provide real relief to some of these worries.

With physical health, the evidence was more circumspect: people were warmer, but the study found 'no direct link between Warm Front measures and better physical health, possibly because their full impact was delayed beyond the study period'. Therefore, there could be 'probable improvements in physical health further down the timeline' (Green and Gilbertson, 2008, p15). One of the interesting questions is the interaction between physical and mental health, as 'poor mental health is a prelude to poor physical health' and the study found a strong association between the two (Green and Gilbertson, 2008, p15). These results imply that investing in the homes of the fuel poor has positive benefits for the NHS, as well as benefits for the occupants.

Financial costs and benefits

The costs of a death or of an illness and the financial benefits of treating or preventing it are all extremely difficult to assess. Even in 1994, the costs of condensation-related ill health meant that:

> ... *adverse housing conditions are responsible for an extra £300 per year per inhabitant in GP [general practitioner] consultations, hospital and medication costs, with an avoidable expense to the NHS well in excess of £1000 million per annum.* (Hunt and Boardman, 1994, p30)

Asthma is a direct result of damp, mouldy homes and the cost of asthma (in all age groups) is a minimum of £847 million per annum (over one quarter of all costs cannot be traced back to an individual illness) (Brambleby et al, 2008, p20). This is just under 1 per cent of the NHS annual budget of £92 billion in 2008. Not all asthma sufferers are in fuel poverty.

Another study (Carr-Hill, Coyle and Ivens, 1993) estimated that of '£2 billion per year as an NHS spend trying to treat conditions caused by poor housing [only] a portion of this ... can be attributed to the effects on health of cold damp housing, although the size of that portion, while unknown, is substantive' (cited in Peters and Stevenson, 2000, p151). In a modelling exercise of the costs to the health service (only) of health conditions related to damp or cold housing, in 1992/93, annual savings were in the range of £44 million to £112 million (Peters and Stevenson, 2000, p149). The DOH has recently stated that: 'for each excess winter death, there is an estimated 8 emergency admissions each winter and over 100 households living in fuel poverty' (DOH, 2009, p1).

The value of the benefits over the 15-year life of an energy-efficiency improvement and including the fuel bill savings were then compared with the costs of the measure and demonstrated that every £1 spent on energy efficiency resulted in 93 pence of savings (Liddell, 2009a, p25). An even wider cost-benefit analysis could be undertaken. There may be days lost from school or work because of illness, whereas the result of the energy-efficiency intervention will have resulted in both additional employment and carbon savings. With the Northern Ireland Warm Homes scheme, the total of all the major benefits could indicate a return that is more than double the investment (Liddell, 2008, p16).

There is a paucity of studies that assess the value to the NHS and the wider economy of improvements in the energy efficiency of people's homes and the reduction in fuel poverty. This is surprising. Around £1 billion is being spent on energy-efficiency improvements through fuel poverty policy (Chapter 6) and the cost to the health service, alone, of cold-related ill health must be more than this. While there might be a slow return to better health as a result of investment in energy-efficiency improvements in the homes of the fuel poor, the returns are there. More importantly, the costs of continuing cold-related ill health will only continue to grow.

Current policies

The DOH does not have a remit to tackle fuel poverty in its obligations, so it has no specific policies. Recently, the DOH has issued a factsheet on *Health and Winter Warmth* (DOH, 2009) and is demonstrating some interest in the relationship between poor-quality housing and ill health. For instance, there are now direct referrals from the health services to the Warm Front programme. However, the major policy in this area is the responsibility of the Department for Communities and Local Government (DCLG).

Unhealthy housing

In support of all this evidence about the health benefits of more energy-efficient housing, there is now a comprehensive methodology to identify the risk of unhealthy housing: the Housing Health and Safety Rating System (HHSRS), introduced into England and Wales in 2006 to replace the previous legislation on unfit homes. Local authorities have a duty to take appropriate action on a category 1 hazard, and one of the most prevalent of these is for excess cold. To avoid this, 'the dwelling should be provided with adequate thermal insulation and a suitable and effective means of space heating so that the dwelling space can be economically maintained at reasonable temperatures' (ODPM, 2006, p27). The mental and health effects of these hazards are both included. No home with a category 1 hazard can be defined as 'decent', the current minimum standard for housing (Impetus, 2008, p8).

The change in definition has had a dramatic effect on the numbers of homes declared non-decent: in England in 2006, 4 per cent of homes would have failed the old fitness standard, whereas 22 per cent had a category 1 hazard under the HHSRS and were declared unhealthy (DCLG, 2008, p244). These were not just for cold, but a variety of causes. Specifically on cold, 2.4 million homes (11 per cent of the stock) would have failed the excess cold hazard. The highest proportions were (DCLG, 2008, pp72–85):

- pre-1919 (26 per cent of that group);
- rural areas (24 per cent);
- detached houses (18 per cent);
- converted flats (17 per cent);
- privately rented (16 per cent);
- pensioners (15 per cent or more, depending on age);
- owner occupied (12 per cent).

There is no defined standard that confirms the absence of excess cold: each local authority can make its own judgement. Originally SAP01 35 was proposed (DCLG, 2006, para 5.27), effectively the same as SAP05 35, and should trigger action by the local authority. SAP05 35 is *de facto* the standard as national indicator 187 (next chapter) uses <SAP05 35 as the indicator of fuel poverty 'to be consistent' with the HHSRS (Defra 2009). Once identified, it is difficult to be certain about the level of improvement that should occur to the energy efficiency of the home. For the Decent Homes Standard (DHS), the figure of SAP01 65 was the aim (not a requirement) to ensure that a household would be unlikely to be suffering from fuel poverty (Defra, 2004, pp4, 46). This is now equivalent to SAP05 65. As shown in Figure 6.3 in Chapter 6, there were no households in fuel poverty with a SAP05 >65 in England in 2006. Therefore, SAP05 35 and 65 are the two boundary triggers for reporting those who are and who are not assumed to be in fuel poverty under national indicator 187 (Chapter 8). As SAP05 38 is the upper limit of a category F property on the Energy Performance Certificate (EPC), there is, effectively, an unofficial consensus that properties in bands F and G are in fuel poverty and unhealthy. The average fuel-poor home was about SAP 38 in England in 2006 (Table 6.1 in Chapter 6). Therefore, about half the fuel-poor homes would have failed the HHSRS.

Many local authorities are not using the HHSRS, as intended, in:

> ... *a clear breach of their duties. Moreover, very few are carrying out their duty, as specified in the Housing Act, to carry out systematic reviews of the housing stock in their area for category 1 and 2 hazards. Given the excess winter death rate in England and Wales and rapidly rising fuel prices ... it is vital that this situation is remedied as soon as possible... Local authorities cannot use a lack of resources as an excuse for not fulfilling an important statutory responsibility.* (Impetus, 2008, p20)

This is despite a recommendation by government that local authorities use the powers that HHSRS gives them in 'their housing renewal and energy strategies' (Defra, 2004, p25). Declaring a house as failing, under the HHSRS, can be an effective intervention, with limited costs to the local authority. The threat is that the home will be compulsorily purchased if no action is taken. The London Borough of Newham, which issues more compulsory purchase orders than all the other London boroughs, found that:

> *There are properties in Newham that have lain empty for some time and are blighting the local neighbourhoods. But in 90 per cent of cases, owners will get them back into use without [us] taking the property from them'.* (Ian Dick, Housing and public health manager) (NRFC, 2007, pp14–15)

The HHSRS and its devolved equivalents (e.g. the Scottish Tolerable Standard) are an extremely important, if underused, piece of legislation. The HHSRS provides the basis for policy on fuel poverty as the worst housing has to be dealt with and all homes have to be surveyed in order to find the worst housing.

In Northern Ireland, there are plans to recruit households for energy-efficiency programmes when people get their flu vaccines from health centres in the most deprived areas. The target group comprises all those with a known respiratory or cardiac risk. Another possible programme will target people being discharged from hospital (Liddell, pers comm).

What is interesting is that current policies on the problem of excess cold do target the worst housing, rather than give people more income.

Conclusions

The number of excess winter deaths in the UK has been above 26,700 in all of the nine years until 2007/08, with no apparent downward trend. Many of these are preventable and more than nine times the number of deaths from road accidents: in 2007/08 there were less than 3000 deaths in Great Britain from road casualties (including pedestrians) (National Statistics, 2009). There is now an acceptance that people get cold in the home, more than outside it, and this risk stems largely from old energy-inefficient properties for people on low incomes. Cold homes are not just correlated with ill health; they cause it.

In 2003, there were some very cold homes among the fuel poor and even after the home was improved through Warm Front, there were still homes where the living room was up to 9°C below the WHO recommended standard. More recent and national data are only available through models. The main health problems are cardiovascular and respiratory disease in elderly people and asthma in children.

Improvements to the home may reduce the risk of ill health and often provide positive mental benefits through a lowering of depression and stress. The effects of fuel poverty on the physical and mental health of children are considerable, but have received little attention. This is one of the few areas where the diverse risks to children of living in homes with inadequate heating can be demonstrated, so it contributes to the debate about the policy priorities of pensioners and families.

Warmth is highly valued, especially by people in cold homes, who will use energy-efficiency improvements to increase the temperature as well as to save money. From an economic perspective, this is beneficial as it limits any potential for a rebound effect – spending the money saved on further energy-using activities.

There is a strong, adequate policy (the HHSRS) requiring local authorities to both find and act on homes that are unhealthy and create a hazard of excess cold: 11 per cent of homes in England in 2006. Very few councils are complying with this obligation; but it provides an immediate legislative route for escalating government action.

The risk of cold-related ill health or mortality is possibly considerable for the group of householders identified as 'I'm not complaining'. The failure to obtain the benefits to which they are entitled, the high cost of not switching fuel suppliers and the failure to self-refer for energy-efficiency programmes means that they could be in severe fuel poverty. This cannot be proved or disproved.

During the 21st century, in the UK, there is considerable suffering caused by the discomfort of living in a cold, possibly damp, home and the problems of subsequent ill health. Even if there were no costs to the NHS, removing this blight would be a justifiable policy objective. Nearly 300,000 people have died, unnecessarily, during the winter in the UK from 2000–2009. The legacy of these cold energy-inefficient homes is ill health and a cumulative burden on the occupants.

There are substantial, but unidentified, costs to the NHS. These will be associated mainly with morbidity, rather than mortality. The annual cost to the NHS of cold-related ill health is almost certainly in excess of £1 billion, and this represents the maximum savings that could be made. In 2009, £1 billion will be spent on energy-efficiency improvements in the homes of the fuel poor. Increased investment to reduce the annual costs to the NHS is likely to be justified. The failure of a substantial policy to tackle fuel poverty would clearly result in hardship, illness, death and considerable avoidable costs. Meanwhile, as fuel poverty increases, the costs to society – and the NHS specifically – will rise.

References

Barnes, M., Butt, S. and Tomaszewski, W. (2008) *The Dynamics of Bad Housing: The Impact of Bad Housing on the Living Standards of Children*, The NatCen Study, National Centre for Social Research, London

Barnett, A. G., Dobson, A. J., McElduff, P., Salomaa, V., Kuulasmaa, K. and Sans, S. for the WHO MONICA project (2005) 'Cold periods and coronary events: An analysis of populations worldwide', *Journal of Epidemiology and Community Health*, vol 59, pp551–557, http://jech.bmj.com/cgi/content/full/59/7/551#T3

BERR (Department for Business, Enterprise and Regulatory Reform) (2008) *Fuel Poverty Statistics: Background Indicators, 2008*, URN08/P31, BERR, London

Bhattacharya, J., DeLeire, T., Haider, S. and Currie, J. (2003) 'Heat or eat? Cold-weather shocks and nutrition in poor American Families', *American Journal of Public Health*, vol 93, no 7, pp1149–1154, www.ajph.org/cgi/reprint/93/7/1149

Boardman, B. (1991) *Fuel Poverty: From Cold Homes to Affordable Warmth*, Belhaven Press, London

Boseley, S. (2008) 'Poverty worries make elderly ill, says report', *The Guardian*, 20 May

Bowie, N. and Jackson, G. (2002) *The Raised Incidence of Winter Deaths*, General Register Office for Scotland, Occasional Paper 7, Scotland

Brambleby, P., Jackson, A. and Muir Gray, J. A. (2008) *Programme-Based Decision-Making for Better Value Healthcare: Second Annual Population Value Review*, NHS National Knowledge Service, Department of Health

Burholt, V. and Windle, G. (2006) 'Keeping warm? Self-reported housing and home energy efficiency factors impacting on older people heating homes in North Wales', *Energy Policy*, vol 34, no 10, pp1198–1208

Critchley, R., Gilbertson, J., Grimsley, M. and Green, G. (2007) 'Living in cold homes after heating improvements: Evidence from Warm Front, England's Home Energy Efficiency Scheme', *Applied Energy*, vol 84, pp147–158

DCLG (Department for Communities and Local Government) (2006) *A Decent Home: Definition and Guidance for Implementation, June 2006 Update*, DCLG, London

DCLG (2008) *English House Condition Survey 2006: Annual report*, DCLG, London, November, www.communities.gov.uk/documents/statistics/pdf/1072658.pdf

Defra (Department for Environment, Food and Rural Affairs) (2004) *Fuel Poverty in England: The Government's Plan of Action*, Defra, London

Defra (2009) *Local Government Performance Framework, NI 187 – Tackling Fuel Poverty – % of People Receiving Income Based Benefits Living in Homes with a Low and High Energy Efficiency Rating*, www.defra.gov.uk/corporate/about/what/localgovindicators/ni187.htm

DETR (Department of the Environment, Transport and the Regions) (2000) *English House Condition Survey 1996: Energy Report*, DETR, London

DOE (Department of the Environment) (1996) *English House Condition Survey 1991: Energy Report*, DOE, London

DOH (Department of Health) (2009) *Health and Winter Warmth: Reducing Health Inequalities*, Regional public health group fact sheet, DOH, updated January

DSD (Department for Social Development) (2003) *Towards a Fuel Poverty Strategy for Northern Ireland – Consultation Paper*, Department for Social Development, Belfast

DTI (Department of Trade and Industry) (2001) *The UK Fuel Poverty Strategy*, DTI, London, November, www.berr.gov.uk/files/file16495.pdf

Gilbertson, J., Stevens, M., Stiell, B. and Thorogood, N. (2006a) 'Home is where the hearth is: Grant recipients' views of England's Home Energy Efficiency Scheme (Warm Front)', *Social Science and Medicine*, vol 63, pp946–956

Gilbertson, J., Green, G. and Ormandy, D. (2006b) *Sheffield Decent Homes: Health Impact Assessment*, Sheffield Hallam University, UK

Government Statistics (2009) *Excess Winter Deaths*, www.statistics.gov.uk/statbase/Expodata/Spreadsheets/D7089.xls

Green, G. and Gilbertson, J. (2008) *Health Impact Evaluation of the Warm Front Scheme*, Centre for Regional Social and Economic Research, Hallam University, Sheffield, UK

GRO (General Register Office for Scotland) (2008) *Increased Winter Mortality in Scotland, 2007/08*, 29 October, www.gro-scotland.gov.uk/statistics/publications-and-data/increased-winter-mortality/increased-winter-mortality-in-scotland-2007-08.html

Hajat, S. and Haines, A. (2002) 'Associations of cold temperatures with GP consultations for respiratory and cardiovascular disease amongst the elderly in London', *International Journal of Epidemiology*, vol 31, pp825–830

Hansard (1998) HC Deb (Session 1997–1998), vol 304, col 305, 14 January

Harrington, B., Heyman, B., Merleau-Ponty, N., Stockton, H., Ritchie, N. and Heyman, A. (2005) 'Keeping warm and staying well: Findings from the qualitative arm of the Warm Homes Project', *Health and Social Care in the Community*, vol 13, no 3, pp259–267

Hong, S. H., The Bartlett School of Graduate Studies, pers comm

Hong, S. H., Oreszczyn, T., Ridley, I. and Warm Front Study Group (2006) 'The impact of energy efficient refurbishment on the space heating fuel consumption in English dwellings', *Energy and Buildings*, vol 38, pp1171–1181

Howden-Chapman, P., Matheson, A., Crane, J., Viggers, H., Cunningham, M., Blakely, T., Cunningham, C., Woodward, A., Saville-Smith, K., O'Dea, D., Kennedy, M., Baker, M., Waipara, N., Chapman, R. and Davie, G. (2007) 'Effect of insulating existing houses on health inequality: Cluster randomised study in the community', *British Medical Journal*, vol 334, p460

Howieson, S. G. and Hogan, M. (2005) 'Multiple deprivation and excess winter deaths in Scotland', *Journal of the Royal Society for the Promotion of Health*, vol 125, pp18–22

Hunt, S. and Boardman, B. (1994) 'Defining the problem', in *Domestic Energy and Affordable Warmth*, Watt Committee, Chapman & Hall, reprinted 2004 by Spon Press, London, pp18–32

Impetus (2008) *Tackling Fuel Poverty Using the Housing Healthy and Safety Rating System*, Report to the Energy Efficiency Partnership for Homes, London, April

Liddell, C. (2008) *The Impact of Fuel Poverty on Children*, Policy briefing for Save the Children, www.savethechildren.org.uk/en/54_7169.htm

Liddell, C. (2009a) *Health Impacts of Strabane District Council's Heating Conversion Programme*, University of Ulster, Coleraine Campus, Northern Ireland

Liddell, C. (2009b) Professor of Psychology, University of Ulster, Coleraine Campus, Northern Ireland, pers comm

Milne, G. and Boardman, B. (2000) 'Making cold homes warmer: The effect of energy efficiency improvements in low-income homes', *Energy Policy*, vol 28, pp411–424

Morris, C. (2007) *Fuel Poverty, Climate and Mortality in Northern Ireland 1980–2006*, Occasional paper 25, Northern Ireland Statistics and Research Agency, Department for Social Development, Belfast, www.dsdni.gov.uk/fuel_poverty_climate_and_mortality_in_ni_1980-2006.doc

Morris, C., Research fellow, University of Ulster, Coleraine Campus, Northern Ireland, pers comm

National Statistics (2009) *Road Casualties*, www.statistics.gov.uk/cci/nugget.asp?id=1208

NEA (National Energy Action) (2009) *NEA backs child poverty campaign*, www.nea.org.uk/nea-backs-child-poverty-campaign/

NRFC (2007) *National Right to Fuel Campaign*, Newsletter

ODPM (Office of Deputy Prime Minister) (2006) *Housing Health and Safety Rating Scheme: Operating Guidance*, ODPM, www.communities.gov.uk/documents/housing/pdf/142631.pdf

Oreszczyn, T., Hong, S. H., Ridley, I., Wilkinson, P. and Warm Front Study Group (2006a) 'Determinants of winter indoor temperatures in low income households in England', *Energy and Buildings*, vol 38, pp245–252

Oreszczyn, T., Ridley, I., Hong, S. H., Wilkinson, P., and Warm Front Study Group (2006b) 'Mould and winter indoor relative humidity in low income households in England', *Indoor and Built Environment*, vol 15, no 2, pp125–135

Peters, J. and Stevenson, M. (2000) 'Modelling the health cost of cold damp housing', in J. Rudge and F. Nicol (eds) *Cutting the Cost of Cold*, E & F N Spon, London

Platt, S., Mitchell, R., Walker, J. and Hopton, J. (2007) *The Scottish Executive Central Heating Programme: Assessing Impacts on Health*, Scottish Executive Social Research, Edinburgh

Press, V. (2003) *Fuel Poverty and Health: A Guide for Primary Care Organisations and Public Health and Primary Care Professionals*, National Heart Forum and others, www.heartforum.org.uk/downloads/FPbook.pdf

Rudge, J. and Gilchrist, R. (2007) 'Measuring the health impacts of temperatures in dwellings: Investigating excess winter morbidity and cold homes in the London Borough of Newham', *Energy in Buildings*, vol 39, pp847–858

Sefton, T. and Chesshire, J. (2005) *Peer Review of the Methodology for Calculating the Number of Households in Fuel Poverty in England – Final Report to DTI and Defra*, www.berr.gov.uk/files/file16566.pdf

Somerville, M., Mackenzie, I., Owen, P. and Miles, D. (2000) 'Housing and health: Does installing heating in their homes improve the health of children with asthma?', *The Society of Public Health*, vol 114, issue 6, pp434–439

Sorrell, S. (2007) *The Rebound Effect: An Assessment of the Evidence for Economy-Wide Energy Savings from Improved Energy Efficiency*, October, UK Energy Research Centre, UK

UKCIP (2009), *UK Climate Projections – UKC09*, UK Climate Impacts Programme, http://ukcp09.defra.gov.uk/content/view/38/6/

White, R. (2004) 'A very British heatwave', *Geography Review*, September, pp21–23

Wilkinson, P., Landon, M., Armstrong, B., Stevenson, S., Pattenden, S., McKee, M. and Fletcher, T. (2001) *Cold Comfort: The Social and Environmental Determinants of Excess Winter Deaths in England, 1986–96*, Report for the Joseph Rowntree Foundation, The Policy Press, Bristol, www.jrf.org.uk/sites/files/jrf/jr101-determinants-winter-deaths.pdf

8

Governance and Budgets

This chapter deals with two big issues: who is responsible for delivering on fuel poverty targets and who is paying? With both there is the related question of what would be a better framework. The chapter picks up several issues that were mentioned in Chapter 1 and begins to extend the debate. With budgets, there are always problems with very large numbers and this is particularly true during a recession. But large numbers equate to substantial employment, so the extent to which this is good or bad is a political and economic decision.

The previous chapters have introduced the ways in which various government departments and their policies interact with the fuel poor. There has been discussion about:

- the Department for Work and Pensions (DWP) and income levels;
- the Department for Business, Enterprise and Regulatory Reform (BERR) and the role of the Office of the Gas and Electricity Markets (Ofgem) in relation to fuel prices and the utilities – a responsibility transferred to the Department of Energy and Climate Change (DECC) since October 2008 (BERR was incorporated within the new Department for Business, Innovation and Skills, or BIS, in June 2009);
- the new DECC (created October 2008) and its advisers, the Climate Change Committee (CCC): the department has responsibility for co-ordinating action on fuel poverty across a range of government departments (DECC 2009, p35). DECC is also now responsible for Ofgem, so some aspects of policy on energy in housing are coming together in one place;
- the Department for Communities and Local Government (DCLG) on housing standards, including decent homes and the social sector and the Energy Performance Certificates (EPCs); local area agreements and the overall framework of local authority performance indicators in England;
- the Department for Environment, Food and Rural Affairs (Defra) transferred responsibility for fuel poverty to DECC in October 2008;
- and throughout, there is the brooding presence of the Treasury.

In addition:

- There is a UK inter-ministerial working group on fuel poverty: it is not clear that the committee is effective or that it meets often. There are no publications.
- There have been policy statements from the prime minister (on 11 September 2008), and announcements that affect policy on fuel poverty in both the most recent pre-budget (November 2008) and budget statements (April 2009).
- Policy on fuel poverty is devolved, but the contributory policies on incomes and fuel prices are not. There are, therefore, parallel teams in each of the devolved administrations dealing with the various aspects of fuel poverty;
- There is the important role of the Fuel Poverty Advisory Groups (FPAGs), one in each UK country, to advise the four governments.

This is a subject that involves considerable ministerial and administrative time. It frequently has a high profile. All members of parliament (MPs) are intimately involved in the problem, as the fuel poor appear in their surgeries with some frequency and desperation. And every time there is a cold spell or a fuel price rise, the media become interested. Even so, policy has not prevented the numbers in fuel poverty from continuing to rise since 2004.

Before proceeding through the various levels of government and decision-makers, there is a discussion about the importance of seeing how they all fit together into one system.

Systematic approach

Much of the problem with current policy-making, in general, is its reductionist approach, which 'attempts to break the problem down into component parts' and then tackle each of them (Chapman, 2002, p18). This results in interactions being missed and reduces the potential for feedback and useful synergies. With a problem, such as fuel poverty, which involves both complex interactions (e.g. between incomes and housing quality) and human beings, it is predictable that the present reductionist method is proving unsatisfactory. A systems approach is particularly important where there is little 'agreement about where the problem actually lies or where improvements can best be made'. Therefore, what is needed is 'a framework within which most or all of the participants can agree an agenda for improvement or a process for moving forward' (Chapman, 2002, p27).

It is 'right for ministers to determine *what* should be the priorities and directions of government policy and action ... but not *how* policies should be implemented'. They 'should be as un-prescriptive about means as possible', but combine this with 'an effective communication system among the different agencies implementing the policy so that what is learned (about what is working and what is not) can be disseminated and adapted to local conditions'.

The latter should be a priority, across different levels of government. 'The ultimate goal is the creation of a system of government that can *learn for itself*, on a continuous basis' and 'clearer expectations that poor performance will be tackled decisively' (Chapman, 2002, pp73–78).

There are two additional features that are important. First, the variations between one jurisdiction and another should be recognized and accepted. Provided the lessons are learned and exchanged: 'Variation will be part of the engine of continuous development' (Chapman, 2002, pp56–57). In addition, the process must include the participants – the householders: 'for complex systems, whether engineered or human activity, the only effective judge of performances is the end user' (Chapman, 2002, p47).

Therefore, with a complex system, the aim should be to establish a clear set of priorities, encourage diversity, monitor and evaluate, learn and promote good practice. Both climate change and fuel poverty are complex systems, so the need for a combined systematic approach must be especially true of them both together. The four governments had a clear set of priorities, in the targets for 2010 and 2016/2018, but did not build them into a coherent administrative framework.

European Union

Much of the UK's energy and environmental policy stems from directives originating in Brussels that relate to traded goods. This applies, for instance, to the EPCs that are required by the Energy Performance in Buildings Directive and the raft of policies to improve the efficiency of many energy-related products, such as fridges, light bulbs and windows (Boardman, 2007, p19). However, much of the benefit of this legislation on products is obtained by better-off households, as people on a low income often buy second-hand equipment rather than new.

The recognition of fuel poverty (or energy poverty, as it is also called) within Europe is beginning, mainly through the recent amendments to the third Electricity Directive ('Fuel poverty elsewhere' in Chapter 1). When discussed by the Parliament, there were 'proposals for an EU definition of energy poverty and the delivery of National Action Plans on Energy Poverty'. The European Anti-poverty Network (EAPN) network is pressing, among other things, for (EAPN, 2008, p3):

- a recognition of the complex causes of fuel poverty and the need for integrated strategies dealing with inadequate income, price regulation and energy efficiency;
- a commitment to develop a common European Union (EU) definition of energy poverty, data and indicators;
- the development of national action plans to fight fuel poverty, with delivery and implementation monitored on social protection and social inclusion;
- the development of an independent social assessment of the impact of liberalization involving people experiencing poverty.

There is also debate in the European Commission about a proposal for a Charter on the Rights of Energy Consumers. The issue of fuel poverty has been recognized in Brussels, so protection through new policies may be forthcoming. The British experience informs the debate, which will be of benefit to the fuel poor in 26 other countries – particularly those known to be suffering badly in Eastern and Central Europe.

One possible definition is that fuel poverty occurs if a household has to spend more than twice the median proportion of its income on all energy services. This links with the original UK definition (Boardman, 1991, p36). Part of the debate within Europe about a universal definition of fuel poverty is whether this would be appropriate. It has a universality that is independent of country-specific conditions, such as the actual proportion of income. The choice of definition will depend upon whether fuel poverty is seen as a relative problem – there will always be some fuel-poor households – in which case twice the median is a useful approach, though a varying number. Alternatively, it will depend upon whether there is an aim to eradicate fuel poverty, which requires some fixed proportion to be identified, so progress can be more easily monitored.

In the traditional way, the EU is preparing for the debate with some EU-wide projects to examine the situation in a range of member states. One of these is the European Fuel Poverty and Energy-Efficiency Project (EEPE), involving France, Belgium, Spain and the UK, among others. An earlier project was APPEEL: Awareness Programme for Policy-Makers in Energy Efficiency in Low-Income Housing.

In mid-2009, however, the European Commission had no direct influence on fuel poverty policy in the UK, although the UK is a contributor to EU policies – for instance, on renewable energy and carbon targets.

UK government and departmental responsibility

The 2000 Warm Homes and Energy Conservation Act (WHECA) has given government an obligation to eradicate fuel poverty where 'reasonably practicable'. Despite the unsuccessful judicial review and appeal, there is still a lack of clarity about the government's responsibilities under the Act, beyond producing the *UK Fuel Poverty Strategy* in 2001.

A Public Service Agreement (PSA) is a cross-departmental objective, but led by a specified department. Taking England as the example, in 2004, Defra was given 'a new Public Service Agreement target to... Eliminate fuel poverty in vulnerable households in England by 2010 in line with the government's *Fuel Poverty Strategy* objectives' (Defra, 2004, p8), known as PSA 07. There is no mention of the 2016 target or WHECA 2000. In its annual report in 2008, the department reported 'slippage' against its fuel poverty target, but did not make any statements about its plans for 2008/09 (Defra, 2008a, pxii). PSA 07 is now a legacy target that the government is monitoring. While responsibility for fuel poverty was transferred to the DECC in October 2008, none of DECC's headline PSAs and Departmental Service Orders (DSOs) mention fuel poverty (Cabinet Office, 2008), although in January 2009, the government was still looking at whether DECC should have a PSA or DSO on fuel poverty (HC 37, 2009, Ev 76, Q324) as a new director general had been appointed to cover domestic climate change and fuel poverty. DECC's main responsibility appears to be to monitor progress in the numbers in fuel poverty (DECC, 2009, p172), until the fuel poverty review is produced.

A DSO is specific to a single department. The present set of 30 PSA and DSOs was established in the comprehensive spending review July 2007, for the period of April 2008 to March 2011 and updated in October 2008, with the creation of DECC.

Despite the plethora of departments with an influence on fuel poverty, none of them have an unequivocal, clear mandate to deliver WHECA 2000. It is a legal obligation without a firm home. This led various campaign groups to propose that government should:

> *Re-establish fuel poverty as a Public Service Agreement (PSA) target. Set up a government Cross Departmental Ministerial Fuel Poverty Task Force with a duty to fulfil the PSA target and meet the government's legal duties on fuel poverty. The task force should be led by a senior fuel poverty minister who sits in the Cabinet and reports directly to the prime minister.* (Fuel Poverty Charter, 2008)

Despite this fragile framework, in England, the minister is sounding proactive:

> *Fuel poverty is an issue which the government takes very seriously... As the majority of fuel poverty households also have the lowest incomes, the government has taken the approach that the most fair and efficient method of identifying vulnerable householders who need help is through the receipt of benefits (primarily means tested).* (Autism Foundation, 2009)

All of this is considerably at odds with the government's policies on, and approach to, ending child poverty. PSA 9 is to 'halve the number of children in poverty by 2010–2011, on the way to eradicating child poverty by 2020'. This target has 26 pages of detailed notes attached to it and includes a reference to fuel poverty under 'tackling poor living conditions' (HMG, 2007, p7). PSA 9 includes the word 'eradicating' and yet bases its definition on a relative formulation of poverty – 60 per cent of median income. Curiously, the government was talking in June 2009 about passing an act to commit government to achieving the child poverty eradication, as if an act had some magic power. There is an additional mismatch between the confidence placed in the 2008 Climate Change Act and the priority accorded to WHECA 2000: an act is only influential if the government supports it with a budget.

In all circumstances, it is extremely difficult to be certain of achieving tough policies, such as the child poverty target, even when the detail is laid out. The failure on fuel poverty is hardly surprising – strong, coherent policies are unlikely to be formulated, let alone achieved, when there is a lack of clear responsibility and leadership within government, despite the legal commitment. This is particularly disturbing since several contributory policies, such as incomes and fuel prices, are not devolved and remain the responsibility of Whitehall.

Country variations

There is a myriad of ways in which the situation in the four countries varies, demonstrating why it is sensible for fuel poverty policy to be a devolved responsibility. Some policies are fully devolved (e.g. the Warm Front range of schemes), whereas others are less so (e.g. the Carbon Emissions Reduction Target (CERT) covers Great Britain, whereas Northern Ireland has its own Energy Efficiency Levy). None of the four administrations is managing to reduce fuel poverty and comply with its target, although England is probably the furthest from having an effective policy. In all four cases, it will be extremely challenging for fuel poverty to be eradicated by 2016, 2018 or any other foreseeable date.

Certain factors are strong indicators of fuel poverty and are common to the four countries: single elderly people, low incomes, homes built before 1919, rural areas, and properties off the gas network. The difference is the proportion in each jurisdiction. Some of the evidence provided is:

- England has the lowest rate of fuel poverty at about 16 per cent in 2008, with Northern Ireland about three times as high (Table 2.5 in Chapter 2).
- The highest increase since 2000 is in Wales, where the number of fuel poor had increased by 150 per cent by 2008 (Table 2.5 in Chapter 2).
- Households with children were more than four times as likely to be in fuel poverty in Northern Ireland in 2006 as in England (Table 2.10 in Chapter 2).
- By 2008, the Scots had to pay the most to have a prepayment meter (PPM) and people in Northern Ireland the least (Table 4.4 in Chapter 4).
- The proportion of the weekly budget spent on fuel is highest in Northern Ireland in 2006/07, at nearly 6 per cent across all households. This was partly because of the lack of natural gas, so households have to buy more expensive fuels, particularly oil (Table 5.6 in Chapter 5).
- Scotland's housing was more energy efficient than England's, in 2006/07, by over 8 SAP05 points (Table 6.3 in Chapter 6), even though a lot of Scottish homes are off the gas grid and a high proportion are solid-walled. This is partly explained by the high proportion of flats (Table 8.1).
- In 2005, it was estimated that 'almost 50 per cent of single pensioners in Scotland and over 40 per cent in Northern Ireland were in fuel poverty

Table 8.1 *Variations in housing characteristics (percentage of homes), by country (2005)*

	England	Scotland	Wales	Northern Ireland	UK
No insulation	7	13	9	–	8
No central heating	9	7	10	2	8
Electric central heating*	8	16	5	6**	8
Pre-1919	18	20	25	15	18
Flats	17	40	12	7	19

Notes: * Of those with central heating. ** 2004.
Source: Utley and Shorrock (2008a, Tables 3E, S, W, N; 5E, S, W, N; 12E, S, W, N; 15E, S, W; 13N; 16E, S, W);
Utley and Shorrock (2008b, Tables 7, 9, 15, 20, 21)

compared with 20 per cent in England. And 20 per cent of urban households in both Scotland and Northern Ireland were in fuel poverty compared with less than 10 per cent in England' (Palmer et al, 2008, p26).

Some of the other housing characteristics vary substantially between the different administrations (Table 8.1), meaning that appropriate targeted solutions are easier when undertaken through devolved responsibility. These are all households, not just the fuel poor; but they are factors that identify the fuel poor in particular.

The devolved administrations have been innovative in many of their policies and provide opportunities for cross-country learning. For instance, both Scotland and Wales are edging policy towards both mandatory minimum standards for housing and to targeting assistance on those with the worst housing conditions, as measured through the EPC. This is exactly the way for fuel poverty policy to progress. Once the innovative programmes are in place, there has to be sensible, honest reporting so that the successes and the failures are evident. Scottish experience of the Central Heating Programme is a good example where the success of the policy meant that it became less effective over time (Scottish Government, 2008, p37).

Northern Ireland

- Electricity PPMs – known as keypad meters – are inexpensive and cost 2.5 per cent below the standard credit rate and 4.9 per cent below the direct debit cost. This is the opposite of the situation, under Ofgem, in Great Britain, where PPMs are usually the most expensive tariff. Over a quarter (29 per cent) of all households have a keypad meter for electricity.
- Because of the widespread use of PPMs, there can be a policy of no electricity disconnections for debt. There is also a voluntary agreement to have no separate standing charge
- The Energy Efficiency Levy is collected from all energy customers (residential and others) and spent 80 per cent on the fuel poor and 20 per cent on community groups. None of it is spent in the homes of the better off.

- These three initiatives result from the combined strength of the Northern Ireland Assembly and the Northern Ireland Energy Regulator – now called the Northern Ireland Authority for Utility Regulation (NIAUR) – and demonstrate what can be achieved by a concern for the disadvantaged.

Wales

- For those on a means-tested benefit, the Welsh Assembly is proposing to limit the Home Energy Efficiency Scheme (HEES) (the Welsh Warm Front) to those in a home rated below E (on the EPC) and to raise it to band C (SAP05 69–80). This is to achieve better targeting of resources.
- For pensioners not on a means-tested benefit, there will be a reduced offer.
- The Welsh government's aim is for there to be no fuel poverty in social housing by 2012.
- New build housing is to be zero carbon by 2011, not 2016 as in England.
- The aim is to generate as much electricity as Wales consumes by 2025 (WAG, 2009, p17).
- Using the experience of Warm Zones, there have been comprehensive area-based activities in Neath Port Talbot (every home in the borough will be visited over a three-year period), Wrexham, and a Heads of the Valley regeneration scheme.

Scotland

- Introduced the Energy Assessment Package from April 2009 with one point of access for advice, benefit entitlement checks, energy-efficiency improvements and additional help for the severely fuel poor. For the fuel poor in properties with a Standard Assessment Procedure (SAP) <39 (bands F and G on the EPC), there are additional insulation and energy-efficiency measures, including renewable heating systems. This is funded by the Scottish Executive and 'represents a major step forward' (Preston, pers comm.). The Energy Assessment Package will be funded by £55.8m per annum from the Scottish government, with additional support from the energy companies through CERT (HC 37, 2009, p45).
- The Energy Assessment Package replaces the successful Central Heating Programme for pensioners and social housing and is better targeted and better funded. The Central Heating Programme ran from 2001 to March 2008, but latterly had difficulty focusing sufficiently on the fuel poor – perhaps only 6000 fuel-poor households received it. A total of nearly £300 million was spent (Fuel Poverty Forum, 2008, p29).
- The Scottish Fuel Poverty Forum has suggested that band F and G properties should be targeted for energy-efficiency improvements.
- The National Home Energy Rating (NHER) system is used for coding the energy efficiency of homes rather than SAP as it includes all uses of energy and the effects of local (colder) climate.

All of these examples illustrate the way in which devolved administrations are producing innovative ideas that could be of benefit to the fuel poor in the other countries, particularly England. Fuel poverty is worse in the devolved adminis-trations, so it is to be hoped they will be more innovative and proactive. Only some of the powers are devolved – much responsibility still stays in Whitehall, including revenue-raising – so the Welsh, Scottish and Northern Ireland governments are dealing with a restricted set of choices. This demonstrates, like the situation with the Northern Ireland regulator, the extent to which political will, determination and concern can be effective. There is a clear role for the UK Inter-Ministerial Group on Fuel Poverty to provide a forum for the exchange of ideas and successful practices. It is unfortunate, therefore, that it appears to be moribund and reactivating it, with each country hosting meetings in turn, would be a useful initiative. This would also demonstrate the benefits of a systematic approach, where combining innovation and learning provides the route to progress.

Regional, local and district authorities

There are similar variations within each of the devolved administrations. The next tier of government comprises the regional authorities (both development agencies and government offices), with few powers but quite substantial responsibilities and budgets. Taking England as an example, there are nine regional authorities with substantially different fuel-poor profiles in 2003:

- Greater London has the lowest proportion of fuel poor (8.3 per cent) and yet the most solid-walled homes and, partly for this reason, the highest number of hard-to-heat properties. This mismatch between the statistics may be because of the inclusion of housing costs as part of income, which is known to disadvantage high-rental areas, such as London. 'London has well-known issues associated with the high proportions of solid wall properties and less attractive profit margins for contractors working there' (CSE et al, 2008, p52). Greater London received the lowest amount from Warm Front per capita of the fuel poor (Table 8.2).
- The north-east had the highest proportion of fuel-poor households in 2006 (16.4 per cent); but the north-west received the greatest expenditure from Warm Front per capita of fuel poor.

The variation in Warm Front expenditure (a factor of four) is much greater than appears justified by the smaller variation in the proportion of fuel-poor households (8.3 to 16.4 per cent). Thus, the definition of fuel poverty and installer profit margins may be determining the rate at which fuel poverty is treated across England. In another example, Scotland is concerned that the proportion of CERT money spent north of the border is disproportionately small; but Ofgem does not collate statistics on where the money is spent, so it cannot be proved.

Table 8.2 *Warm Front spending and fuel poverty, by region, England (2006)*

Region	Average spend per fuel poor household, 2006–2007 (£ per annum)	Households in fuel poverty, 2006 (%)
North-west England	390	14.2
West Midlands	311	13.7
Yorkshire and Humber	284	12.7
North-east England	249	16.4
East Midlands	189	12.9
South-west England	166	11.6
East of England	116	9.7
South-east England	118	8.5
Greater London	96	8.3

Source: CSE et al (2008, p52); BERR (2008a, Table 37)

The levels of concern for fuel poverty shown by the various management groups also vary: in a search of Regional Housing Strategies, the words 'fuel poverty' appeared 29 times in the north-east's report and once in the strategy from the east of England (NEA, 2007, p28). Thus, while there are benefits of requiring the regional housing authorities to take responsibility for fuel poverty, this has to be in a context of clear definitions and targets, with both rewards and penalties. It cannot be left to chance and goodwill.

The South-east England Development Agency (SEEDA) undertook a study of the ways in which both fuel poverty and climate change could be tackled in the region (CSE et al, 2008). The proposed strategy would demonstrate the synergies that come from a focus on the energy efficiency of the housing stock through two concurrent objectives:

- a 20 per cent reduction in carbon dioxide emissions by 2016, relative to 2003;
- eliminate fuel poverty, where practically possible, by 2016, through improving all homes (whether fuel poor or not) to a minimum standard of efficiency (i.e. SAP 65).

The proportion of fairly efficient homes (SAP >65) more than doubled between 1996 and 2005, partly demonstrating the way in which this number is affected by the construction of new homes (Table 8.3). The proportion of really inefficient homes (SAP <35) dropped by less than 40 per cent, at an annual rate of 20,000 properties a year. At this rate, it will take more than 20 years to tackle the remaining 400,000 homes with a SAP <35 in the south-east.

The role of the regional authorities is to bridge the divide between central and local government. They could establish how many fuel poor there are thought to be in total in their region by summing the estimates from individual local authorities, and ensuring that, across the regions, these add up to the national total. Those calculations would depend on a clear definition of fuel

Table 8.3 *Proportion of homes in south-east England, by energy efficiency (1996–2005)*

	1996	*2001*	*2005*
Percentage SAP01 <35	18.4	12.8	11.5
Percentage SAP01 >65	11.8	21.6	23.3
South-east England total (millons)	3.1	3.3	3.4

Source: CSE et al (2008, p12)

poverty. This would be the first step in disaggregating responsibility for the elimination of fuel poverty – a similar approach to the useful exercise, several years ago, which divided up the target for renewable energy generation according to the commitments individual regions were prepared to make.

The role of the regions is either being ignored or underestimated, undoubtedly with sub-optimal results: 'No one [in Whitehall] has a clear picture of what might be the result or benefits of such consideration; no one is asking for it to be considered and no one is checking whether it had been considered. It simply is not a routine feature of policy-making or programme delivery' (Roberts, 2008, p12).

Local Area Agreements and fuel poverty

Below the regional authorities are the counties, the district councils, metropolitan boroughs and unitary authorities. The counties have no housing responsibilities, but the 450 others do. These local authorities combine to form 150 Local Strategic Partnerships (LSPs) in England, formed, for instance, from one county and its five co-terminus district councils. There are similar Single Outcome Agreements (SOAs) in Scotland. Since June 2008, each LSP has had to enter into a Local Area Agreement (LAA) as part of the new local government performance framework. LAAs set out the priorities for a local area agreed with central government and the LSP. Each LSP is judged on all 198 performance indicators, but of these each LAA chooses 35 local improvement targets on which they will primarily be monitored. Since the 2000 Local Government Act established LSPs:

> ... participation has become central to the work of local authorities, not only to identify community needs, but also as a means of addressing them. Arguably, local policy-making has never looked more vibrant as a result. (Jenkins, 2008, p21)

National performance indicators

Of the 198 performance indicators, several relate to climate change (e.g. National Indicator (NI) 186 covers per capita carbon emissions, and 148 of the 150 LAAs include at least one of them, demonstrating that local authorities are signing up to the climate change agenda.

For fuel poverty, NI 187 has been adopted as a priority in 40 out of 150 LAAs (Defra, 2008b). This requires the strategic partnership to report the numbers of households on income-related benefits with a SAP05 <35 and >65 each year. By implication, this is the range that the government believes determines whether a household is at real risk of being in fuel poverty or that there is a strong likelihood it has been removed from fuel poverty. The government's method of identifying the fuel poor is, therefore, becoming tighter and is focusing on the combination of low incomes and energy-inefficient homes. As discussed (p42), while it is an improvement on the present definition, it may be too narrow, especially as the target group for NI 187 does not include those on tax credits or disability living allowance (DLA), i.e. it does not include everyone who is eligible for Warm Front or the CERT Priority Group. The focus on means-tested households only reinforces the policy split between the 58 per cent of fuel-poor households covered by free energy-efficiency programmes and the 42 per cent who are not. The latter will both be outside of policy and unmeasured. As can be seen from Table 6.1 in Chapter 6, in England in 2006, half the fuel poor had a SAP05 <38 and slightly over 30,000 properties had a SAP05 >65. So, there are a lot of properties to be shifted from one end of the distribution to the other. The numbers of fuel poor have increased since 2006, thus making the task even greater. The SAP05 35 is linked to the Housing Health and Safety Rating System (HHSRS) (Chapter 7) as indicative of a property that would fail. Thus, through NI 187, there is some coherence developing in policy in relation to the worst housing. However, as demonstrated in Chapter 6, a higher standard of SAP05 81 is now needed to minimize the risk of a household being in fuel poverty at the higher prices existing in 2009. Getting a fuel-poor household's home to SAP05 65+ is only the first stage.

The 40 LSPs that have included NI 187 in their LAAs come from all regions of the country (Defra, 2008b) – there is one in the east of England, but eight in the south-west (the region with the warmest climate) and a relative low proportion of fuel poverty (Table 8.2). Many other local authorities, undoubtedly, still give an emphasis to fuel poverty, even though NI 187 is not one of their identified priorities. However, there appears to be no correlation between concern and the prevalence of fuel poverty.

Another performance standard (NI 186) is based on the per capita carbon emissions of all the residents within the LAA jurisdiction and was included as a priority in 100 out of the 150 LAAs:

> *Action by local authorities will be critical to the achievement of the Government's climate change objectives. Local authorities [LAs] are uniquely placed to provide vision and leadership to local communities by raising awareness and to influence behaviour change. In addition, through their powers and responsibilities (housing, planning, local transport and powers to promote well-being) and by working with their Local Strategic*

Partnership, LAs can have significant influence over emissions in their local areas. (Defra, 2008c)

With these two performance indicators, the government is enrolling the local authorities in national objectives and devolving responsibility to them, with funding linked, weakly, to success in achieving these self-set goals. The method of measurement is defined by the government, but the target for achievement is set by each individual LAA. There is no information about how challenging these targets are – that is a matter for local specification. Responsibility for both NI 186 and NI 187 has been transferred to DECC.

The use of the SAP may cause problems when SAP09 is introduced inasmuch as the new scale will have neutralized the effect of fuel price rises. This devolution of responsibility for fuel poverty to LSPs appears to be both sensible and suspect:

- The local authorities are well placed to assess fuel poverty in their area.
- Only just over one quarter of LAAs give NI 187 priority. Fuel poverty is less of an issue for the other 110 out of 150.
- The funding link provides neither a strong financial incentive nor a strong penalty for the local authorities in achieving their goals.
- The goal in the LAA is set by the LSP. This may or may not be a tough target. It is not publicized or identified.
- The proposed method of monitoring is expensive (annual surveys linked to postal questionnaires). Previous policies have failed because of inappropriate monitoring (e.g. Home Energy Conservation act – HECA).

In summary, it is not clear how much this new approach of LAAs will contribute to lowering fuel poverty, though it should be a step in the right direction. A larger step would be if there is a requirement to report on the total number of fuel poor within each housing authority and make sure that this gives the same aggregate national total as the Building Research Establishment's (BRE's) fuel poverty model. However, it is an interesting development by central government in England to incorporate other levels of government into the eradication of fuel poverty.

Other players

There are a great many other contributors to policy on fuel poverty – for instance the utilities, FPAGs and primary care trusts; but none of them have any defined responsibilities to reduce fuel poverty. There is even the suggestion that the pension funds might be interested in providing the capital for energy-efficiency investment programmes. The utilities are particularly interesting because they are now providing more money for energy-efficiency improvements in the homes of the disadvantaged than the government, which brings them considerable power:

As they [the utilities] become executors of obligations or policies (for example, the Renewables Obligation or the Energy Efficiency Commitment), they become more important to governments in delivering policies. As a result, they become involved in the development of such policies. (Mitchell, 2008, p52)

People and communities

In relation to climate change, local communities throughout the UK are choosing to get on with providing solutions, through transition towns, carbon reduction action groups (CRAGs) and in a host of other ways (Howell, 2009). In Oxfordshire alone there are over 50 groups. Most of these groups are only known about in a local context – they are not usually part of a formal mass movement, but they do demonstrate a strong desire for, and commitment to, grassroots action.

It is unlikely that the problem of climate change will be solved, even partly, through relying on an up-swelling of local initiatives; but they may be an essential component of future success, together with involving the individual householders and citizens. There has to be a 'personal motivation to act. You simply cannot regulate or innovate enough to tackle the problem without first stimulating a genuine desire to take action' (Spencer, 2007). People:

- are still confused about whether climate change is a serious problem, thanks in particular to media coverage;
- are uncertain about the best ways to reduce their own footprint, while wanting to preserve their lifestyle: 'the public is torn between competing and conflicting mindsets. As citizens they want to avert climate change, but ... as consumers they want to go on holiday, own a second home, a big car and the latest electronic goods' (Downing and Ballantyne, 2007, p6);
- believe that there is no urgency because the climate changes have not yet occurred and will affect future generations more than themselves (Downing and Ballantyne, 2007, p4);
- think that industry is the main culprit (including power stations) and thus dissolve their own responsibility: 'only 4 per cent [of the public] perceive they have a large influence to combat climate change, while 33 per cent feel they have none' (Downing and Ballantyne, 2007, p5).

The conclusion is that 'a range of measures, simultaneously, on a number of fronts and allied with political leadership and vision, will be required to encourage, engage and enable the public to act' (Downing and Ballantyne, 2007, p6).

The government has a considerable task to mobilize the population. One possible policy is the introduction of personal carbon allowances, as described in Chapter 5. The personal carbon allowance is a policy that could combine action on climate change with reducing fuel poverty. Although it is a relatively simple concept, it can only be introduced as an entity or not at all – like a congestion charge, you cannot have a partial scheme or even a trial at a small scale (Fawcett et al, 2007).

Sadly, there have been very few studies of what it is like to suffer from fuel poverty and most of these have been linked to feelings of comfort or the size of the fuel bills. The study on 'I'm not complaining' (Smith, 1986) is still one of the rare examples. The importance of engaging people in the debate about what should be done to make their homes more energy efficient has been demonstrated by the Warm Zone schemes: several visits may be required to ensure that the householder is happy with the chosen options and to ensure that they will not opt out to avoid the hassle. This is no small problem:

> *... there will be a number of households who will not accept assistance when it is offered to them. Preliminary results from the evaluation of Warm Zones have shown that, even with repeat visits, around 20 per cent of households refuse energy efficiency advice and/or measures.* (Defra, 2004, p12)

Sometimes these are people for whom it is just an inconvenient time – a new baby has been born, the house has been redecorated, someone has lost their job. A return visit, after a few months, can meet with a different response and genuine welcome. The experience in Newark and Sherwood, where they have had a long-term rolling programme of improvements to social housing, is that the number can be reduced to below 2 per cent (Pickles, pers comm). There is clearly a potential link between the reluctant participants and the 'I'm not complaining' group, which demonstrates why complete coverage and 100 per cent involvement is important. It may be that a community focus on improving the environment within which they live can be sufficient to enrol even the reluctant. Otherwise, many of the severely fuel poor may never be found and helped.

Self-selection is not a good way of ensuring that the fuel poor in the least energy-efficient homes do access the available grants. Programmes that are inclusive will be of the greatest benefit to them and can, therefore, be justified on both economic efficiency and equity grounds (Sefton, 2002, p396).

Costs

In 2008, approximately £1 billion was spent on 100 per cent grants for energy-efficiency improvements in low-income homes in the UK (Table 6.13 in Chapter 6). This is in addition to the £3 billion spent on income supplements for pensioners through winter fuel payments in the same year (Table 3.4 in Chapter 3). The total of £4 billion is insufficient to prevent fuel poverty from rising, partly because it is so poorly targeted: only one quarter (i.e. £1 billion) is being spent on the fuel poor and the remainder is being spent on non-fuel poor households.

The government has no overall strategy that includes an estimate of the costs of eradicating fuel poverty by 2010 or 2016. In their first annual report, the FPAG recommended that the government 'should now provide more thorough estimates of the costs or at least a range of the possible costs of meeting the targets' (FPAG, 2003, p14). The government provided a background paper for FPAG in which:

> *Initial results suggest that around £1.8 billion to £2.2 billion might need to be spent, from all sources, on vulnerable fuel-poor households (ignoring price and income movements) to remove them from fuel poverty. The majority of this money needs to be spent in private housing – around £1.5 billion to £1.9 billion. Around £0.3 billion to £0.4 billion needs to be spent in social housing.* (DTI, 2003, pp3–5)

The costs per household varied from £1200 to £2600. This was just vulnerable households, when fuel prices were at their lowest, so numbers of fuel poor were low. They did not include administrative costs and assumed perfect targeting (i.e. all expenditure was on the fuel poor).

More recent documents, written for the FPAG but apparently not made publicly available, established that there would be 1.1 million vulnerable households in fuel poverty in 2010 in England, of whom 100,000 would refuse help. Of the remaining 1 million, the numbers that could be taken out of fuel poverty are (FPAG, 2006):

- 22 per cent through the installation of cavity wall and loft insulation and gas central heating, at a cost of £700 million;
- 50,000 pensioners through claiming pension credit, to which they are entitled, but not claiming, and getting the associated council tax and housing benefits;
- 16 per cent through access to a heating system with the same costs as gas, either through a gas network extension, community heating or renewables for around £900 million;
- 14 per cent through the replacement of the existing old gas central heating boiler with a modern efficient one, at a cost of £1100 million;
- 25 per cent (half the remainder) as a result of adding £1000 to income (e.g. from benefit entitlement checks) or reducing the cost of fuel by £100 (because only 10 per cent is spent on fuel);
- alternatively, 17 per cent could have their solid walls externally insulated at a cost of £2100 million;
- 4 per cent through installing solar water heating for a cost of £700 million, though this would remove more households from fuel poverty if modelled earlier in the process.

Table 8.4 *Relationship between targeting and programme cost, UK*

Targeting accuracy (% going to fuel poor)	Cost per house	Numbers treated	Total cost	Annual cost (2010–16)
25	£7500	20 million	£150 billion	£21.5 billion
50	£7500	10 million	£75 billion	£10.7 billion
100	£7500	5 million	£37.5 billion	£5.4 billion

Source: Author

This would still leave 23 per cent (230,000) vulnerable households in fuel poverty after a capital expenditure of £5.5 billion (or £5500 per house). The above extrapolation results in costs that are underestimates because the:

- Costings assume perfect targeting (i.e. all expenditure is on vulnerable fuel-poor households and no one else).
- The cost of the management overheads of the scheme are additional – perhaps an extra 10 to 20 per cent.
- The costs of the measures have increased since 2005.
- The proportion of people in fuel poverty requiring more expensive measures may now be higher than in 2005, as many of the easiest and cheapest interventions have been done in the interim.

Thus, the amount of money required to lift a household out of fuel poverty may now be higher, even assuming perfecting targeting, say a present estimate of £7500 per property. There are 5 million households in fuel poverty in early 2009, so the remaining question is how successful the targeting of the assistance could be (Table 8.4), assuming that the 2016 target is sacrosanct.

A rough assessment of the likely costs was given in *Home Truths* (Boardman, 2007) on a per household basis (Table 8.5) and also, from separate analysis, came to a figure of £7500 per house. This was not the full cost as administrative costs were not included. There are, however, economies of scale included, as the property would be in a low-carbon zone (next chapter). The concentrated action reduces the cost per house, both from the number of measures undertaken and because neighbouring houses are being treated at the same time, so the contractors' costs are lower too. In order to achieve the economies of scale, more than the homes of the fuel poor are treated: the costs would be recouped in a variety of ways to suit the needs of the individual home-owner. The aim would be to achieve a SAP05 81 level. The costs are difficult to confirm – some pilots that take fuel-poor homes up to SAP05 81 are needed. The Sustainable Development Commission (SDC) has estimated that the cost of external solid wall insulation is £6500 (SDC, 2009, p8). If this includes all of the scaffolding, then the price of installing solar thermal would be lower, by about £1000. Other additional costs would be to install the community combined heat and power (CHP) scheme along the street.

Table 8.5 *Estimated cost, per household, in a low-carbon zone*

Measure	£
Solar thermal, including scaffolding	3000
Solid wall insulation, marginal cost only, as scaffolding there	1900
Connection to an existing community combined heat and power (CHP) scheme	1000
Insulating the loft, repairs, some double glazing – a nominal	1600
Total	7500

Note: based on costs from the Energy Saving Trust.
Source: Boardman (2007, p89)

Depending on the numbers involved, the total cost could be £10,000 per household, rather than the £7500 used in Table 8.4.

It is difficult to estimate how precise targeting could be, though as the numbers in fuel poverty grow, so does their concentration in any geographical area. In Newcastle Warm Zone, about one third of the homes are in fuel poverty (Connor, pers comm). It would seem unlikely that any scheme would hit the 50 per cent target, so that annual expenditure in the range of £15 billion to £20 billion is likely to be needed for the next nine years, provided that fuel prices do not rise further.

The government has rejected the proposal to bring all fuel-poor homes up to a standard of SAP 81, describing it as unrealistic because:

> ... the cost of bringing a property up to the band C rating would be between £10,000 and £20,000, depending on the type of property. We think that to bring all properties currently occupied by fuel-poor households to at least SAP 81 ratings, or indeed SAP 69 rating for hard-to-treat homes, would cost in the region of £50 billion... [We still accept] the imperative to make a step change in domestic energy efficiency to meet both our climate change and fuel poverty agendas. (Hansard, 2009).

The overall cost to fuel poverty proof homes through energy-efficiency measures across the UK would be in the region of £50 billion, according to the government, or in excess of this, based on an extrapolation of advice given to the FPAG. The remaining question is whether it should be found.

The government has a commitment to eradicate fuel poverty by 2016 and has known about this commitment since 2000. Its failure to prevent fuel poverty increasing is a result of the lack of appropriate funds and policies, independently of any cost-effectiveness calculation. It would now be a travesty if the government is to say that over the remaining seven years it is not 'reasonably practicable' to eradicate fuel poverty just because the expenditure has become more concentrated. Any delay also increases the suffering of the present fuel-poor occupants.

All of the technologies required to achieve a SAP05 81 are in existence, are known about and have been piloted. They may be expensive; but policy can reduce these costs – for instance, through area-based approaches. In all cases, they could be proved to be cost effective depending on the parameters taken.

Cost effective and reasonably practicable

There has been no clarification from the government about what it deems to be cost effective or reasonably practicable, despite the judicial review. The definition of cost effective is not straightforward as it can include a range of costs, a variety of benefits, and it can use different rates of interest and payback periods:

> ... sometimes it might be thought worthwhile spending a little bit more now, for something extra later... At root, there is almost no disagreement that least costs is the preferred option. It is the timing over which any option is valued that is contested; as is what is contained within the calculation; and how that calculation is made. (Mitchell, 2008, p38)

The cost effectiveness of an energy-efficiency measure varies with the level of energy efficiency of the dwelling it is installed into:

> ... the less energy efficient the dwelling is to start with, the more cost effective it is to improve the energy efficiency of that home (i.e. the higher the ratio of potential savings to costs). (Sefton, 2002, p374)

To this should be added two other issues. First, the rebound effect – the fuel poor take much of the benefit of an energy-efficiency improvement as additional warmth, rather than as a fuel saving. This may be confusing for climate change policies, but in reality it is beneficial: there is less money for the household to spend on other energy-using activities and demonstrates that a focus on the fuel poor and targeting the least energy-efficient homes is a sensible economic policy.

Second, the Stern Review, demonstrating a useful approach to cost effectiveness, found that early action is still the least costly route to a low-carbon future. Any delay increases the costs and the risks:

> Mitigation – taking strong action to reduce emissions – must be viewed as an investment, a cost incurred now and in the coming few decades to avoid the risks of very severe consequences in the future. (Stern, 2006, pi)

This is using future benefits over a long time period as part of the equation. Using the Stern analysis, the spending figures quoted in *Home Truths* could be justified (Boardman, 2007, p102). These included the £10.5 billion investment in energy-efficiency measures and the £2.4 billion of tax relief to give an annual total of nearly £13 billion for the whole housing stock. There is a strong focus on fuel poverty alleviation in the proposals, but also effective targeting. The sum of £13 billion was based on having nine years to eradicate fuel poverty. Frm 2009 there are only seven years, so the annual budget has naturally increased. In *Home Truths* there was a wide range of fiscal incentives to motivate all types of householders to take action: most policies on fuel poverty will work best if set in a context where everyone is trying to reduce their carbon footprint.

The government has produced some cost estimates of the degree of improvement needed in fuel-poor homes, but did not accompany this by a statement of cost effectiveness and certainly not one that reflected Lord Stern's approach. A calculation that compares the costs and benefits on a household basis will arrive at different assessments than one that compares costs and benefits on a societal basis. The latter would add in the benefits of reduced carbon emissions, lower National Health Service (NHS) costs, reduced cold and suffering and the benefit of the UK complying with its international targets. With some of these (e.g. the 15 per cent of energy that has to come from renewable sources by 2020), failure results in a potentially significant fine from the European Commission.

At the core of this debate are attitudes to investment in the housing stock. The latter is a national asset, worth around £4 trillion in the UK (26 million × £150,000) that is poorly equipped to cope with the challenges of climate change. Investment to reduce energy demand in our homes should be placed on a par with investment to increase supply in our power stations and grid. This is particularly important for low-income fuel-poor households, many of whom are in rented accommodation. The investment has to be with someone else's capital – they have no savings.

Current expenditure and future funds

The government states that £20 billion has been spent on fuel poverty policy during 2000 to 2008 (BERR, 2008b). The details are not presented; but this appears to be the sum of expenditure on Warm Front, Energy Efficiency Commitment (EEC)/CERT, the Decent Homes Standard (DHS) and the winter fuel payment (some in Great Britain; some in England only). Perhaps as much as £18 billion went on winter fuel payments (Table 3.4 in Chapter 3) and barely £5 billion towards energy-efficiency improvements (Table 6.13 in Chapter 6). Some of the £5 billion (about £1.5 billion) came from utility funding, the rest from government and the taxpayer. Thus, a lot of money is being spent on fuel poverty policy, but barely one quarter of it reaches the fuel poor (Table 6.14 in Chapter 6). Further expenditure is needed in order to comply with the legal obligation under WHECA 2000.

Householders, in general, spend a lot on their homes at the moment. In 2005, £23.9 billion was spent on repair, maintenance and improvement works in UK housing and much of this work represents a missed opportunity for low-carbon refurbishment (Killip, 2008, p12). Getting some proportion of this expenditure more clearly focused on making the home low carbon would contribute to the required Green Revolution: 'Many energy-efficiency measures would be particularly effective as part of a fiscal stimulus, as they could be implemented quickly and would be relatively labour-intensive' (Bowen et al, 2009, p3).

During a recession, these costs will be lower than they would have been because there is spare capacity at the manufacturers and within the construction industry. Also, creating employment reduces the cost to government of welfare support, such as unemployment benefit. So there is:

> ... the potential of energy-efficiency measures to deliver a fiscal stimulus and to help deliver climate change objectives. They are also useful from the point of view of enhancing energy security and reducing fuel poverty. (Bowen et al, 2009, p13)

To the extent that these energy-efficiency programmes are subsidized (e.g. for low-income homes), the money can either come from taxpayers or through the utilities. While it is easier for the government if the utilities fund an increasing share of the energy-efficiency improvements – as suggested by the CCC – this is harmful to the fuel poor. All low-income households pay utility bills. The fuel poor probably contribute less to the Treasury through value added tax (VAT) and certainly only a small proportion pay income tax. Thus, utility-funded programmes re-enforce fuel poverty, whereas government-funded schemes should be more successful at alleviating it.

The CCC is expecting substantial amounts of investment in energy-efficiency improvements, but is assuming that these are mainly funded by the utilities. These would impact upon the fuel poor and are the reason why the CCC expects fuel poverty to increase substantially, by about 1.7 million households. This aspect of their proposals should be reconsidered.

There are some additional sources of funding available – for instance, through other charges on the utilities that are not passed through to customers. The government raises VAT on all fuel prices and the amount has been increasing healthily since fuel prices starting rising in 2004 – an estimated additional £400 million per annum. There are other potential sources:

> To help kick-start a massive national programme of home energy efficiency and renewable energy, a windfall tax on the £9 billion of unearned profits the energy companies gathered under the European Emissions Trading Scheme (EU ETS) may well be justified. A longer-term funding solution is required, however, and the auctioning of carbon permits under the EU ETS should be used to help sustain this fuel poverty programme. (Fuel Poverty Charter, 2008)

An increasing number of the EU Emissions Trading Scheme (EU ETS) permits are being auctioned, with less given away as free permits. These cover about 50 per cent of the UK's carbon emissions and the proportion is rising – for instance, aviation is due to be included. The sums raised from the partial auctions are relatively modest: about £300 million per annum (ENDS, 2008, pp15–16); but this is expected to increase as the targets become tighter.

Another, rarely mentioned, sum of money is the £15 billion a year of unclaimed benefits and tax credits that the Treasury has to budget for but are not paid out (Chapter 3). These should be available to fund capital improvements in the homes of those poor households who are not accessing this income benefit. This would be similar to what the utilities are doing: raising money through fuel bills to fund capital investments.

Conclusions

On governance, there is an Act of Parliament, the WHECA 2000, but no clarity about who is responsible for delivering it. If there is uncertainty about who is responsible, it is not surprising if there is little clarity about delivery mechanisms and budgets. To recap:

- The UK governments have a legal obligation to eradicate fuel poverty for the vulnerable by 2010 and for all households by 2016 (2018 in Wales), where reasonably practicable (a phrase that has not been defined).
- Of the major English departments involved, the PSA which defines its responsibilities in relation to fuel poverty, is weak for Defra (a legacy), non-existent for DCLG and DWP and not yet defined for DECC. BERR (now BIS) has ceased to have responsibility for energy.
- The regional authorities have no obligations in relation to fuel poverty.
- All local authorities have to report on NI 187, the fuel poverty indicator; but of the 150 LAAs entered into by local authorities, only 40 have accepted that this is one of their main priorities and that their performance on it will be linked to funding. Each chooses its own reduction target. If the other 110 LSPs focus on fuel poverty, they do so, effectively, as a subsidiary activity.
- Neither Warm Front nor CERT is required to tackle fuel poverty and none of their evaluation is linked to it.
- The winter fuel payment for pensioners is barely related to fuel poverty.
- Of the £20 billion nominally spent by the government on fuel poverty over 2000 to 2008, less than 25 per cent has gone to the fuel poor.
- Current annual expenditure is £1 billion for energy-efficiency improvements (raised from both the government and the utilities) and £3 billion for income support. Both amounts are rising.
- Fuel poverty continues to increase and no one is responsible.
- The approximate cost of improving the energy efficiency of the homes of the UK fuel poor to a SAP05 81would be about £75 billion to £150 billion,

depending upon the effectiveness of the targeting. This is £10 billion to £20 billion per annum between 2010 and 2016. The government has rejected this as unrealistic.

- The government has never produced a clear costed statement of a fuel poverty programme that would enable it to comply with its legal obligations.

Central government is beginning to devolve responsibility for fuel poverty to the housing authorities, particularly through LAAs and NIs of performance. This trend should be reinforced using the policies that are already there – for instance, the HHSRS and the DHS. It would not be a major step for the government to link all of these layers of responsibility and different initiatives into one coherent strategy. It would still be possible to eradicate fuel poverty by 2016, as required under the act.

The challenge of a systems approach is to combine the needs of fuel poverty policy, so that there is a clear hierarchy of responsibilities. These would include for each of the four administrations:

- a new PSA on fuel poverty, led by DECC in England, that confirms the obligation to eradicate fuel poverty by 2016 and defines 'reasonably practicable';
- a cross-departmental ministerial fuel poverty task force to ensure that the PSA is delivered; the task force should be led by a senior fuel poverty minister who sits in Cabinet and reports directly to the prime minister. This would replace the UK inter-ministerial group on fuel poverty, which appears to be moribund;
- all senior civil servants working on fuel poverty to spend an induction period (at least a month) with the various agencies (Energy Action Grants Agency (Eaga), utilities, local authorities, Warm Zones, money advisers) that deliver the policies to the fuel poor; this would include representatives from the DWP and NHS, as well as the more obvious departments;
- a strengthening of the powers of the FPAGs so that they have a firm voice in reporting on what is happening in their country, in a way that makes the governments respond positively; these new powers may be similar to those given to the CCC;
- an obligation placed on all the regional authorities to coordinate data collection and monitoring on rates of fuel poverty in their areas – this will, at a minimum, mean that all the fuel poor can be identified down to the local authority level; this monitoring must tally with the government's own fuel poverty model, so there is consistency of knowledge on the size of the problem and the speed with which it is being dealt with. This will enable a more accurate allocation of financial resources;
- the definition being used in NI187 should be the starting point, as all local authorities have to quantify the number of means-tested benefit recipients in a home with a SAP05 <35;

- introducing a special bonus for local housing authorities that deliver excellent progress on the eradication of fuel poverty in their area.

The government's failure to make progress on eradicating fuel poverty and fulfilling its legal obligations must be strongly linked to the absence of a systematic, coherent structure for decision-making and responsibility. There is no-one clearly charged with the delivery of the WHECA 2000. There has never been a comprehensive assessment and statement of the likely costs. These failings represent negligence, on the part of the government, and a dereliction of humanity towards the fuel poor.

References

Autism Foundation (2009) 'Minister Joan Ruddock responds to UKAF on autism and fuel poverty, UK', *UK Autism News*, http://ukautismnews.blog.co.uk/2009/04/22/minister-joan-ruddock-responds-to-ukaf-on-autism-and-fuel-poverty-uk-5988716/

BERR (Department for Business, Enterprise and Regulatory Reform) (2008a) *Fuel Poverty Statistics, Detailed Tables 2006*, Annex to Fuel Poverty Strategy Report, 2008, URN 08/P33, BERR, www.berr.gov.uk/files/file48038.pdf

BERR (2008b) *What Is Fuel Poverty?*, www.berr.gov.uk/energy/fuel-poverty/index.html

Boardman, B. (1991) *Fuel Poverty: From Cold Homes to Affordable Warmth*, Belhaven Press, London

Boardman, B. (2007) *Home Truths: A Low-Carbon Strategy to Reduce UK Housing Emissions by 80% by 2050*, research report for the Co-operative Bank and Friends of the Earth, London, www.foe.co.uk/resource/reports/home_truths.pdf

Bowen, A., Fankhauser, S., Stern, N. and Zenghelis, D. (2009) *An Outline of the Case for a 'Green' Stimulus*, Policy brief, Grantham Research Institute on Climate Change and the Environment, LSE, London, February

Cabinet Office (2008) *Machinery of Government: Economy, Business, Climate Change, Energy and Environment*, London, October

Chapman, J. (2002) *System Failure*, Demos, London

Connor, D., Director, Newcastle Warm Zone, pers comm

CSE, ACE (Centre for Sustainable Energy and Association for the Conservation of Energy) and Moore, R. (2008) *Retrofitting the Existing Housing Stock in the South East – A Strategy to Reduce Carbon Emissions and Alleviate Fuel Poverty: 2008–2011*, CSE, ACE, www.seeda.co.uk/publications/sustainable_prosperity/docs/SE_Strategy.pdf

DECC (Department of Energy and Climate Change) (2009) *Annual Report and Resource Accounts 2008-09*, DECC, HC 452, www.decc.gov.uk/en/content/cms/publications/annual_reports/2009/2009.aspx

Defra (Department for Environment, Food and Rural Affairs) (2004) *Fuel Poverty in England: The Government's Plan of Action*, Defra, London

Defra (2008a) *Departmental Report 2008*, Defra, Cm 7399, www.defra.gov.uk/environment/business/reporting/pdf/ghg-cf-guidelines-annexes2008.pdf

Defra (2008b) *Local Area Agreements 2008*, www.defra.gov.uk/corporate/about/what/localgovindicators/laa-2008.htm

Defra (2008c) *Local Government Performance Framework,* NI 186 – Per capita reduction in CO_2 emissions in the LA area, www.defra.gov.uk/corporate/about/what/localgovindicators/ni186.htm

Downing, P. and Ballantyne, J. (2007) *Tipping Point or Turning Point? Social Marketing and Climate Change,* Ipsos MORI, www.ipsos-mori.com/DownloadPublication/1174_sri_tipping_point_or_turning_point_climate_change.pdf

DTI (Department of Trade and Industry) (2003) *Estimating the Costs of Tackling Fuel Poverty in England, Paper for FPAG,* October, www.berr.gov.uk/files/file16163.pdf

EAPN (European Anti-poverty Network) (2008) *Network News 1261,* EAPN, April–June

ENDS (2008) 'UK's Carbon Allowance auction raises £54m', 407, December, p15

Fawcett, T., Bottrill, C., Boardman, B. and Lye, G. (2007) *Trialling Personal Carbon Allowances,* UK Energy Research Centre, Research Report, December, www.ukerc.ac.uk/Downloads/PDF/T/Trialling_Personal_Allowances.pdf

FPAG (Fuel Poverty Advisory Group) (2003) *Fuel Poverty Advisory Group for England: First Annual Report – 2002/2003,* Department of Trade and Industry, London, February

FPAG (2006) *FPAG 121(06): Costs of Tackling Fuel Poverty in England,* FPAG, London

Fuel Poverty Charter (2008) Supported by a coalition of Age Concern; Association for the Conservation of Energy; Barnado's; Centre for Sustainable Energy; Child Poverty Action Group; Disability Alliance; energywatch; Friends of the Earth; Help the Aged; National Energy Action; National Right To Fuel Campaign; WWF, www.foe.co.uk/resource/press_releases/Fuel_Poverty_Charter_08092008.html

Fuel Poverty Forum (2008) *Review of Fuel Poverty in Scotland,* Scottish Government, May, www.scotland.gov.uk/Topics/Built-Environment/Housing/access/FP/fuelpovertyreview

Hansard (2009), HC Deb (Session 2008–09), vol 489, col 1206, 20 March

HC 37 (2009) *Energy Efficiency and Fuel Poverty,* Third report of session 2008–2009, Environment, Food and Rural Affairs Select Committee, Stationery Office, London

HMG (2007) *PSA Delivery Agreement 9: Half the Number of Children in Poverty by 2010–11, On the Way to Eradicating Child Poverty by 2020,* Her Majesty's Government, www.hm-treasury.gov.uk/d/pbr_csr07_psa9.pdf

Howell, R. (2009) *The Experience of Carbon Rationing Action Groups: Implications for a Personal Carbon Allowances Policy,* Final report for UK Energy Research Centre, Demand Reduction Theme, www.eci.ox.ac.uk/publications/downloads/howell09crags.pdf

Jenkins, D. (2008) Chief Executive, Dorset County Council, in S. Cooke and D. Vyas (eds) *Votes and Voices: The Complementary Nature of Representative and Participatory Democracy,* NCVO, Local Government Association, www.ncvo-vol.org.uk/uploadedFiles/NCVO/What_we_do/Policy/Civil_Society_and_Participation/votes%20and%20voices%20FINAL.pdf

Killip, G. (2008) *Building a Greener Britain: Transforming the UK's Existing Housing Stock,* Report for the Federation of Master Builders, ECI, University of Oxford, Oxford, UK

Mitchell, C. (2008) *The Political Economy of Sustainable Energy,* Palgrave Macmillan, Basingstoke, UK

NEA (National Energy Action) (2007) *Regional Housing Boards: Promoting Affordable Warmth,* NEA Guidance Note, Newcastle, UK

Palmer, G., MacInnes, T. and Kenway, P. (2008) *Cold and Poor: An Analysis of the Link between Fuel Poverty and Low Income*, New Policy Institute, London, www.npi.org.uk/reports/fuel%20poverty.pdf

Pickles, D., Sustainable Energy Manager, Newark and Sherwood District Council, pers comm

Preston, I., Centre for Sustainable Energy, Bristol, UK, pers comm

Roberts, S. (2008) *On the Same Map? A Snapshot of the Relationships between UK Energy Policy and the English Regions*, Report to the Department for Business, Enterprise & Regulatory Reform, from Centre for Sustainable Energy, Bristol, UK

Scottish Government (2008) *Review of Fuel Poverty in Scotland*, May

SDC (Sustainable Development Commission) (2009) *A Sustainable New Deal*, SDC, London

Sefton, T. (2002), 'Targeting fuel poverty in England: Is the government getting warm?', *Fiscal Studies*, vol 23, no 3, pp369–399

Smith, K. (1986) *'I'm Not Complaining': The Housing Conditions of Elderly Private Tenants*, Kensington and Chelsea Staying Put for the Elderly Ltd, in association with SHAC, London

Spencer, M. (2007) BBC News, 4 May 2007

Stern, N. (2006) *Stern Review Final Report*, Treasury, www.hm-treasury.gov.uk/stern_review_report.htm

Utley, J. I. and Shorrock, L. D. (2008a) *Domestic Energy Fact File (2007): England, Scotland, Wales and Northern Ireland*, Building Research Establishment, Watford, www.bre.co.uk/page.jsp?id=879

Utley, J. I. and Shorrock, L. D. (2008b) *Domestic Energy Fact File 2008*, Building Research Establishment, www.bre.co.uk/page.jsp?id=879

WAG (Welsh Assembly Government) (2009) *One Wales: One Planet: The Sustainable Development Scheme of the Welsh Assembly Government*, WAG, May, www.assemblywales.org/bus-home/bus-guide-docs-pub/bus-business-documents/bus-business-documents-doc-laid/gen-ld7521-e.pdf?langoption=3&ttl=GEN-LD7521%20-%20One%20Wales%3A%20One%20Planet%20-%20The%20Sustainable%20Development%20Scheme%20of%20the%20Welsh%20Assembly%20Government

9

Solutions

This book is designed to ensure that future UK fuel poverty policy, especially over the years up to 2016, can be based on a sounder understanding of where existing policies have failed and why, so that there is a better chance of eliminating this blight for all the fuel poor.

The following proposed set of solutions is based on what has been learned in the previous chapters about the underlying problems, so that an alternative route to the eradication of fuel poverty can be found. It would be difficult to do worse than the present situation: 42 per cent of fuel-poor households are not eligible for the 100 per cent energy-efficiency grants and of the support that is given, only one quarter reaches the fuel poor. The rest goes to subsidize the non-fuel poor. The total cost of these 'fuel poverty' policies is around £4 billion in 2008, so that only £1 billion is reaching the fuel poor. In addition, all of the households helped through Warm Front are also eligible for the Carbon Emissions Reduction Target (CERT) Priority Group, so some households have two options, while others have none.

The government has a legal obligation to eradicate fuel poverty among vulnerable households by 2010 and for all fuel poor by 2016, where reasonably practicable. In mid 2009, fuel poverty is still rising and is affecting about 5 million households in the UK, so the 2010 target is clearly impossible. The second target could be achieved, as the government aspires: 'We intend to put ourselves on a trajectory to meet the 2016 target' (HC 37, 2009, Ev 75, Q319). It is difficult to have any confidence that this will occur with current policies and poor targeting. The government's forthcoming review of fuel poverty will, therefore, have to provide radical new policies and initiatives.

Some of the answers will require political decisions on relative priorities – for instance, on whether to focus on pensioners or families with children and whether to provide short-term income support or capital for long-term energy-efficiency improvements. There are good opportunities to combine fuel poverty and climate change policies; but conversely there are risks: additional income helps the fuel poor, but enables them to use more energy in highly polluting homes; any form of carbon policy that increases fuel prices would increase fuel poverty. Generally, though, it is the introduction of a climate change focus that reinforces the solutions on fuel poverty: for both reasons, an emphasis on capital investment in the energy efficiency of the housing stock is the best answer.

Many issues have to combine to eradicate fuel poverty because many factors combine to cause the problem. What is certain is that this is an interactive problem, covering factors as disparate as definitions of comfort and world oil prices. In that, it is a true reflection of our daily lives: complex, interwoven and providing us with varying degrees of control. And for the fuel poor, they have few options that they can control. As a result, they were spending in 2006 only about half of what would be needed for them to have adequate energy services (based on Tables 3.1 and 6.1 in Chapters 3 and 6 respectively). This gap widens when there is a fuel price rise and for those already in the most severe fuel poverty. The situation for the fuel poor is dire and causing great hardship, discomfort and ill health.

The proposed framework

The proposed solutions, described in more detail below, would, ideally, involve the following:

- Confirmation that policy is designed to eradicate fuel poverty by 2016 in the UK, or 2018 in Wales, in compliance with the 2000 Warm Homes and Energy Conservation Act (WHECA) and other legislative and policy commitments.
- The limitation of 'as far as is reasonably practicable' is no longer an appropriate excuse. With political will, the remaining seven years from 2009 are sufficient. There are substantial costs involved; but the problem of fuel poverty is too great for the government to use limited budgets or limited time as a justifiable restriction.
- A new fuel poverty strategy is required to bring all the elements together, including clear channels of responsibility for delivering the solutions and penalties for failure. Several departments of central government and other levels of government should be involved, particularly the local authorities with housing responsibilities. This should be a costed plan with clear targets, which is updated annually – not just reported upon. Any shortfall in a year will have to be identified and made up as soon as possible, similar to the reports required on compliance with the 2008 Climate Change Act.
- The strategy would be a policy package combining greater income with improved energy efficiency.
- The increased income goes beyond present entitlement to benefits. It would introduce a new element so that householders are compensated for their high heating costs, according to the energy efficiency of the property they are living in, based on the bands on the Energy Performance Certificate (EPC).

- All energy-efficiency interventions would be focused on achieving a level of SAP05 81 in any home likely to be lived in by a low-income household.
- These interventions would be incorporated into an area-based approach, to tackle areas of concentrated fuel poverty first: one low-carbon zone in each local authority.
- The government and the energy regulators (Office of the Gas and Electricity Markets, or Ofgem, and the Northern Ireland Authority for Utility Regulation, or NIAUR) would combine to ensure that the energy utilities introduce a series of policies to reduce energy costs for the poorest people. These would include reverse tariffs (unit prices increase with usage levels), low-cost prepayment meters (PPMs) (cheaper than standard credit and direct debit, as happens in Northern Ireland already) and some social tariffs. Price regulation may have to be reinstated by Ofgem in Great Britain because of the way in which the companies have contributed to the creation of fuel poverty among the disadvantaged. The liberalized market does not work for the poor and institutional change will be required to redress this failure;
- The new strategy will be written on the assumption that fuel prices will continue to rise. It will take a precautionary approach, acknowledging from the start that there is a risk of future price increases causing further fuel poverty and identifying how policy will combat the rising numbers of fuel poor.
- The high levels of expenditure required by this new strategy will be funded by sources of money that do not create extra costs for the fuel poor. The amount funded by consumers, through the utilities directly, will be held to a minimum and preferably less than the £80 per customer, being paid in 2009 (Table 4.3 in Chapter 4).
- This activity has to occur in the context of a radical new approach to the energy efficiency of the whole housing stock: all of us have to be working towards low-carbon homes, and in this setting the work on fuel poverty becomes inclusive, essential, acceptable and not stigmatizing.
- The resultant expenditure will help to create 'green jobs', providing employment for out-of-work construction teams and a stimulus to the economy to limit the impact of the recession.

If all these are achieved, there will be improved energy security, cuts in the costs of cold-related ill health to the National Health Service (NHS), reduced carbon emissions from the housing stock and immeasurable improvements to the lives of millions of householders though the progressive eradication of fuel poverty.

Targeting homes and people

A major spur to writing this book was the recognition of the mismatch between the definition of fuel poverty and eligibility for assistance:

- 42 per cent of fuel-poor households do not qualify as eligible for the existing free energy-efficiency programmes. None of them are on means-tested benefits, disabled living allowance or tax credits but half of them are in the vulnerable categories (Table 3.5 in Chapter 3).
- Less than 25 per cent of the £4 billion of annual expenditure under fuel poverty policy is received by the fuel poor; the rest goes to people on a means-tested benefit or who are vulnerable, but not in fuel poverty, or to pensioners of all incomes (Table 6.14 in Chapter 6).

There clearly needs to be a realignment of definitions and eligibility. It is always acknowledged that fuel poverty is caused by a combination of low incomes and energy-inefficient housing, but this is not reflected in the criteria for eligibility of fuel poverty policies. No aspect of the three main schemes – winter fuel payments, Warm Front and CERT – links to the calibre of the housing. This has to change by combining data on the worst housing with that of the poorest people. It is the interaction of these that causes fuel poverty, so the recognition in policy of both sets of factors is a necessary pre-requisite to better targeting. At the moment:

- It is possible to identify someone on a means-tested benefit on the doorstep when offering an energy-efficiency improvement for free, but not to identify if they are in fuel poverty.
- It is possible to identify someone who is old, young, ill or disabled on the doorstep, but not to identify if they are in fuel poverty.

One of the important findings from the book is to confirm that no one criterion identifies the fuel poor accurately and the scale of the problem:

- 50 per cent of the fuel poor are pensioners, but these pensioner households only represent 19 per cent of all pensioners;
- 58 per cent of the fuel poor are in receipt of a means-tested benefit, DLA or tax credit, but they represent only 22 per cent of all households receiving an income-related benefit.

There are similar problems with targeting the worst homes, which need to be acknowledged:

- The poorest households live in homes that are slightly more energy efficient than the average (SAP05 54 instead of 52).
- The fuel poor live in homes that are considerably less energy efficient than the average (SAP05 39 instead of 52) or, indeed, the non-fuel poor (SAP05 54).
- The poor and the non-fuel poor have the same level of energy efficiency of their homes (SAP05 54); it is the fuel poor who predominantly occupy the least energy-efficient homes.

This confirms two things: there is a distinct difference between the poor and the fuel poor, and the energy inefficiency of the home is a major contributor to fuel poverty and therefore the route to its permanent eradication. The difference between the poor and the fuel poor, as stated in the Preface, is the role of capital equipment. This is reconfirmed. In an energy-efficient home, the effect of a fuel price rise is minimal; in an energy-inefficient home, it can be a catastrophe.

The new policy approach would start with those households in an energy-inefficient home, initially identified as an F- or G-rated property on the EPC. The emphasis has to be on the least energy efficient first.

The problem with the least efficient homes is that any policy to target the worst houses (F and G bands, with a SAP05 below 38) will reach about half of the fuel poor. But these fuel-poor households represent only 27 per cent of all the homes in these two bands. So, would targeting the worst houses result in a better fuel poverty policy? There are several components to an answer to this question:

- One third of the fuel poor have to pay more than 15 per cent of their income on fuel and are in some of the least efficient homes, averaging SAP05 32 (BERR, 2008, Table 7). Thus, tackling the worst homes would reach many of those in the greatest fuel poverty.
- There is a strong relationship between the severity of fuel poverty and the energy inefficiency of the housing stock (Figure 2.3 in Chapter 2).
- With a policy to target the worst homes, those who are non-fuel poor are also living in really energy-inefficient properties that should be improved. Getting these better-off households to take action would be good for the environment and for reducing carbon emissions. Thus, even where fuel poverty policy fails, there are beneficial environmental effects. The measures do not have to be given for free to these better-off households.
- It is extremely easy to identify all pensioners – the government has a centralized database, as it is already providing them with the state pension. To deliver winter fuel payments involves minimal administrative costs. However, the location of the least energy-efficient homes is not known.
- The proposal is, for a variety of policy objectives, that each local authority assembles an address-specific database of the energy efficiency of all the properties in its jurisdiction (Boardman, 2007, pp49–50). The primary justification is to find all the fuel-poor households (assuming they are those with the lowest levels of energy efficiency).
- The database will enable the worst homes to be identified and improvements to occur.
- The energy efficiency of a property is a stable entity; it does not vary as income levels do. The energy-efficiency rating can be improved, as measures are added. Progressively improving the energy efficiency of the housing stock can be measured with some confidence and accuracy and mapped. At any point in time, the least energy-efficient homes can be found once there is a database.

- Meanwhile, the least energy-efficient homes are mainly older properties, built at the same time, in tight geographical areas (e.g. Victorian terraces). They are relatively easy to identify and would be known by every local environmental health and housing officer.
- The major benefit of targeting the worst housing is that this is a one-off expenditure (if done to a high standard) that permanently improves the home. It is not a recurring cost – once a home has been dealt with, this is recorded on the database and the occupants are hopefully out of fuel poverty. Further expenditure is not needed to make the property fuel poverty proofed at present fuel prices.
- The other contribution of a housing approach is towards climate change policy: these properties are the most polluting in the UK. The extent to which there are reductions in emissions from these properties will depend primarily on the scale of the improvements and the present indoor temperature: for the fuel poor, relatively small upgrades (a few SAP points) will often result in the householder taking most of the benefit as extra warmth. The real savings occur when the energy-efficiency improvements enable the householder to have both adequate warmth and reduced energy consumption.

In conclusion, targeting fuel poverty policy on the worst homes permanently reduces fuel poverty and contributes to climate change commitments. The targeting may, initially, be as inaccurate as present policies, such as the winter fuel payment. But accurate solutions are easier to develop – for instance, with the creation of property databases. Targeting the worst homes is therefore the core of the proposed solutions.

'I'm not complaining'

There is one more reason why a comprehensive approach – which can only be achieved through an area-based policy on housing – is necessary. The reason is to help the group which has been identified throughout this book as the 'I'm not complaining group'. These are people who are self-contained and retiring, who do not claim all the benefits they are entitled to, who do not switch energy suppliers to get a cheaper tariff, who do not self-refer themselves for energy-efficiency improvements, and who may well be in the most severe fuel poverty. Their housing conditions are like those found among elderly fuel-poor households in Wales who 'had lower incomes, resided in older properties, and lacked double glazing and central heating' (Burholt and Windle, 2006, p1205).

We cannot rely on them coming forward for help as they are fearful of the consequences and believe that they must cope, despite their own suffering. It is not possible to prove, or disprove, this group exists, nor how large it might be; but the evidence collected in the 1980s (Smith, 1986) is likely to be indicative of a similar group today. They desperately need our help, but are hidden from view. Only a fully inclusive approach to the energy efficiency of the housing stock will uncover their plight in an acceptable way.

What standard?

The next issue to be discussed is the appropriate standard to be achieved in homes if they are to be fuel poverty proofed. British homes are some of the least energy efficient in Europe: the UK has a legacy of leaky homes. At the same time, the UK is one of the most unequal societies in Europe, with the incomes of the poorest households decreasing relative to the general UK population (Table 3.2). As fuel poverty results from a combination of low incomes and energy-inefficient homes, it is not surprising that fuel poverty is traditionally a British phenomenon. Only recently are other countries, notably in Eastern and Central Europe (ECE), experiencing similar problems.

The aim is for any property to be sufficiently energy efficient that it would provide affordable warmth (and other energy services) for any low-income household that moves into it. A SAP05 of 81 is the required level at the fuel prices current in early 2009 for a home of 85 square metres occupied by a family with an income below £9000 per annum (Table 6.15 in Chapter 6). The calculation has taken into account the required expenditure on those uses of energy not included in the SAP (all appliances, cooking and non-fixed lighting) and the cost of the electricity standing charge. There are virtually no low-income households living in homes at this level of energy efficiency (bands A and B on an EPC) in the UK in 2009. The task is huge because the problem is deep, extensive and worsening.

The average home of the fuel poor has a SAP05 of 38, so an average upgrade of 43 points is required. The level of energy efficiency of the poorest households is SAP05 54, so they still require to be improved by 27 points. The average home visited by Warm Front was upgraded by 23 points in 2007/08 (from 38 to 61), less than is needed by either group. Because of the design of the EPC and SAP, moving a household from a category G to a category F rating on the EPC results in as great a money, energy and carbon saving as moving a household from a D to an A category. Tackling the worst housing has real benefits if linked to EPC bands.

There is already a policy that requires the local authorities to intervene with the worst housing (approximately bands F and G) as much of it is deemed to be unhealthy. Few local authorities are fulfilling their duties under this legislation in an effective way, so there is an easy and quick policy route for government to require action. This requirement may have to be backed by additional funds, though action by owners on empty, unhealthy homes can often be generated both quickly and cheaply with some pressure from the local authority.

The standard of SAP05 81 will cease to be valid if there are future fuel price rises, though the calculation is difficult to make because of the way in which the SAP scale is adjusted in different versions to neutralize energy price rises.

Implicit in this approach to a SAP05 81 standard is the need for a debate about how it is reached. This is not about the technologies to be used – they all exist; rather, it is a discussion about the installation of individual measures or a holistic approach (outputs versus outcomes). The two main programmes – Warm Front and CERT – take a piecemeal, measure-by-measure approach. Neither of them is required to achieve a certain level of energy efficiency, however minimal. Only Warm Zones attempt to lift people out of fuel poverty; but they are often unable to because the appropriate measures will not be funded by the existing schemes. There are administrative costs and hassle for the household attached to this piecemeal approach, which may not be much greater if the household has a substantial upgrade in one go, rather than over several visits. Once in the home, the programme should install as many measures as necessary.

Package 1: The first 50 per cent

To eradicate fuel poverty by November 2016 means that half of the homes have to be treated in half the available time: the first 50 per cent should have been taken out of fuel poverty by 2013. Some of the fuel poor will live in fairly concentrated areas of fuel poverty and these are tackled first, because they should be easiest to find and to treat. The other 50 per cent are likely to be scattered, so are the focus of the second package.

The evidence from a variety of sources is that the most successful approach to eradicating fuel poverty is a holistic one, not just in relation to the property, but to the lifestyle of the occupants as well. It is the combination of increased incomes, through benefit entitlement checks, with energy-efficiency improvements and advice that is most successful. Just as it is the combination of problems that is the most disastrous – for instance, a single person on a low-income living in (and probably under-occupying) an energy-inefficient house has over a 97 per cent chance of being in fuel poverty at 2007 fuel prices. For both these reasons a packaged approach is proposed through low-carbon zones (Boardman, 2007, p88). Such an approach has been endorsed by Secretary of State for Energy and Climate Change Ed Miliband:

> We also need, over the coming years, to move towards a much more house-by-house, street-by-street approach ... the transition to North Sea gas is perhaps the right model to think about – every house was visited and switched over. We need the same approach in relation to energy efficiency because that can make a huge difference to families' bills and to carbon emissions. (Hansard, 2009)

The low-carbon zone would:

- Take an area-based approach, similar to Warm Zones and to the government's proposed Community Energy Saving Programme (CESP), but be more ambitious. There will be a red line on a map that encircles the zone.

- There will be at least one low-carbon zone in each housing authority area to encompass at least 50 per cent of fuel poor living in that jurisdiction (i.e. on average, 5000 fuel-poor households). If the fuel poor represent one third of all households in the low-carbon zone, the total size of the low-carbon zone is 15–20,000 properties.

- The first task will be to maximize the income of the household through benefit entitlement checks that not only establish what they should be receiving, but take them right through the process to make sure the money is actually being received. This also increases the likelihood that the household will be eligible for free installation of measures through receipt of the passport benefits.

- Every household in the low-carbon zone will be brought out of fuel poverty by a combination of measures, but primarily energy-efficiency improvements. These will include the standard insulation measures, low- and zero-carbon technologies (particularly solar thermal and photovoltaics) and the development of combined heat and power (CHP) schemes to provide community heating and low-cost electricity. The CHP could be fired by biomass or green gas (Boardman, 2007, p65).

- The design of the proposed feed-in tariff should be focussed on the needs of the fuel poor and the measures installed in the low-carbon zone should maximize these benefits: they are a future income for the residents.

- There will be economies of scale from treating all the homes in one area at the same time – for instance, from the multiple use of contractors' equipment, rather than moving it around from site to site and the economies achieved at the household level from an extensive refurbishment (e.g. only one set of scaffolding).

- It is anticipated that all the existing schemes (Warm Front, CERT PG and decent Homes Standard (DHS)) will continue, whether inside or outside the low-carbon zone.

- There is the ever-present targeting problem if only about one third of the homes are likely to be fuel poor. Providing that there is a range of flexible methods of funding the work (so the better-off are not subsidized, or not through fuel poverty policies), this becomes a positive asset. The activity encompasses all incomes and tenures and the inclusion of all the properties means that there is no poverty stigma attached to the receipt of measures, which can be a reason for refusal. The aim is to develop a groundswell of enthusiasm and commitment, throughout the community and population.

- It is taken as a given that all the energy-efficiency improvements are provided at nil cost to the fuel-poor occupants. Money can be raised from the landlord, if appropriate; but the fuel poor, with no savings, cannot contribute to the costs. A request to them to do so will result in the scheme failing the fuel poor.

Package 2: The second 50 per cent

The second package is required to identify and treat the remaining, scattered, fuel-poor homes, as well as to support the effectiveness of low-carbon zones. While the first low-carbon zones are being implemented, each local authority is preparing to treat the other half of the fuel poor. This primarily requires an address-specific energy-efficiency database to be assembled of all the properties in that local authority area and all tenures. Some further detail about how to do this was provided in *Home Truths* (Boardman, 2007, p50):

- The database has to be 100 per cent complete before the end of 2013 so that the remaining G- and F-rated properties, at least, can be identified for action. The present assumption is that ensuring there are no fuel-poor households in F- and G-rated properties is the main step towards eradication. More detail should emerge by 2013 as to where the remaining fuel poor are living: one third of the fuel poor are in E-rated properties (Table 6.1 in Chapter 6), so dealing with the Fs and Gs is only the beginning.
- This new database will be used by the Department for Work and Pensions (DWP) to provide an income supplement to all recipients of means-tested benefits to reflect the extra costs of the property's energy inefficiency. Based on an 85 square metre property and February 2009 fuel prices, this would range from an additional £5 per week for a household in a C-rated property (SAP05) to £25 per week for a G-rated property. In 2009, all 5 million fuel-poor UK households would receive this supplement, at an average of about £20 per week, for this size property, though most of the fuel poor, and certainly those in the deepest fuel poverty, live in bigger homes (BERR, 2008, Table 7). This policy could initially be grafted onto the process of providing cold weather payments: eligibility is confined to the recipients of means-tested benefits (Chapter 3)and the present payment level is £25 per qualifying week. The new supplement can be paid automatically through this route and refined once the energy efficiency of the individual's home is known. One of the advantages of this energy-inefficiency supplement is that it incorporates the DWP's huge expenditures into the fuel poverty equation and makes it in its interests to contribute to solving the problem. At the moment, the DWP is not affected by the success of fuel poverty policy.
- The total cost of the new supplement, at £20 per week for 5 million households would be £5.2 billion, if paid throughout the year. This is about twice the current level of winter fuel payments, which should be subsumed into the commitment.

Several existing policies are revitalized and mean that a useful level of action can occur quickly:

- The Housing Health and Safety Rating System (HHSRS) is reinforced strongly in all local authorities. This provides the legislative basis for the energy-efficiency databases as it requires the local authority to undertake a systematic review of the housing stock in their area for category 1 and 2 hazards. Second, the local authority needs to become proactive on requiring action on those homes identified as failing the category 1 hazard of excess winter cold (i.e. those in G- and F-rated bands). Neither duty is being complied with.

- All Local Strategic Partnerships (LSPs) have to report on the level of fuel poverty among households in receipt of a means-tested benefit in their area under National Indicator (NI) 187 even if it was not selected as one of their priority measures. If these reports are collated by the appropriate regional authorities and cross-checked with the government, it should be possible to establish how many fuel poor are living in each housing authority and that it is the same as the number in the fuel poverty model. If the total, for England, is more than 3.5 million (as estimated for 2008; Table 2.3 in Chapter 2), this is quite possibly accurate, as at least two methods of calculating the numbers come up with a figure of 4 million in England in 2008 (pp50–51, 156). There may be even more fuel poor than the English government has projected.
- A second DHS is introduced, requiring all social housing to achieve SAP05 81 by 2016.
- Private landlords are not yet incorporated within the fight against fuel poverty. The government's Landlord's Energy Saving Allowance (LESA) is not well known. It should be enhanced (a bigger annual allowance to cover more measures – for instance, a boiler), widely advertised and tapered down over time. This would encourage landlords to take action now while the LESA is still in existence. The standard of the privately rented sector needs to be linked in securely with any proposed minimum standards and the HHSRS.

The renewed activity on the fuel poor is in the context of wider housing and climate change policies. For instance, there would be a clear government policy statement – and wide publicity – about mandatory minimum standards for the whole housing stock, clarifying when it will become impossible to resell an unimproved G-rated property (Boardman, 2007, p53). Thus, everyone will recognize the importance of an energy-efficient home, supported by other policies (e.g. financial incentives) to stimulate general activity on the worst homes.

Much of this policy is necessary if the UK is going to achieve the required reductions in residential carbon emissions and matches the level of activity implied in the government's ambition for the Great British Refurb, so that by 2020 'up to 7 million homes will have had the opportunity to take up … "whole-house" changes' (DECC, 2009, p17). That is nearly 700,000 properties a year, about the same as the 714,000 homes that have to be improved if all 5 million fuel-poor households in the UK are to be treated. This is an enormous task and every month that passes makes the task more difficult because there are more fuel poor and less time. However, the two packages proposed here ensure that low carbon and low income become synonymous, as fuel poverty is eradicated.

Costs

Any programme that is looking at spending thousands of pounds on millions of homes will have a price tag in the billions of pounds: it is mathematically unavoidable. When this is combined with the ever-shortening timescale imposed by the WHECA 2000, the result is a large, annual budget. Current expenditure on all fuel poverty policy is around £4 billion, so that existing policy is in the right ball-park. There are several principles that have to be respected in paying for these new proposals:

- It is extremely difficult to identify the fuel poor (except on paper);
- There is no need to subsidize the rich;
- Any programme should be at no cost to the poor.

The targeting problem is a major hurdle: the size of the total budget depends upon the accurate identification of the fuel poor and the non-fuel poor, but this could only be achieved by invasive and detailed questions about the financial circumstances, savings and assets of every household involved. These audits would be extremely expensive, time-consuming and possibly counter-productive: people do not like to discuss their wealth or their poverty.

On the other hand, every household lives in a home, which is a substantial financial asset. The proposal, therefore, is to focus on the capital asset that is the property and to ignore the income of the occupant. The difference is important with privately rented property and non-existent with privately-owned and occupied homes. With registered social landlords, there are mechanisms, for instance through the Homes and Communities Agency, for both requiring and funding action.

The assumption is that there is a range of financial options for funding the improvements in the home and that the discussion with the home owner about financing would be in private, behind the front door. The home owner chooses which of the different financial packages is the most appropriate, for instance:

- Pay in cash;
- Raise an additional mortgage;
- Take out a low-interest loan, provided by the government, similar to the KfW scheme in Germany (Boardman, 2007, p51);
- The default mechanism would be a charge on the property;
- Nothing is provided for free;
- The recent discussions about a pay-as-you-save scheme would only be relevant in owner-occupied dwellings, where the home is already warm. It would not be appropriate for the fuel poor, as much of the benefit of the

energy-efficiency improvement would be taken as additional warmth, not lower energy bills.

The choices need to be attractive, simple and clear so that most, if not all, homes within an area join into the low-carbon zone to achieve the greatest economies of scale. A piecemeal approach increases the costs for all homes.

Both Kirklees and Harrogate local authorities have developed schemes that involve the costs being repaid by a charge on the property, when it is sold. In both cases, the local authority pays the interest on the loan until the property is sold, which could represent a substantial financial burden, if the loan exists for several years. If the householder has a large mortgage already, then the loan is not offered, as it could result in negative equity for the householder.

There are problems with private landlords, as they may never sell the property. In these cases, it may be necessary to put a time limit on the completion of the work: for instance the next five years. This was the time period provided for conversion of the heating system when a zone was declared under the 1956 Clean Air Act.

The national context is crucial to the successful delivery of the low-carbon zones. It has to be clear to all home-owners that energy-inefficient properties have to be improved and that energy-efficient homes have a higher market value. Then the home-owner can appreciate that the investment is a sound one as it will increase the value of the property. At the moment, too many elderly people might refuse such a scheme, if it were seen as reducing the value of their estate and their legacy to the children. Similarly, the private landlord has to be confident of obtaining a return on the investment, independently of the lower fuel bills of the occupants. If it is widely accepted in society that F- and G-rated properties are unhealthy, have to be treated and are a financial liability in their present condition, then it will be easier to persuade householders to release equity or take out loans.

If the government make the decision to continue with the present method of funding energy-efficiency improvements through the utilities (i.e. CERT) and taxpayers money (i.e. Warm Front and winter fuel payments), then the cost will be substantial. The minimum would be £5.4 billion per annum for energy efficiency improvements alone (Table 8.4), assuming perfect targeting. Instead, the costs should be raised without further impact on the fuel poor to avoid a vicious circle of some households being pushed into fuel poverty in order to raise the money to help take others out of it. This would imply the use of new sources of funding such as the income from European Union Emissions Trading Scheme (EU ETS) auctions and the introduction of reverse tariffs, so that only high energy users contribute to the costs (both covered in Chapter 4).

A more likely scenario is that the present inaccurate targeting continues and the cost is closer to £22 billion each year to treat 20 million homes. There are only 26 million homes in the UK, so this would be a policy of doing virtually every home, for free. The choice facing government is almost between everything for free, or nothing.

Incomes

With the present wide definition of fuel poverty (i.e. going beyond those on income-related benefits), then the role of incomes is similar to that in general society: the poorest and most vulnerable households need more money (relative to other households). This can only be achieved by the government adopting positive redistributive policies. The situation is more specific for those defined as poor through the benefits they receive. Marginal improvements to the incomes of the fuel poor through the benefits they already receive are possible; but they are marginal, particularly in comparison with the size of recent fuel price increases.

A strong emphasis has to be placed on benefit entitlement checks in order to make sure that all of those who are eligible are claiming their benefits. This would bring some of the excluded 42 per cent into eligibility for free energy-efficiency policy, as well as increasing their incomes. The proportion that could be captured is not known.

In addition to the benefit-entitlement checks and a new energy-inefficiency supplement, increasing benefits quickly after a major fuel price rise would be one of the most useful improvements so that the poor do not wait up to 18 months for additional money. Increasing the minimum wage to prevent those in part-time work slipping into fuel poverty, is another useful, contributory policy to support higher incomes for the fuel poor.

Finally, providing households with extra income is important because it is the only effective short-term solution. But these fuel poor are living in energy-inefficient homes, so that the extent to which this extra income is spent on additional warmth and energy services means that additional carbon dioxide is emitted at a time when the UK has stringent reduction targets. The measures on additional incomes will alleviate fuel poverty for some households, but it would be too expensive to use incomes to eradicate fuel poverty. Only capital investment in the energy efficiency of the homes can do that. For the 17 per cent in the most severe fuel poverty, additional income and a SAP05 81 will both be needed.

Another development that is required is that the winter fuel payments should cease as a fuel poverty policy. If the payments are to continue, then it is because they are clearly labelled a pension supplement or are converted into the energy-inefficiency benefit. Over 80 per cent of this nearly £3 billion is going to the non-fuel poor in 2008. At a time of budgetary constraint, it is not fair to deprive the really fuel poor of assistance in order to continue with the winter fuel payments, many to well-off pensioner households.

Fuel prices

The electricity and gas industries in the UK are fully liberalized – that is, they compete for customers. There are no monopoly fuel suppliers, except in Northern Ireland. Competition between the companies inevitably focuses on those people who use the most fuel, do not have debts and pay regularly (i.e. better-off households who create profits, not costs). As a result, more households are currently being forced into fuel poverty by fuel price rises than are being taken out of it by government policies and a large proportion of these fuel price rises are avoidable, as they are specifically targeted to disadvantaged householders by the utilities. The fuel poor have to pay unnecessarily high energy prices as a result of government policy on liberalization, utility profit maximization and the regulator's passivity in Great Britain. All of these will have to be counteracted if energy prices are to be reduced for the fuel poor to a fair level. Competition and the market are not delivering for them. There is a need for strong regulation to deliver strong social priorities, but this has to be led by government (Mitchell, 2008, p140; Scrase et al, 2009, p241):

- The government has both to require Ofgem to give priority to the fuel poor and to ensure that this ruling is enforced. Ofgem already has an obligation to consider the vulnerable and future generations, so the basis for action is there.
- Some focus is now being placed, belatedly, on these social issues. Ofgem has relinquished control over prices, so it can do very little that is meaningful about the situation. It will probably be necessary to take back control of prices in order to prevent the market manipulation that is taking place.
- Fuel prices – and therefore fuel poverty – in Great Britain are being increased through government policies, funded through the utilities, on emissions trading, the Renewables Obligation (RO) and energy-efficiency investment programmes. These already increase the cost per household by £80 per annum. This sum should be capped for the fuel poor, or reduced.
- It is undoubtedly convenient for the government to have large energy-efficiency programmes funded by the utilities, but not when these, in turn, increase fuel poverty. The funding for CERT PG is regressive: the fuel poor pay £200 million towards the scheme, but receive about £125 million back.
- The regulator in Northern Ireland has the same mandate as Ofgem, but has managed to deliver policies that are much more supportive of the fuel poor – for instance, no disconnections, no premium for the PPM and an Energy Efficiency Levy that is solely spent on the fuel poor or community groups. It can be done if there is the motivation and inclination.
- New initiatives, such as smart meters and reverse block tariffs, will only provide benefits for the poor if they are consciously designed in, for instance, by making sure that all-electric homes are protected.
- Lower fuel prices for the fuel poor will help to alleviate fuel poverty, but will not eradicate it. Many of the additional costs being levied on the fuel poor should never have been imposed by the utilities, or allowed by Ofgem. It would, therefore, be a travesty if the utilities are 'rewarded' with kudos for bringing in social tariffs to offset these higher charges: social justice requires the utilities to reduce their prices for the fuel poor, anyway.

Contributory policies

There is a range of other policies that will contribute to the eradication of fuel poverty. It is such a tough task that probably every one of the following is needed to make a contribution. The development of a systems-based approach to fuel poverty would be a major step towards this incorporation so that all players and layers of government know their responsibilities and the size of the task. The government cannot deliver the eradication of fuel poverty with the present centralized approach: only the four governments have any legal obligations.

The four countries need to compare notes on the effectiveness of policy, frequently and honestly. While there are major differences between the circumstances in each authority, there are also similarities so that the parallel experiments will be informative. The Welsh government's plan for One Wales and the Scottish Energy Assessment Package both seem particularly helpful since they target both the worst homes and the poorest people.

Extending or strengthening some existing policies would bring results quickly. These include:

- Enforcing the HHSRS, perhaps with additional funds for local authorities;
- Publicizing and extending the LESA and increasing the allowance from £1500 per annum to a sum that would allow a boiler to be included;
- Making the results of the EPCs publicly available;
- Announcing a second round of the DHS, with a target of SAP05 81 by 2016 in all social housing.

With new construction, the amount of new social housing being built each year is gradually increasing, as is much needed. The main task is to ensure that this is kept for renting and is available to help the fuel poor get out of the worst homes. Similarly, many of the fuel poor are under-occupying their homes and this creates a demand for fuel expenditure that is difficult to meet from one or two meagre incomes. Providing a good range of smaller properties, designed for older people, might help some of them choose to downsize.

The choice of heating systems encouraged or allowed through the fuel poverty schemes has a substantial impact upon fuel poverty and carbon emissions. Homes that are hard to heat, all electric or in rural areas should be given priority and brought up to an exceptionally high standard of energy efficiency, particularly if the heating fuel cannot be changed. Where there is no gas supply, the installation of solar thermal, biomass and CHP should all be evaluated.

The use of SAP for fuel poverty policy should be minimized because of the way in which fuel prices are fixed in the short term and neutralized between different versions. An alternative would be to build on the fuel poverty model's approach – and that of the National Home Energy Rating (NHER), as used in Scotland – to incorporate the cost of all uses of energy, as in the definition of fuel poverty. The regional climate variation is also important. SAP covers 85 per cent of the energy used in the home, but only 58 per cent of the expenditure and 68 per cent of the carbon (Table 6.2 in Chapter 6). The proportion excluded by SAP will grow in importance as homes become more energy efficient in their production of warmth. A new methodology would have the additional benefit of preparing for the Code for Sustainable Homes (CSH), level 6, which requires new homes to recognize all uses of energy in the home.

There should be a greater emphasis on scrappage programmes, funded by the utilities, that replace, old, inefficient appliances with new efficient ones, for a nominal cost (e.g. the price of a second-hand appliance). The Fridgesavers scheme was very successful and should be reintroduced, as a minimum. The inefficient use of energy in lights, appliances and cookers is just as much a drain on the purse as leaky windows and walls.

Definition

While there are deficiencies with the present UK definitions of fuel poverty, the basic perspective is still sound: all energy needs within the home should be achievable for a defined proportion of income. Beyond that, the household is in fuel poverty. This clearly includes all energy services in the home, not just heating. These are assumed to provide accepted, defined standards of energy service (warmth, hot water, lighting, etc.) that have to be achievable and are based on society's norms, not some reduced standard because these are low-income households. It is the amount of money that 'needs' to be spent, not what is actually spent that is of importance.

The definition of income should exclude housing costs in societies where there is a wide geographical variation between, particularly, the rents paid. At the moment, including income received to help with rents, as in the UK, penalizes those living in high rent areas, such as London. A household could be taken out of fuel poverty just because the rent goes up: the increased housing benefit shows as increased income. There is a risk that a household will cease to be deemed to be in fuel poverty despite becoming poorer.

The proportion of income that defines fuel poverty can be fixed (like the 10 per cent in the UK). This does simplify the problem and policy target; but if set at a historically high level, it is unjust at times of rapid fluctuations in fuel prices. That is the recent experience in the UK.

Alternatively, the trigger expenditure level can be related to what the average household is spending, which takes into account fuel price fluctuations. The academic basis for the original 10 per cent figure was that it represented twice the median expenditure. Twice the median (or average) is deemed to represent a disproportionate level of expenditure and would be an appropriate level for a floating proportion. A varying proportion of income will make policy more complex because it could change annually, but does accurately reflect the level of a relative hardship faced by the fuel poor. A relative approach is taken for policy on child poverty in the UK.

For monitoring purposes, the definition of income can be adjusted (equiv-alized) according to the number of people in the household or based on some minimum income standard. In both cases, considerable detail is required to reflect the various permutations in society and to avoid further crude approxi-mations. These link with the definitions of poverty – for instance, being in receipt of less than 60 per cent of median incomes. All of these methods have their benefits and disadvantages. They are mainly useful for monitoring and analysis over time. They are less useful for targeting, particularly if people have to be identified in their homes. Receipt of a means-tested benefit and owner-ship of the relevant passbook make this the easiest method in practice.

The most important point is that fuel poverty and eligibility for assistance are defined on the same basis. It is this mismatch that has caused so much money to be wasted in the UK. The category of 'vulnerable' households has to be dropped as part of the official definition. It was introduced to frame the 2010 target (i.e. whom should we help first); but this target is now defunct, so the definition can go. It is far too extensive and covers the majority of all UK households. As a result it is too loosely related to fuel poverty.

A new strategy

All of these new solutions need to be brought together in a clear and costed plan, a new UK Fuel Poverty and Energy-Efficiency Strategy. In particular this new strategy has to answer some political questions, particularly if policy continues to be similar to the present system:

- Does the government accept the legal obligation to eradicate fuel poverty by 2016 (as the minister has implied) and will, therefore, implement the necessary policies and expenditure?
- How should any expenditure be split between income support and energy-efficiency investments? The current proportions are roughly three-quarters on winter fuel payments and one quarter on energy-efficiency improve-ments. How should this vary over time? This is effectively a choice between symptoms (and immediate amelioration) and causes (and permanent reduction).
- What proportion of the expenditure should come from the utilities and energy bill payers (which includes all of the fuel poor) and what proportion from the government and taxpayers (a smaller contribution from the fuel poor) and what proportion from new, identified sources?
- If there is a new philosophy to redefine eligibility in terms of both the worst houses and the poorest people, identify what the relative political priorities are for pensioners, families with children, people in rented accommodation, etc., as this determines what level of assistance is given and the definition of fuel poverty used for monitoring.
- Which system of monitoring who is fuel poor is to be used?

- In the context of other policies – for instance, on climate change – is the aim to target the fuel poor more accurately and thus make 'fuel poverty' expenditure more effective? Or is it best to have an extensive poorly focused programme that fulfils other objectives and increases public awareness and support, with the expenditure implications that this indicates?
- What are the boundaries for any cost-benefit analysis undertaken – for instance, are NHS costs and building industry employment opportunities included or excluded? If there are limitations on the budget, how is the government defining the basis for setting these limitations?

The new strategy would:

- Be based on a stated level of expected fuel price rises and demonstrate how people will be kept out of fuel poverty, despite these potential increases.
- Confirm the level of energy efficiency (e.g. SAP rating) to be achieved in each house and whether there are any cost limits on this.
- Identify the additional financial support to be given to those homes where the required level of energy efficiency has not been reached, how these households are to be identified and how the payment level is to be set.
- Identify the budget available, the sources of money (government, utility, home-owner, etc.) and the expected timescale for achieving specified standards. The timetable should align fuel poverty targets with those for climate change, as, in the short term, policies to improve incomes and reduce the cost of energy for the fuel poor would increase consumption. The roll-out of the low-carbon zones will have to be prompt to offset this.
- Align government targets and the targets of those involved in delivering (i.e. all to be framed in terms of reductions in fuel poverty). The present mismatch between the outputs required of installers and the outcomes that government is legally required to comply with demonstrates the lack of coherence in present policies.
- Confirm which layer of government has what level of responsibility for delivery and what additional funds are available and what the sanctions are for failure. For instance, what are the respective responsibilities of each housing authority, the regional housing boards and the Housing and Communities Agency?
- Be clear about which institution has responsibility for monitoring the government's progress, on a similar basis to the Climate Change Committee (CCC). Is this an enhanced role for the four Fuel Poverty Advisory Groups (FPAGs)?

In the absence of such a plan, it is not possible for government to establish where it is in relation to its legal obligation and whether it is on the necessary trajectory.

As fuel poverty is becoming a widespread problem within the EU, this new strategy could provide a template for the other member states for the reports required under the Electricity Directive (2009/72/EC) from mid 2011. The UK could lead the way on both climate change and fuel poverty eradication.

Finally, fuel poverty is inevitably a complex interdisciplinary problem; but it does not have to be this complex. The government's new strategy should ensure that there is a simplified approach, with clear targets, assumptions and monitoring procedures. This will enable more people to be involved and to encourage the delivery of successful policy. It is the least that we owe to the fuel poor.

It is now nearly eight years since *The UK Fuel Poverty Strategy* was published in November 2001, and yet there are more households in fuel poverty than there were then. It is as if the targets had never been set and the WHECA 2000 had never been passed. The problem of fuel poverty is a real and growing problem that affects nearly one in five households by mid 2009. This complex social problem has not been honoured with firm, coherent and just policies. The hope is that this book will make that more likely in future so that there is a possibility, just, that fuel poverty can be eradicated by 2016.

References

BERR (Department for Business, Enterprise and Regulatory Reform) (2008) *Fuel Poverty Statistics, Detailed Tables 2006, Annex to Fuel Poverty Strategy Report*, 2008, URN 08/P33, BERR, London

Boardman, B. (2007) *Home Truths: A Low-Carbon Strategy to Reduce UK Housing Emissions by 80% by 2050*, Research report for the Co-operative Bank and Friends of the Earth, London, www.foe.co.uk/resource/reports/home_truths.pdf

Burholt, V. and Windle, G. (2006) 'Keeping warm? Self-reported housing and home energy efficiency factors impacting on older people heating homes in North Wales', *Energy Policy*, vol 34, no 10, pp1198–1208

DECC (Department of Energy and Climate Change) (2009) *Heat and Energy Saving Strategy: Consultation*, DECC, February, http://hes.decc.gov.uk/consultation/consultation_summary

DTI (Department of Trade and Industry) (2001) *The UK fuel pvoerty strategy*, DTI, London, November, www.berr.org.uk/files/file16459.pdf

Hansard (2009) HC Deb (Session 2008–2009), vol 388, col 978, 5 March,

HC 37 (2009) *Energy Efficiency and Fuel Poverty*, Third report of session 2008–2009, Environment, Food and Rural Affairs Select Committee, Stationery Office, London

Mitchell, C. (2008) *The Political Economy of Sustainable Energy*, Palgrave Macmillan, Basingstoke, UK

Scrase, I., Kern, F., Lehtonen, M., MacKerron, G., Martiskainen, M., McGowan, F., Ockwell, D., Sauter, R., Smith, A., Sorrell, S., Wang, T. and Watson, J. (2009) 'Energy policy implications', in I. Scrase and G. MacKerron (eds) *Energy for the Future: A New Agenda*, Palgrave Macmillan, Basingstoke, UK, Chapter 14

Smith, K. (1986) *'I'm Not Complaining': The Housing Conditions of Elderly Private Tenants*, Kensington and Chelsea Staying Put for the Elderly Ltd, in association with SHAC, London

Index